F Minus

F Minus

BY TONY CARRILLO

**Andrews McMeel
Publishing, LLC**

Kansas City

F Minus is distributed internationally by United Feature Syndicate, Inc.

07 08 09 10 11 WKT 10 9 8 7 6 5 4 3 2 1

ISBN-13: 978-0-7407-6839-2
ISBN-10: 0-7407-6839-5

Library of Congress Control Number: 2007925290

www.andrewsmcmeel.com

Introduction

I had already been drawing my cartoons on a regular basis for a couple of years when I got the news that *F Minus* was going to be syndicated. The idea of producing comic ideas every day for possibly several years was daunting, but I felt up to the task. After several weeks of doing nothing, I decided it was time to get back to work making comics. So I cleaned off my desk, sharpened my pencils, adjusted my seat to the proper height for creative development, put on a tie, and started thinking.

By day seven, my paper was still blank. I came to the conclusion that I had somehow lost the ability to come up with funny cartoons. In my depression, I began to eat an alarming amount of licorice with little regard for my own health.

Days passed by, and I became more and more certain that my brain was no longer capable of creating comic ideas. Then something happened. You might call it a miracle. I do.

One clear morning, I was walking down the street, discussing my mental block with my girlfriend. Riding up the street toward us on a bicycle was a friend and *F Minus* fan I'll call "Scott." We waved hello as he approached, and Scott waved back. Suddenly, like an angel from heaven, a large black bird dropped from the sky. We saw the bird descend upon Scott's head and attack it like a scrap of bread tossed by an old woman in a park. We could only watch, stunned, as Scott rolled past us, flailing wildly at the great winged beast. He disappeared down the street, still swatting at the bird. To this day, I do not know if he survived.

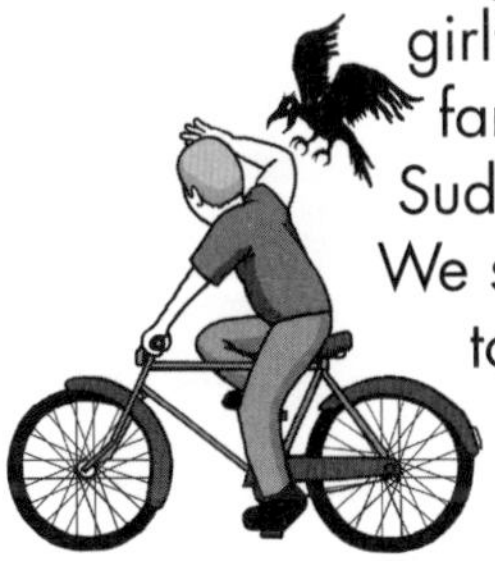

When I got back home and sat down at my desk, I realized that something had happened in my brain. Whatever it was that had not been working before suddenly got switched back on. This event I witnessed, although tragic, allowed me to get back to creating *F Minus* comics.

This book is a collection of the first year of *F Minus*, and includes a selection of 'toons from the college years (see pages 7–12). I hope you enjoy them.

And thank you, Great Black Bird of Comedy. May you continue your good works.

This book is dedicated to my mom, who taught me how to draw, and to my dad, who taught me what was funny.

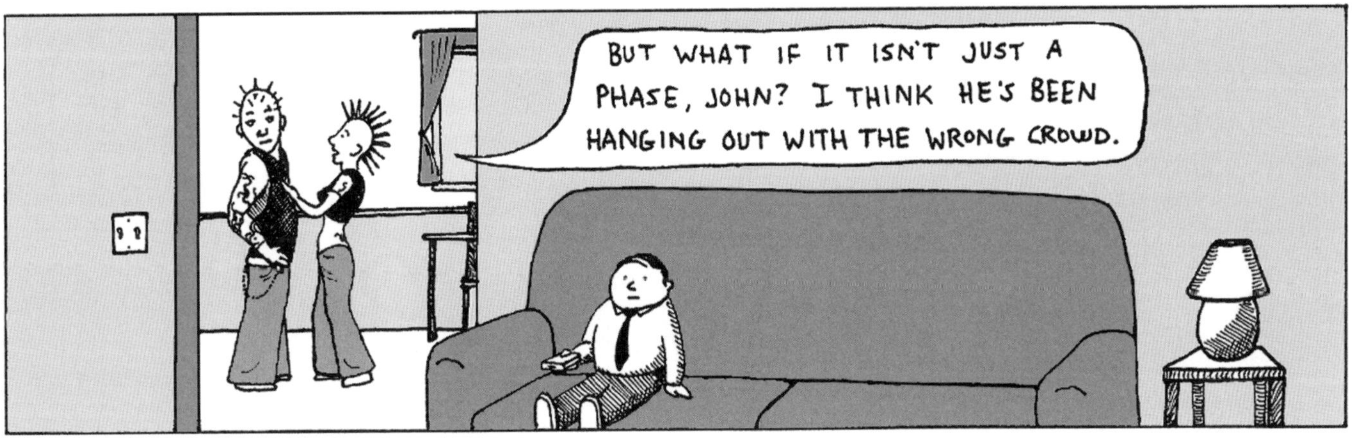
BUT WHAT IF IT ISN'T JUST A PHASE, JOHN? I THINK HE'S BEEN HANGING OUT WITH THE WRONG CROWD.

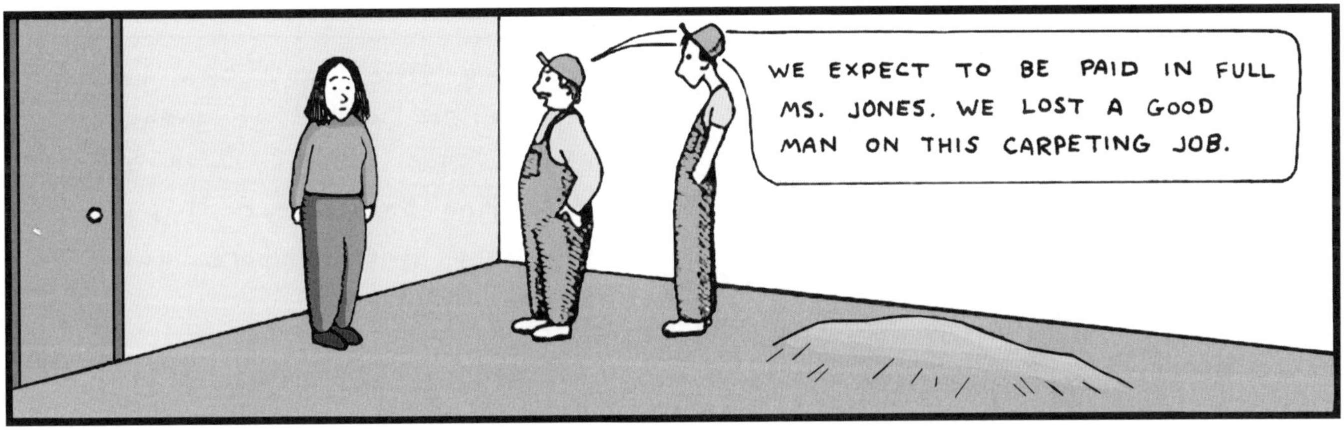
WE EXPECT TO BE PAID IN FULL MS. JONES. WE LOST A GOOD MAN ON THIS CARPETING JOB.

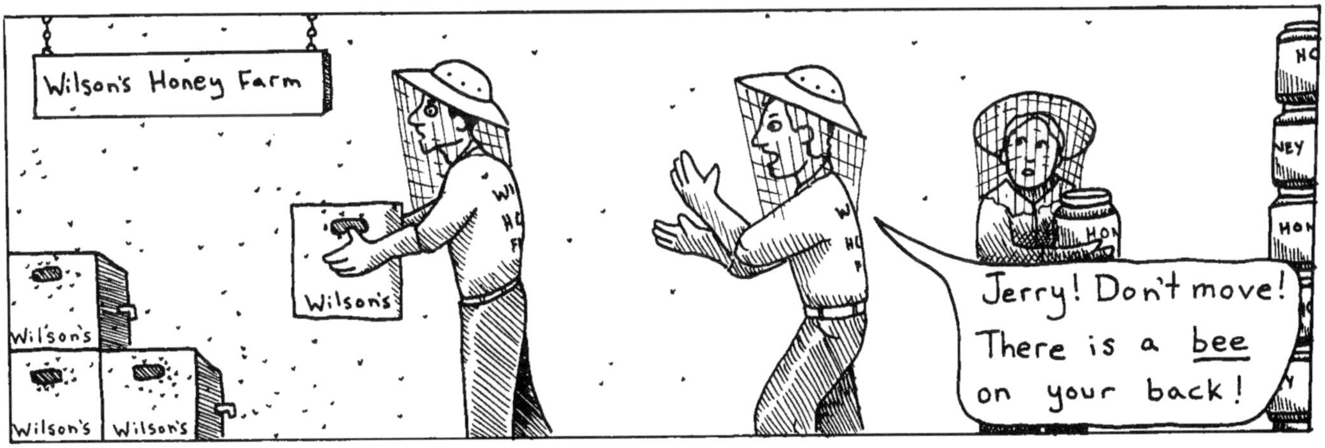
Wilson's Honey Farm
Wilson's
Wilson's
Wilson's
Wilson's
Jerry! Don't move! There is a bee on your back!

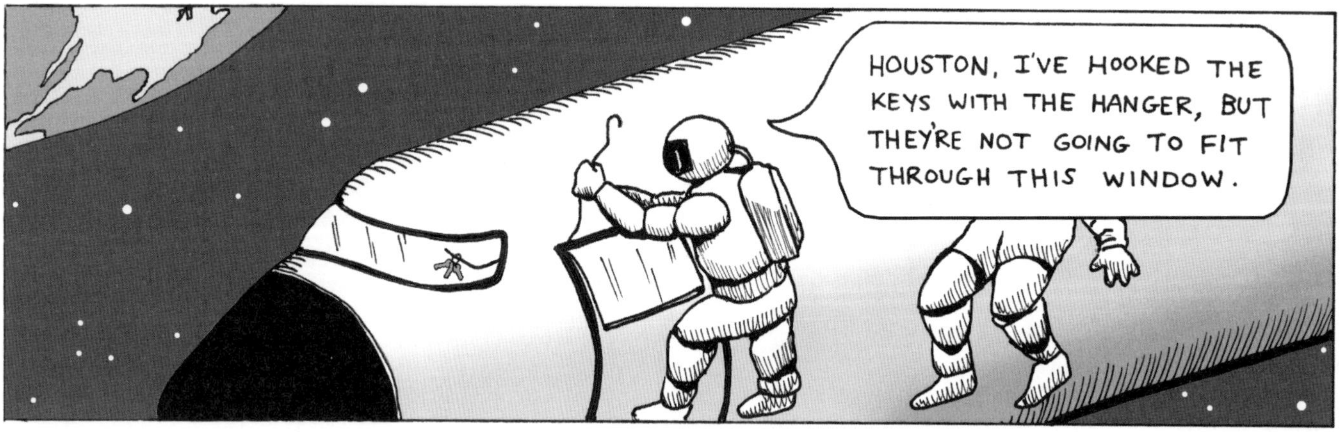
HOUSTON, I'VE HOOKED THE KEYS WITH THE HANGER, BUT THEY'RE NOT GOING TO FIT THROUGH THIS WINDOW.

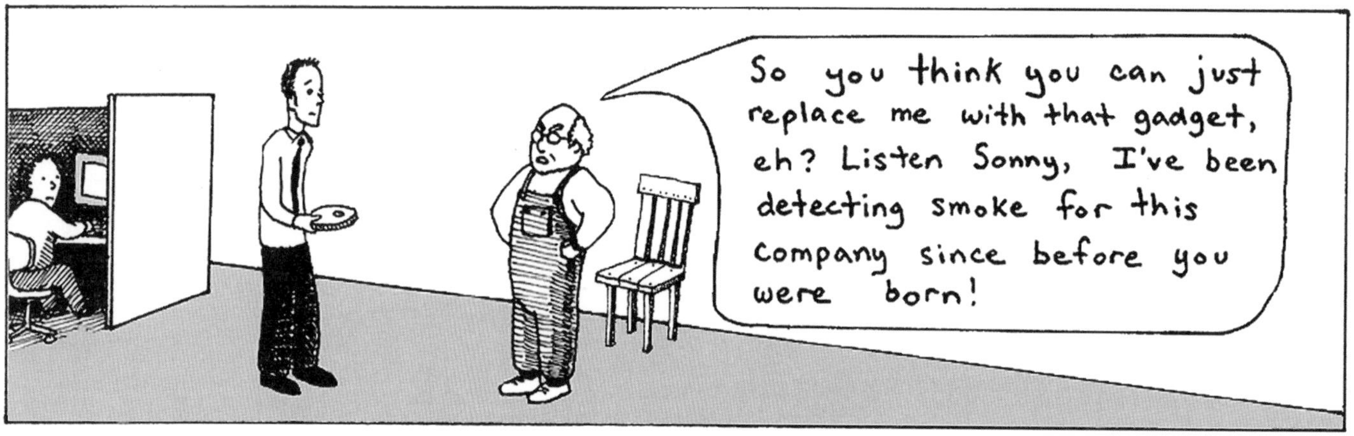
So you think you can just replace me with that gadget, eh? Listen Sonny, I've been detecting smoke for this company since before you were born!

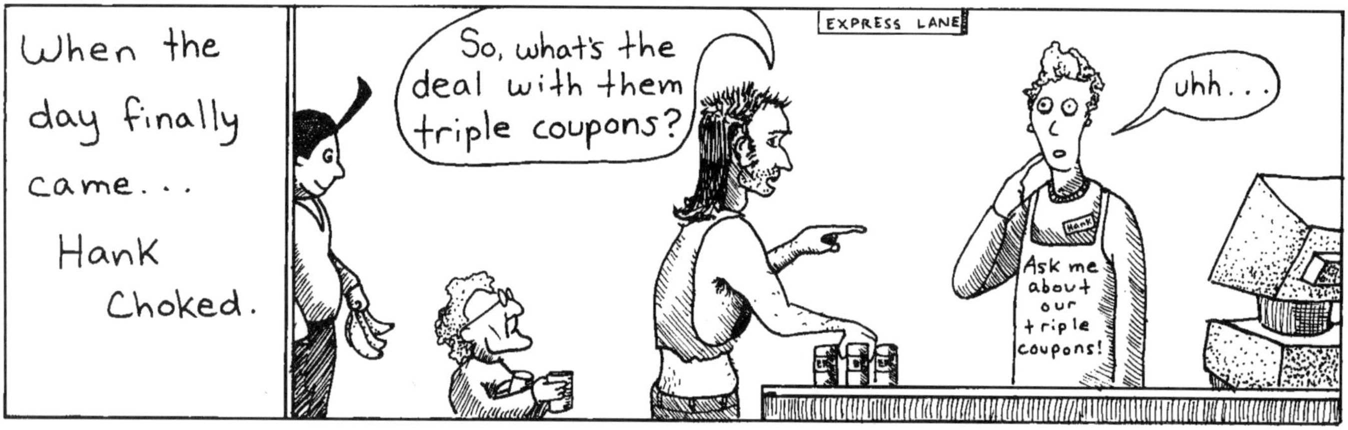
When the day finally came...
Hank Choked.
EXPRESS LANE
So, what's the deal with them triple coupons?
uhh...
Hank
Ask me about our triple coupons!

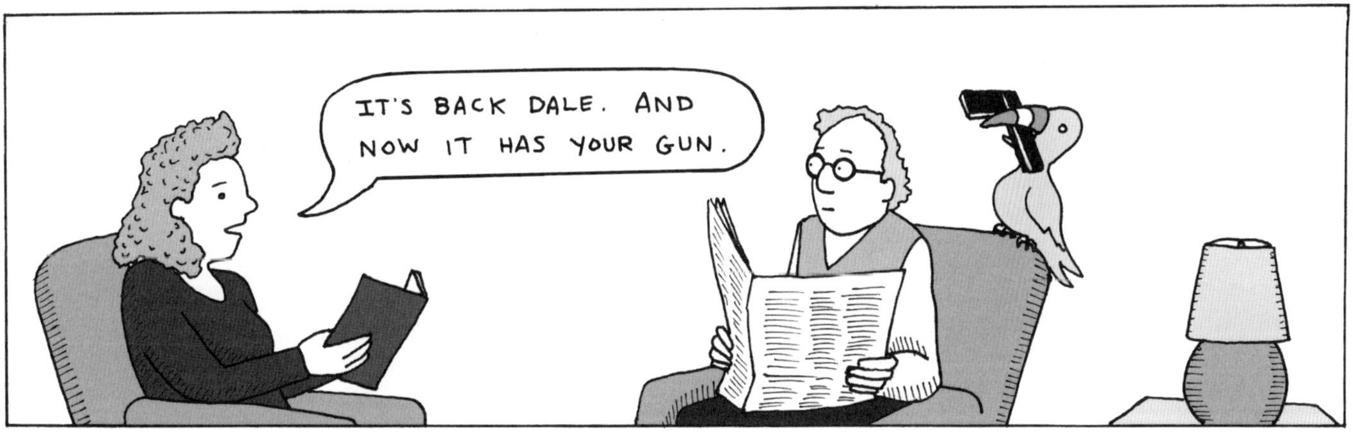
IT'S BACK DALE. AND NOW IT HAS YOUR GUN.

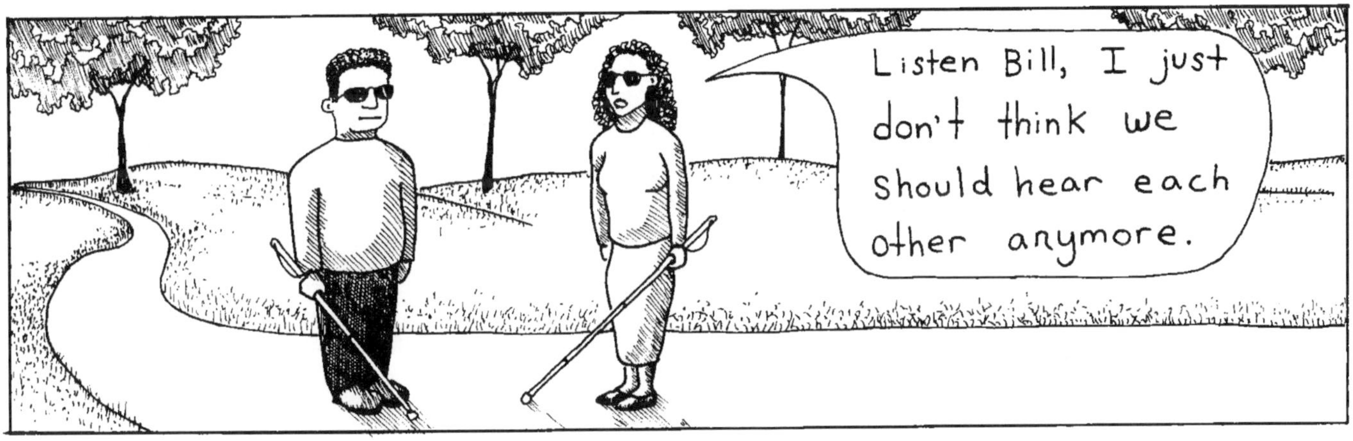
Listen Bill, I just don't think we should hear each other anymore.

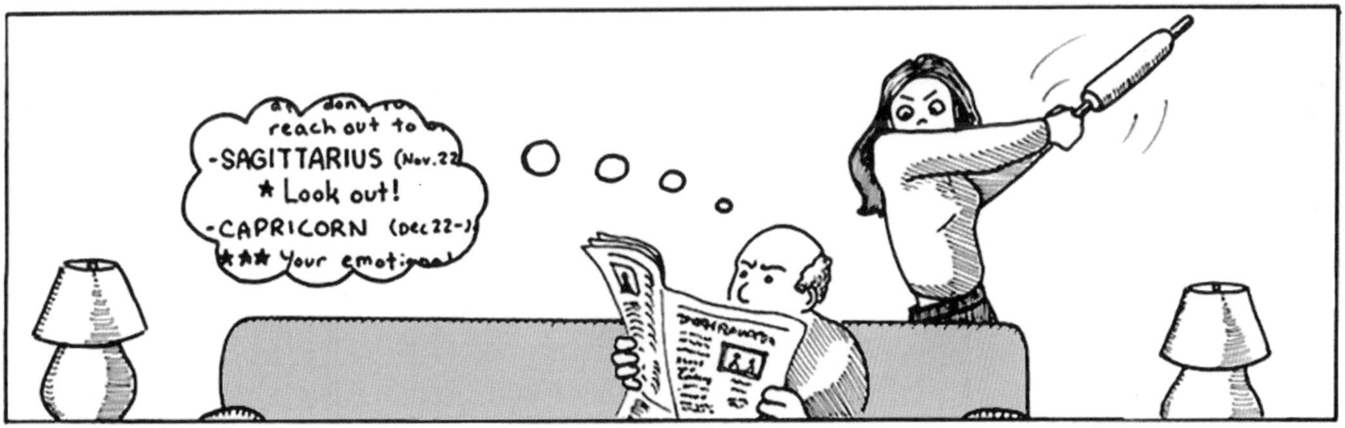
reach out to
-SAGITTARIUS (Nov.22
★ Look out!
-CAPRICORN (DEC 22-
★★ Your

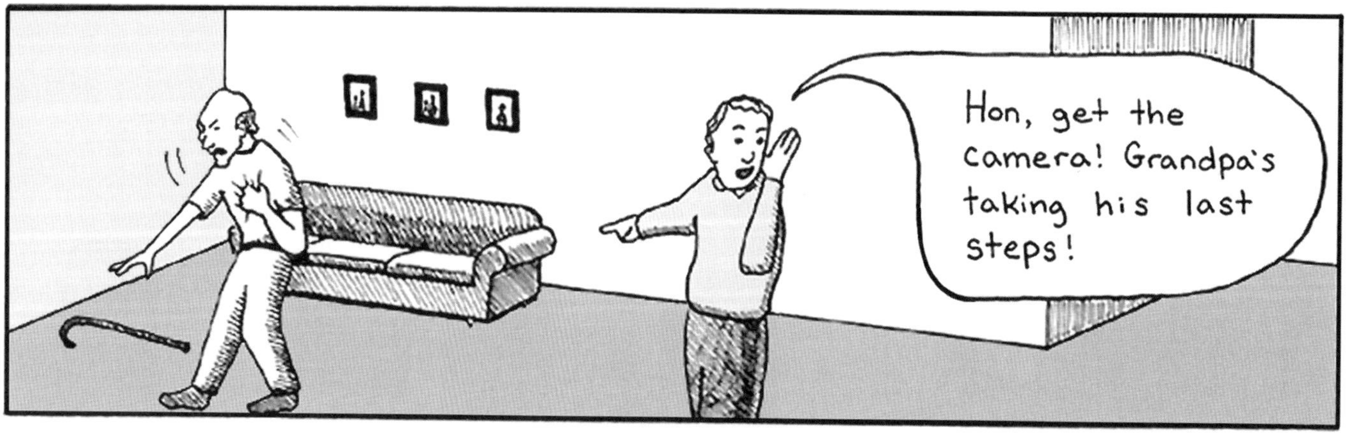
Hon, get the camera! Grandpa's taking his last steps!

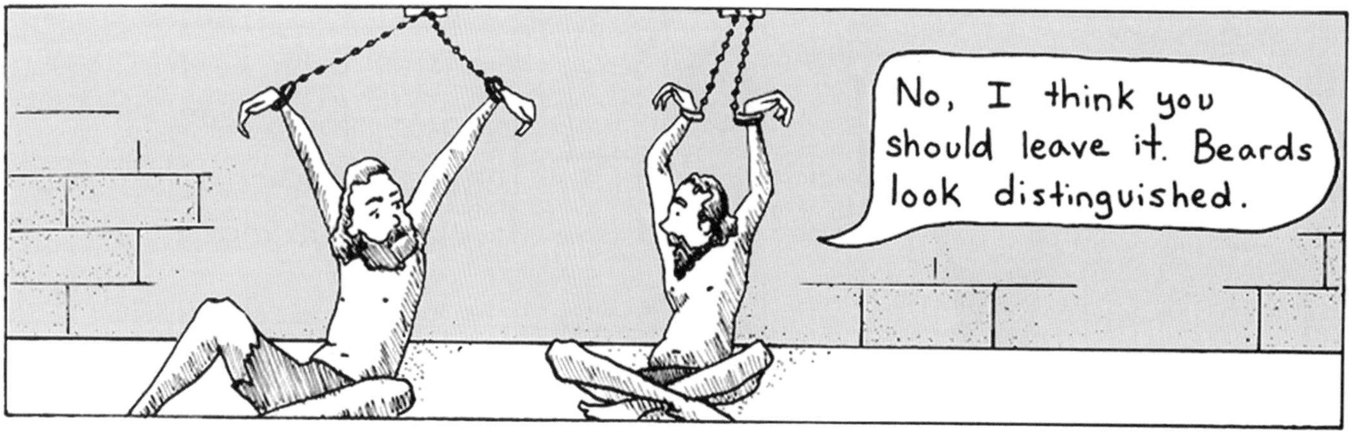
No, I think you should leave it. Beards look distinguished.

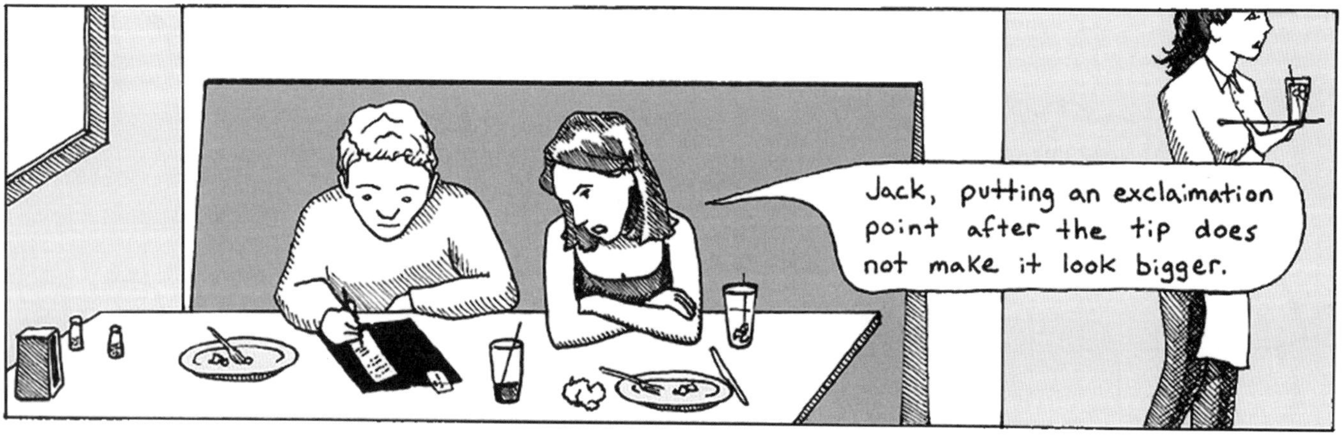
Jack, putting an exclamation point after the tip does not make it look bigger.

F Minus presents:

One of life's precious moments

Mugger and victim share a laugh when she accidentally douses him with perfume instead of her pepper spray.

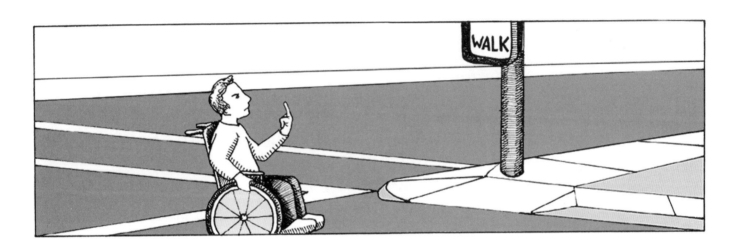

Mitch, I think that we should see other people.

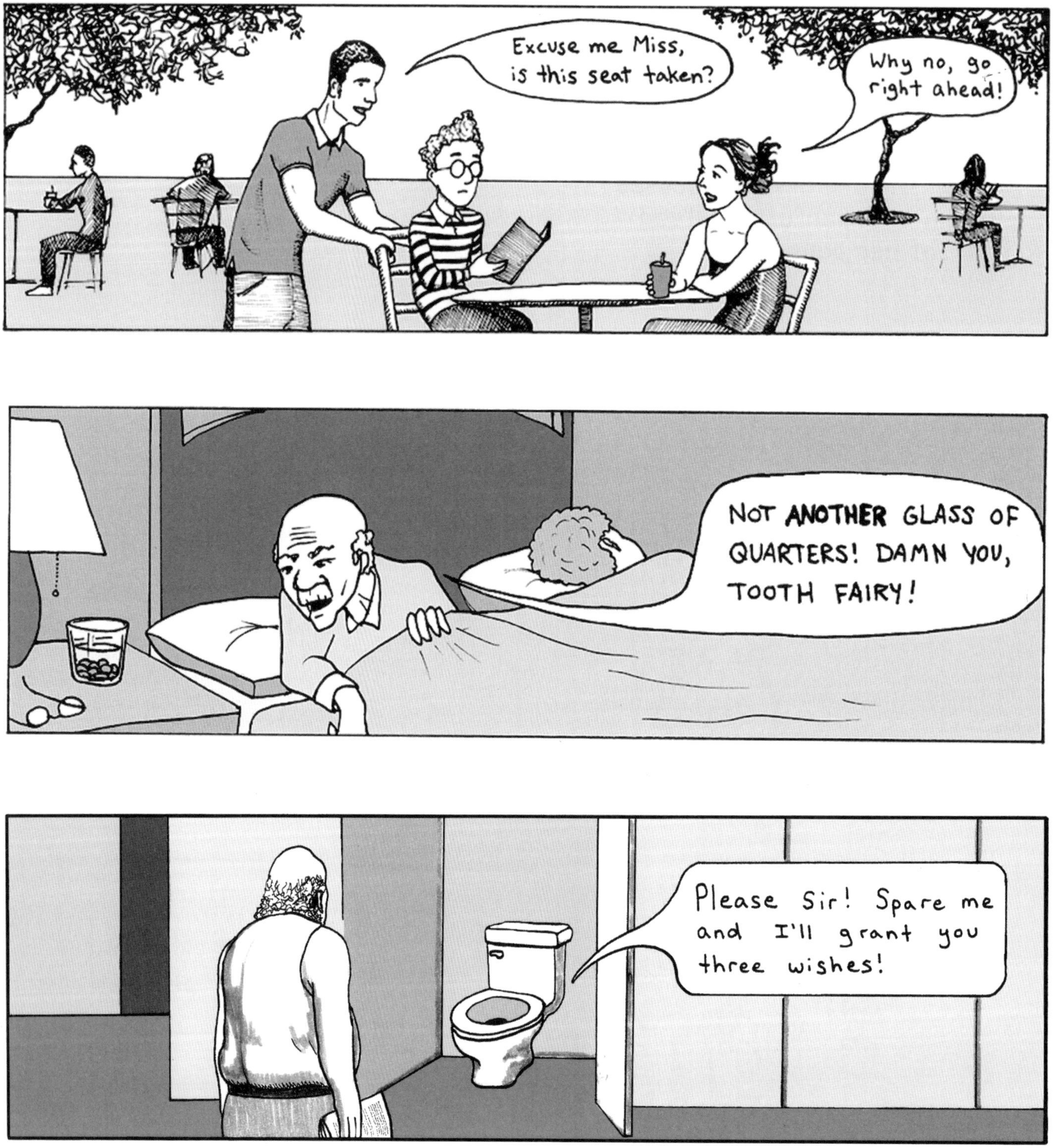
Excuse me Miss, is this seat taken?
Why no, go right ahead!
NOT **ANOTHER** GLASS OF QUARTERS! DAMN YOU, TOOTH FAIRY!
Please Sir! Spare me and I'll grant you three wishes!

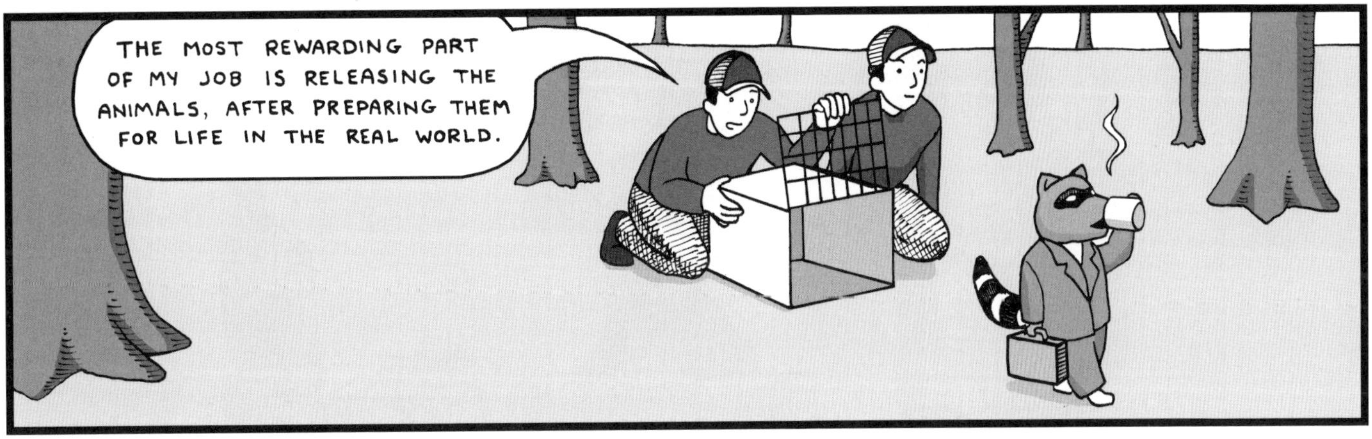
THE MOST REWARDING PART OF MY JOB IS RELEASING THE ANIMALS, AFTER PREPARING THEM FOR LIFE IN THE REAL WORLD.

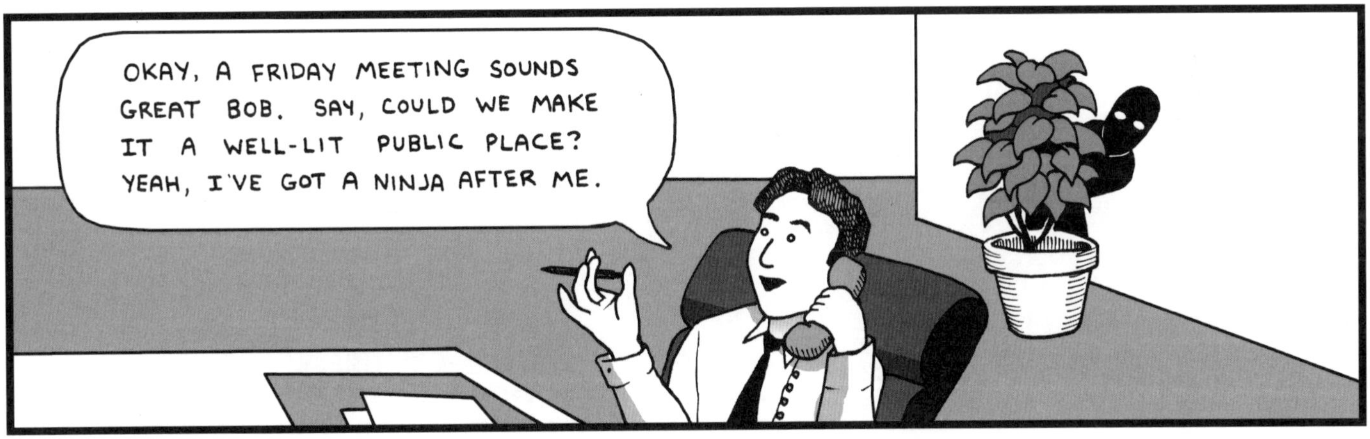
OKAY, A FRIDAY MEETING SOUNDS GREAT BOB. SAY, COULD WE MAKE IT A WELL-LIT PUBLIC PLACE? YEAH, I'VE GOT A NINJA AFTER ME.

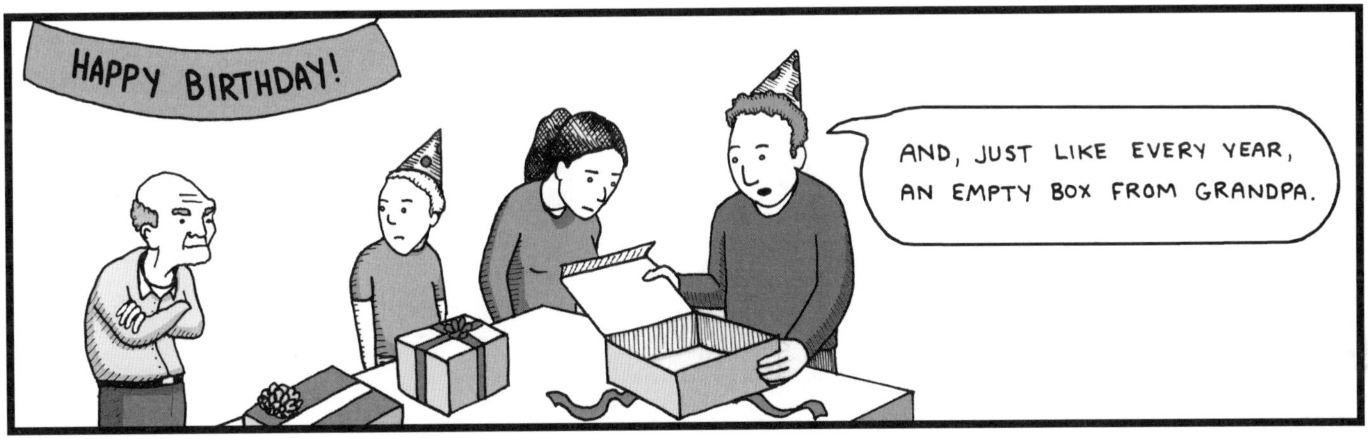
HAPPY BIRTHDAY!
AND, JUST LIKE EVERY YEAR, AN EMPTY BOX FROM GRANDPA.

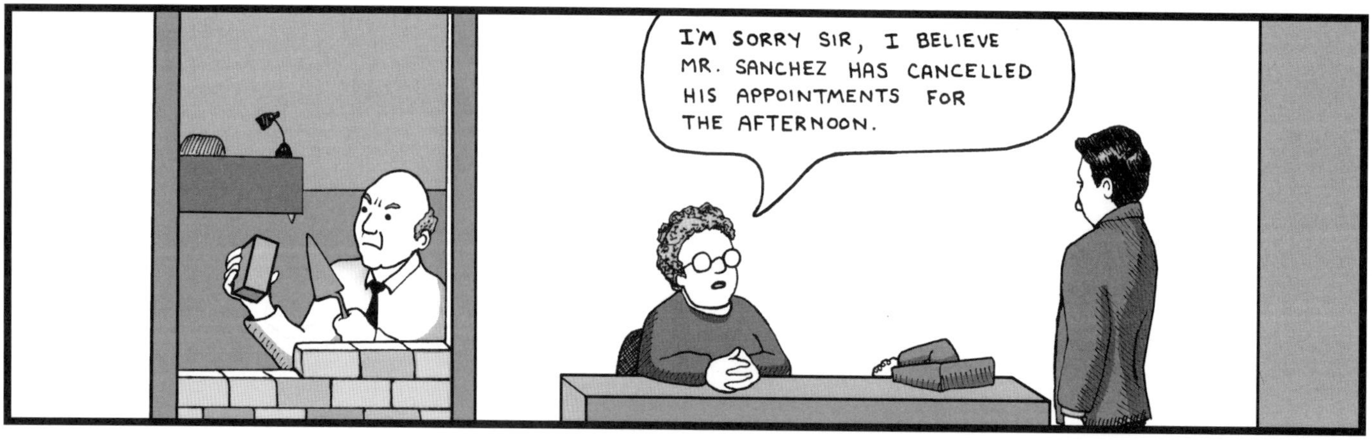
I'M SORRY SIR, I BELIEVE MR. SANCHEZ HAS CANCELLED HIS APPOINTMENTS FOR THE AFTERNOON.

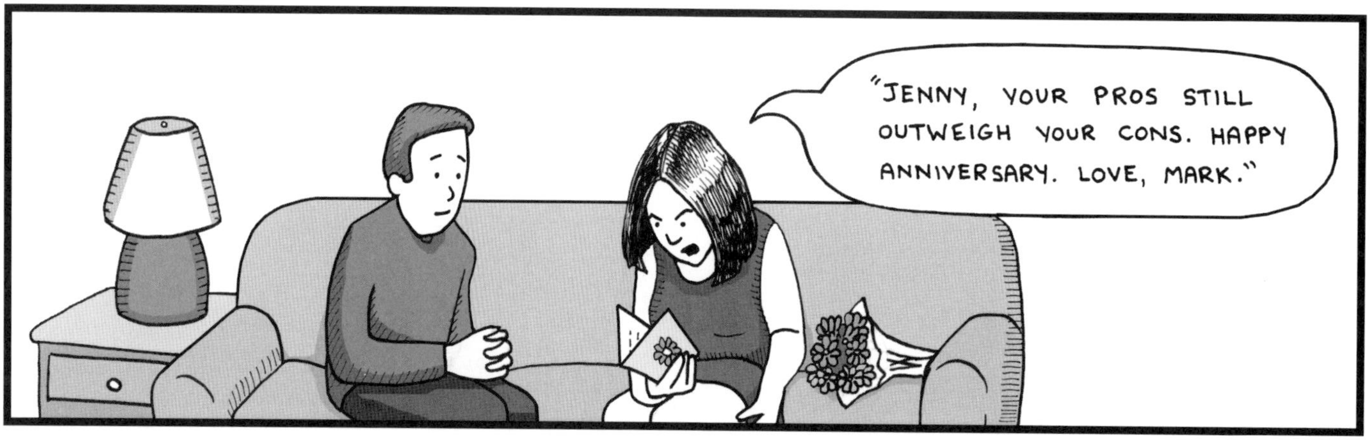
"JENNY, YOUR PROS STILL OUTWEIGH YOUR CONS. HAPPY ANNIVERSARY. LOVE, MARK."

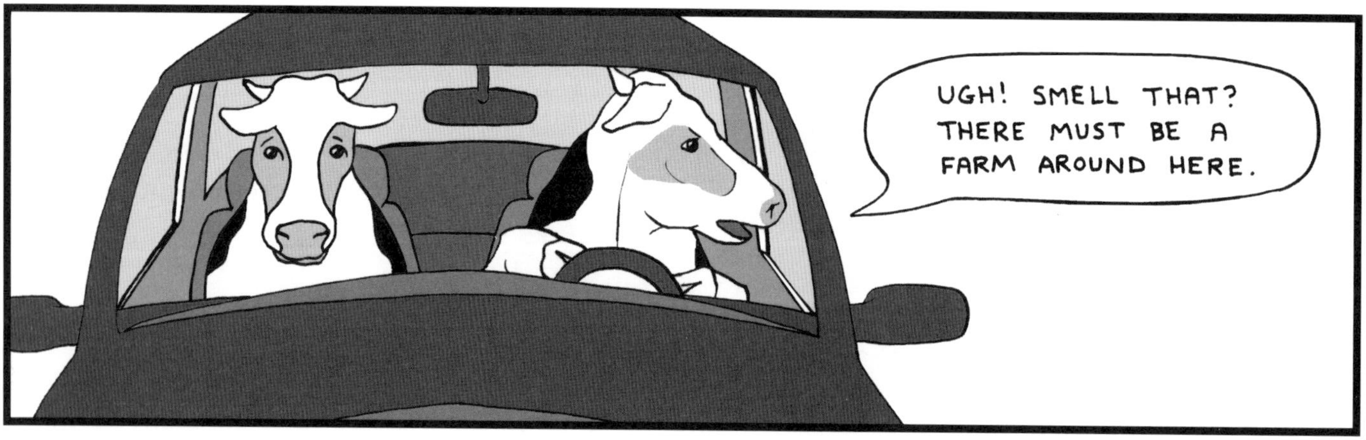
UGH! SMELL THAT? THERE MUST BE A FARM AROUND HERE.

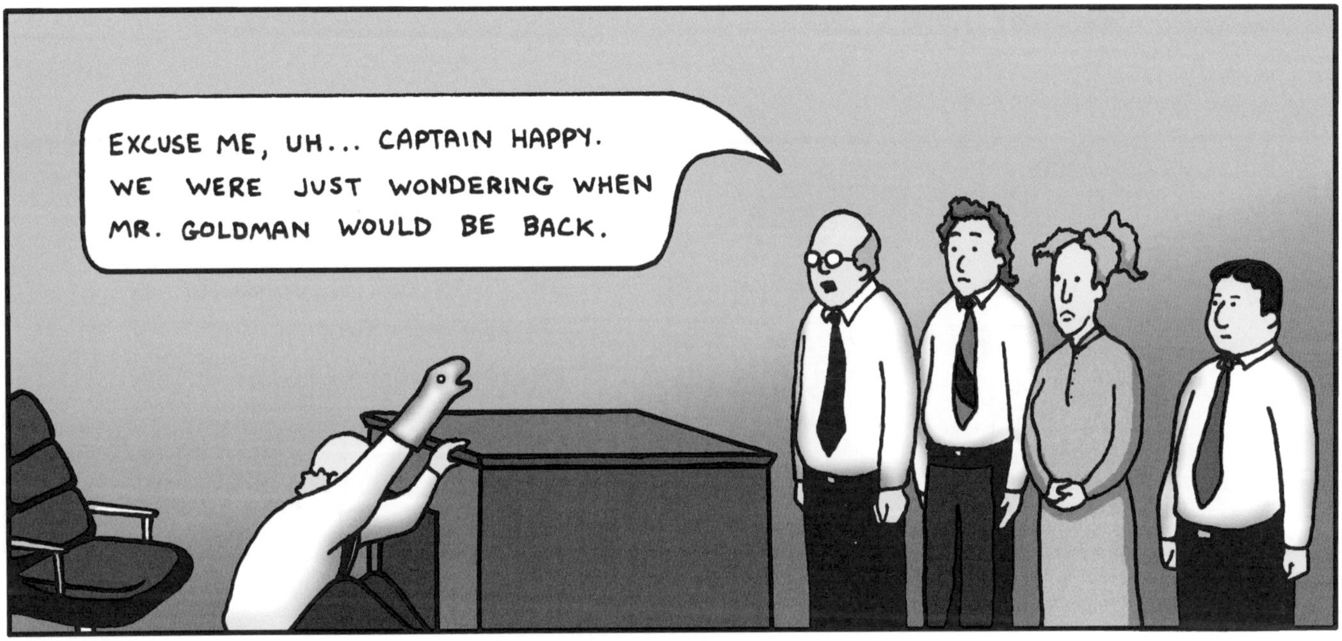
EXCUSE ME, UH... CAPTAIN HAPPY. WE WERE JUST WONDERING WHEN MR. GOLDMAN WOULD BE BACK.

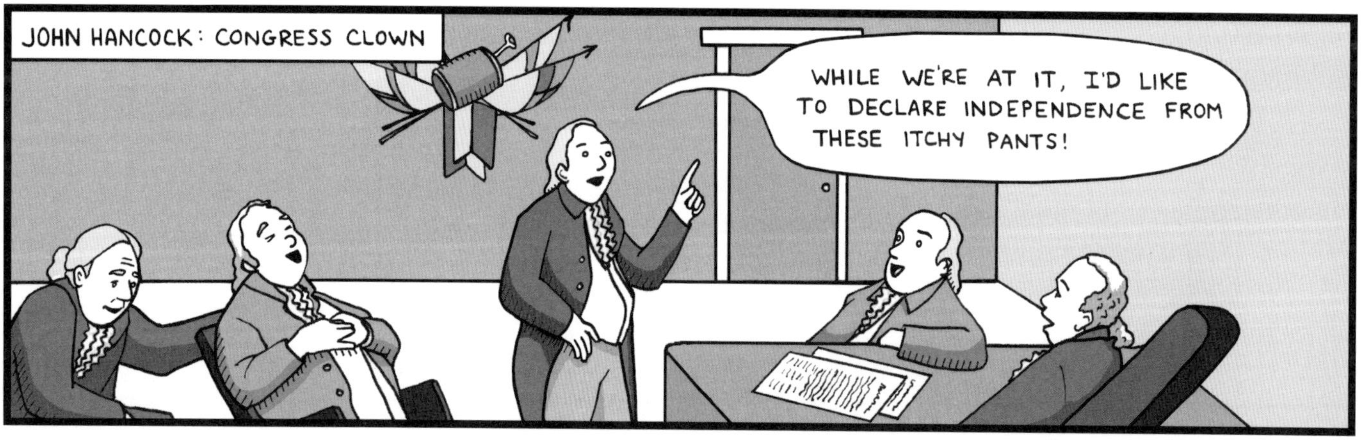
JOHN HANCOCK: CONGRESS CLOWN
WHILE WE'RE AT IT, I'D LIKE TO DECLARE INDEPENDENCE FROM THESE ITCHY PANTS!

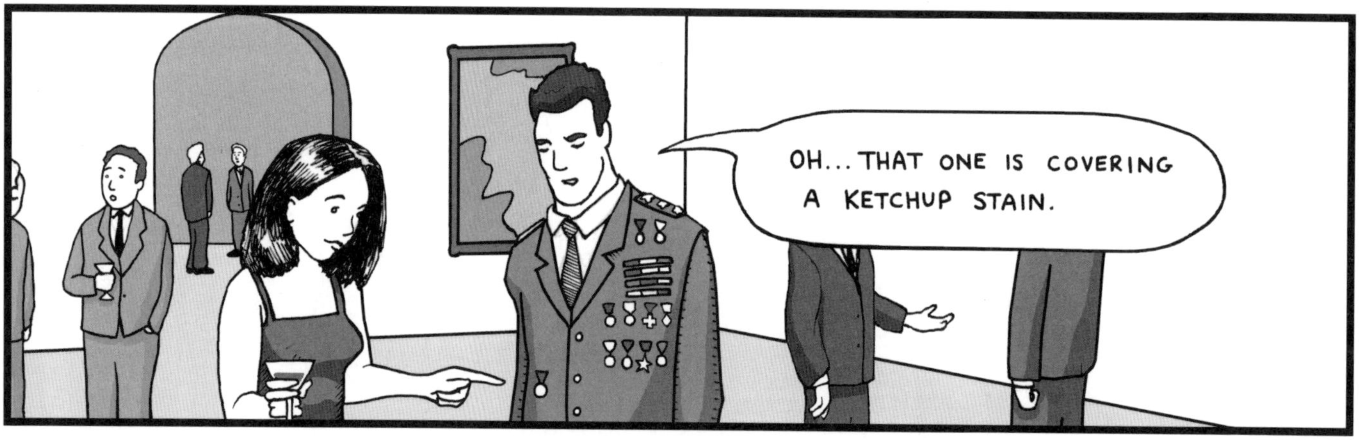
OH... THAT ONE IS COVERING A KETCHUP STAIN.

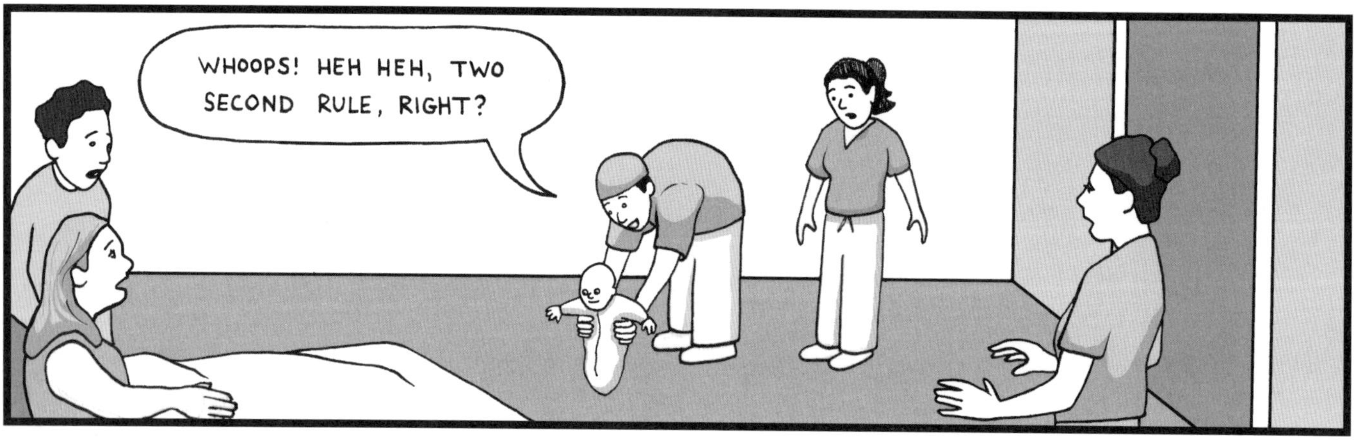
WHOOPS! HEH HEH, TWO SECOND RULE, RIGHT?

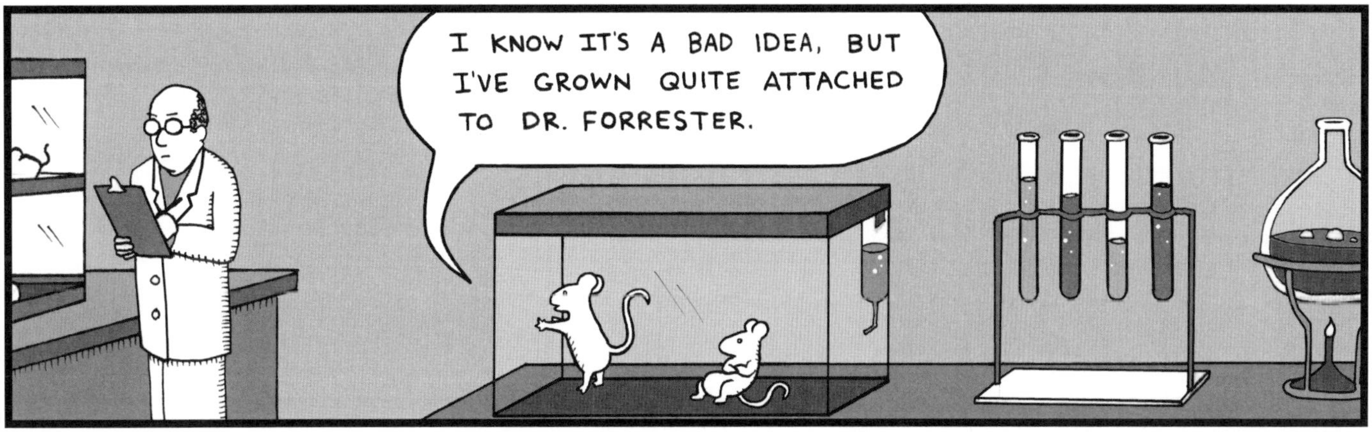
I KNOW IT'S A BAD IDEA, BUT I'VE GROWN QUITE ATTACHED TO DR. FORRESTER.

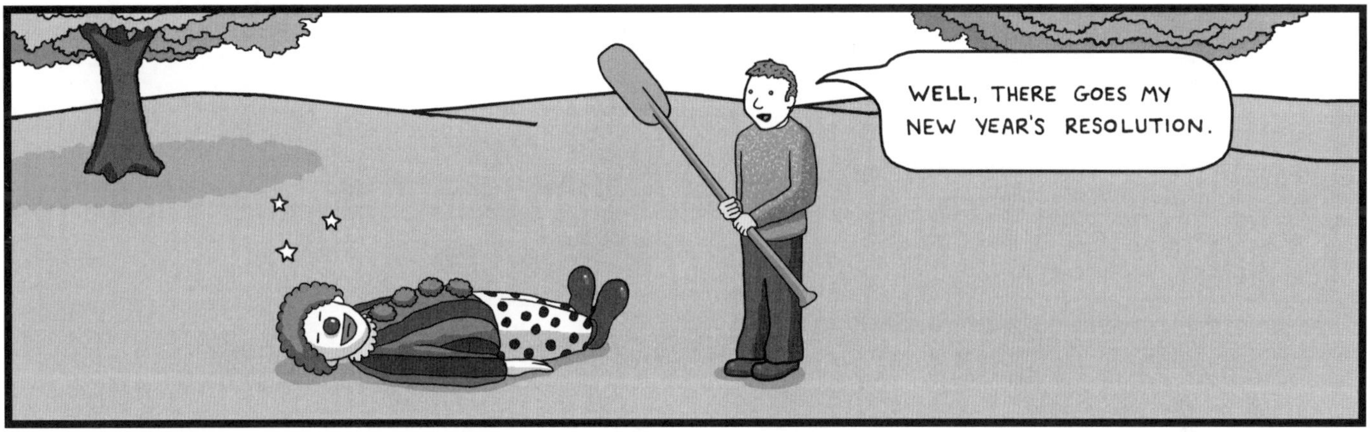
WELL, THERE GOES MY NEW YEAR'S RESOLUTION.

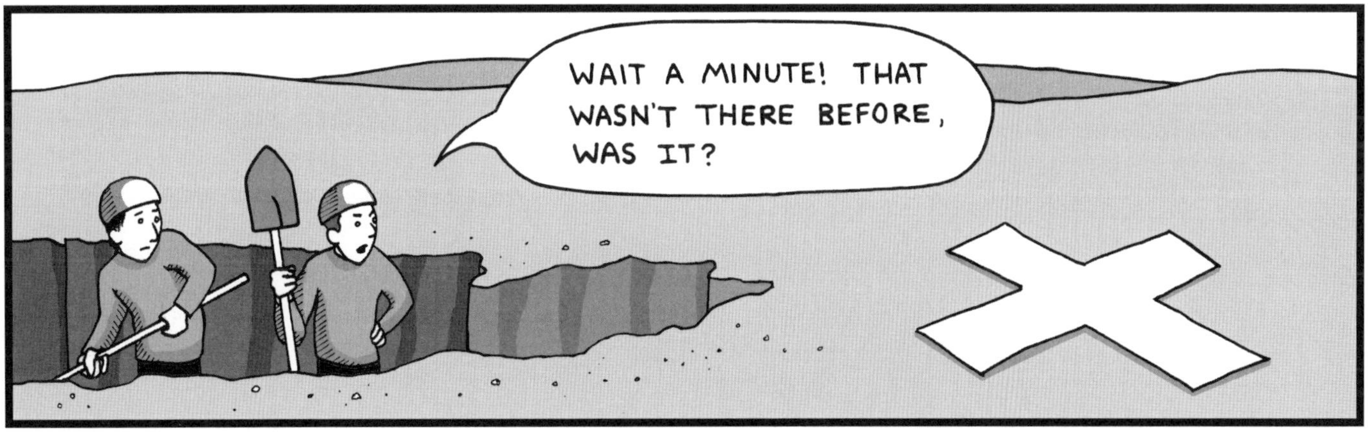
WAIT A MINUTE! THAT WASN'T THERE BEFORE, WAS IT?

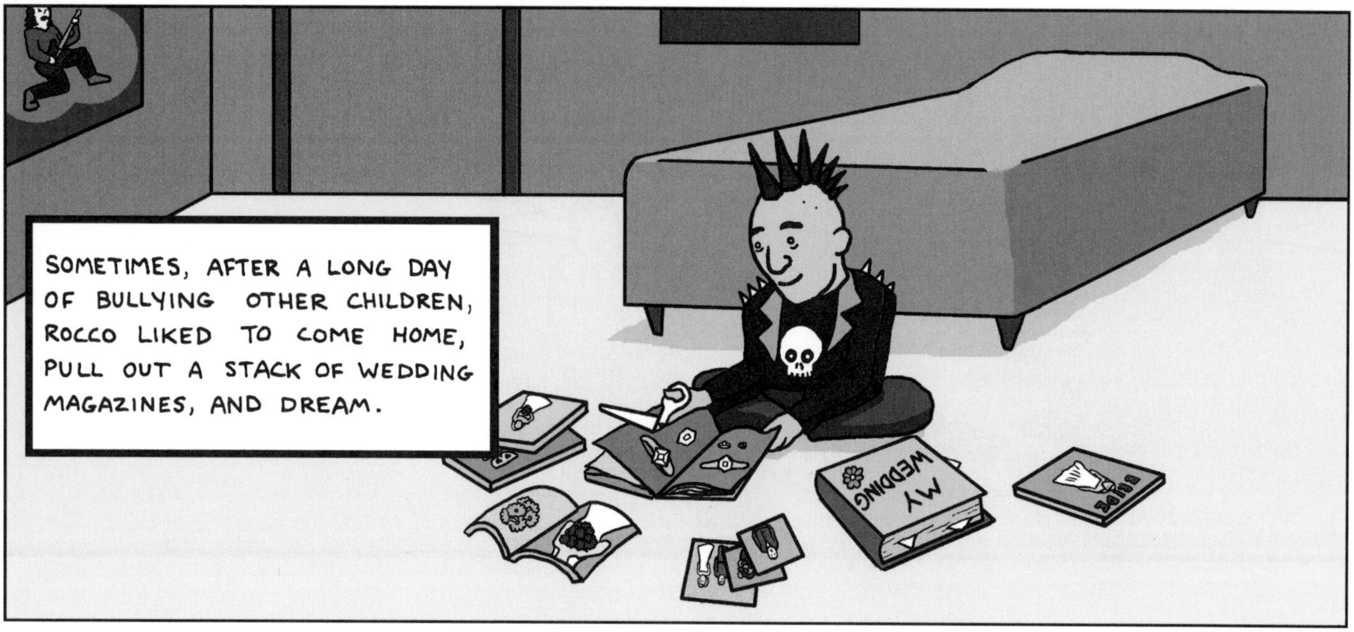
SOMETIMES, AFTER A LONG DAY OF BULLYING OTHER CHILDREN, ROCCO LIKED TO COME HOME, PULL OUT A STACK OF WEDDING MAGAZINES, AND DREAM.
MY WEDDING
BRIDE

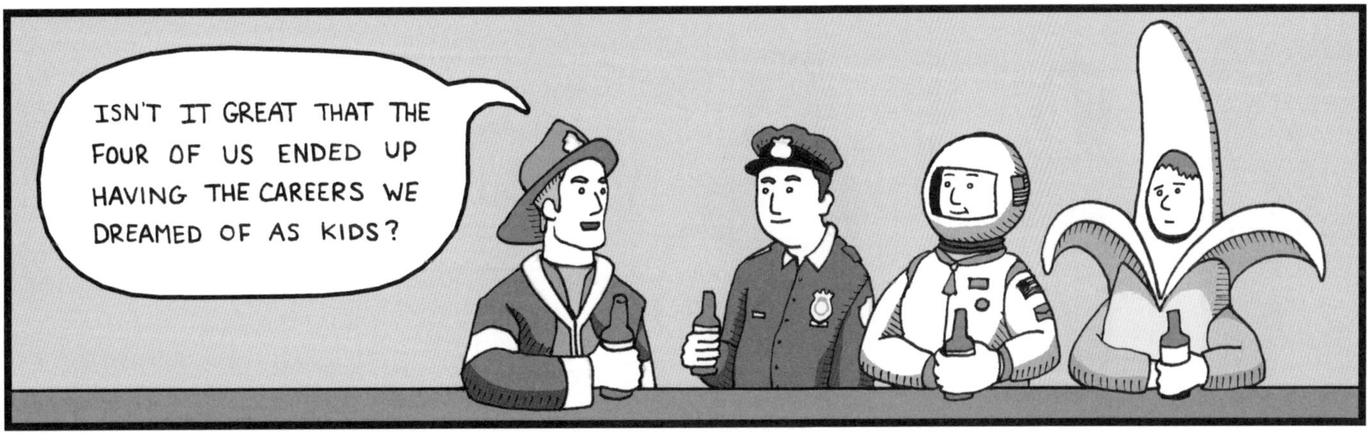
ISN'T IT GREAT THAT THE FOUR OF US ENDED UP HAVING THE CAREERS WE DREAMED OF AS KIDS?

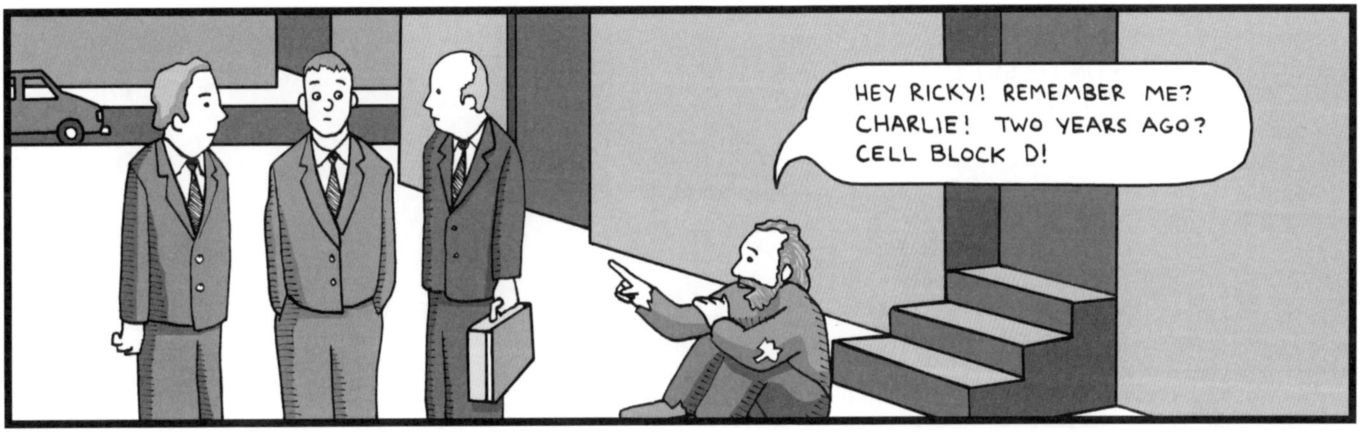
HEY RICKY! REMEMBER ME? CHARLIE! TWO YEARS AGO? CELL BLOCK D!

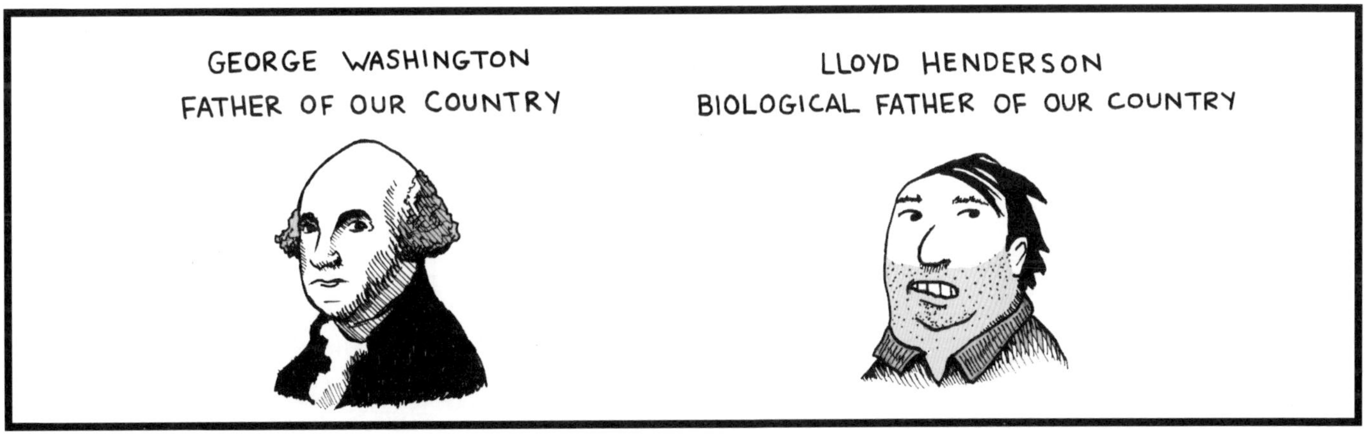
GEORGE WASHINGTON
FATHER OF OUR COUNTRY
LLOYD HENDERSON
BIOLOGICAL FATHER OF OUR COUNTRY

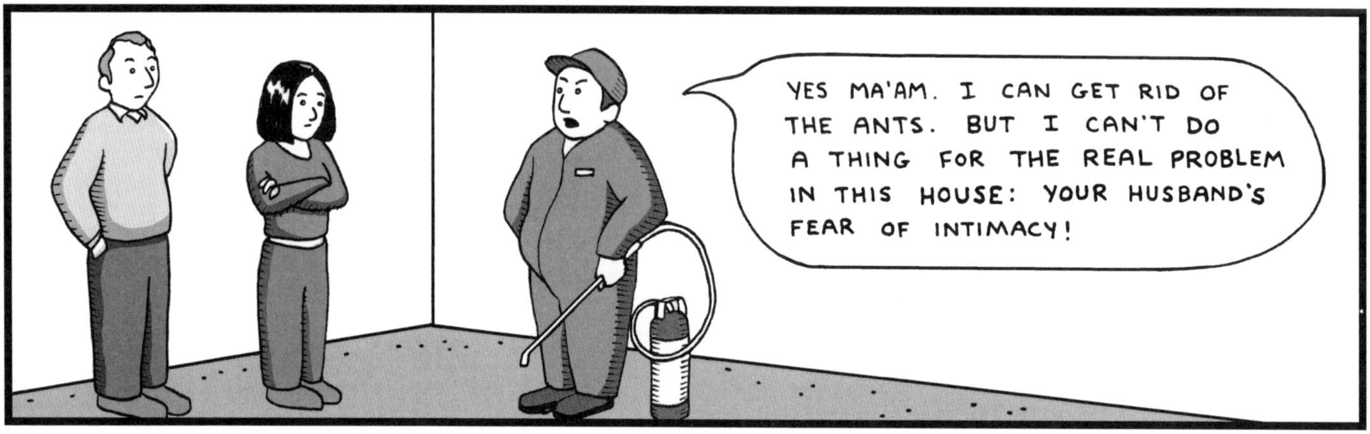
YES MA'AM. I CAN GET RID OF THE ANTS. BUT I CAN'T DO A THING FOR THE REAL PROBLEM IN THIS HOUSE: YOUR HUSBAND'S FEAR OF INTIMACY!

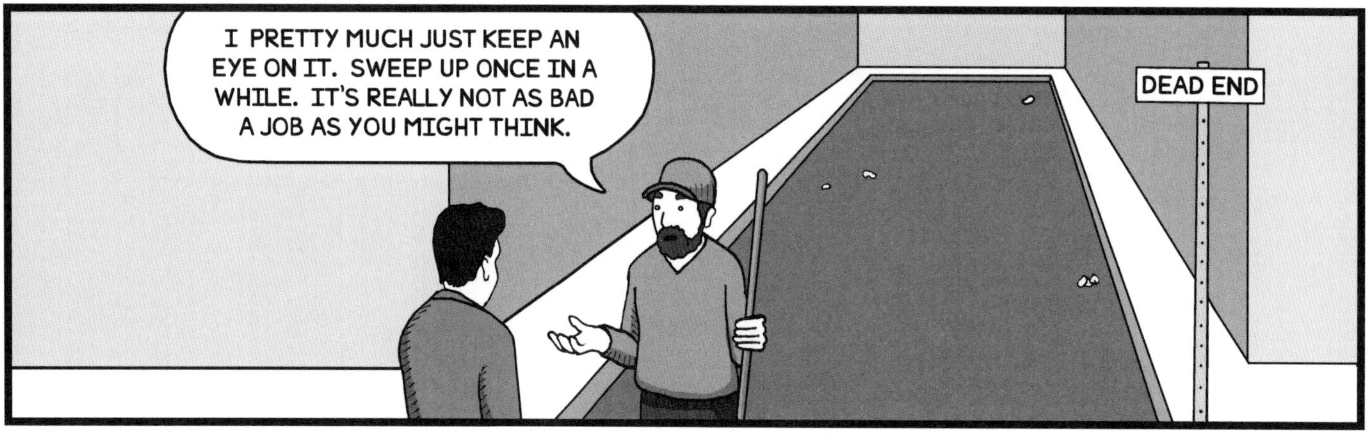
I PRETTY MUCH JUST KEEP AN EYE ON IT. SWEEP UP ONCE IN A WHILE. IT'S REALLY NOT AS BAD A JOB AS YOU MIGHT THINK.
DEAD END

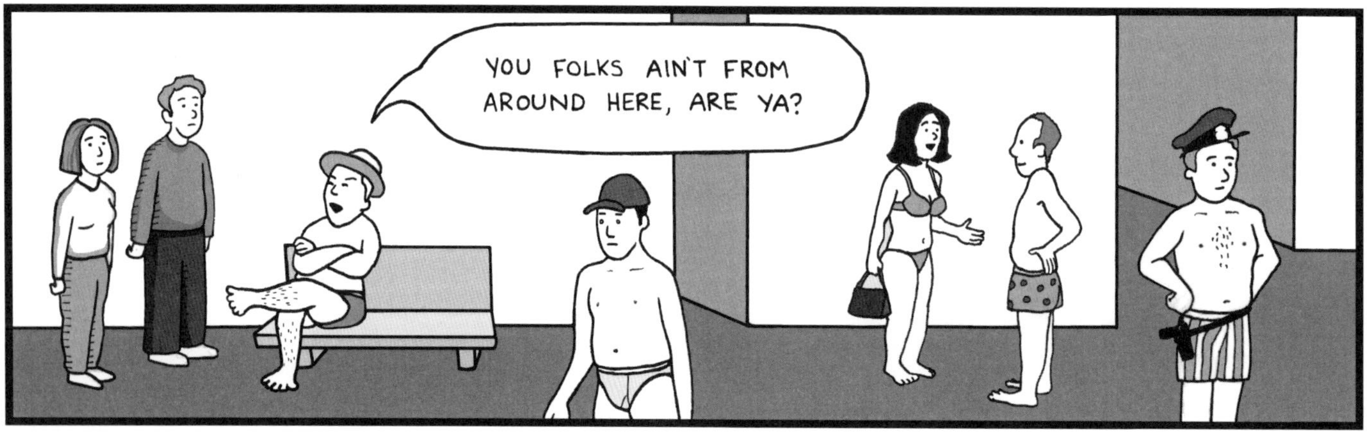
YOU FOLKS AIN'T FROM AROUND HERE, ARE YA?

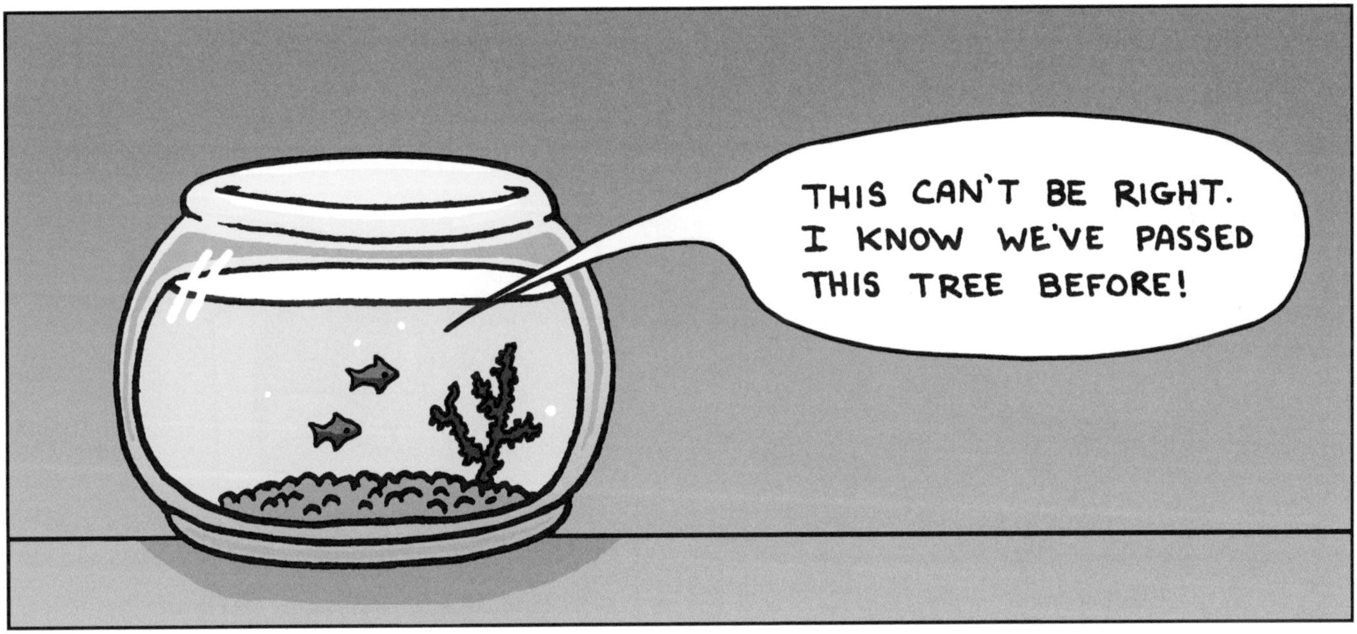
THIS CAN'T BE RIGHT. I KNOW WE'VE PASSED THIS TREE BEFORE!

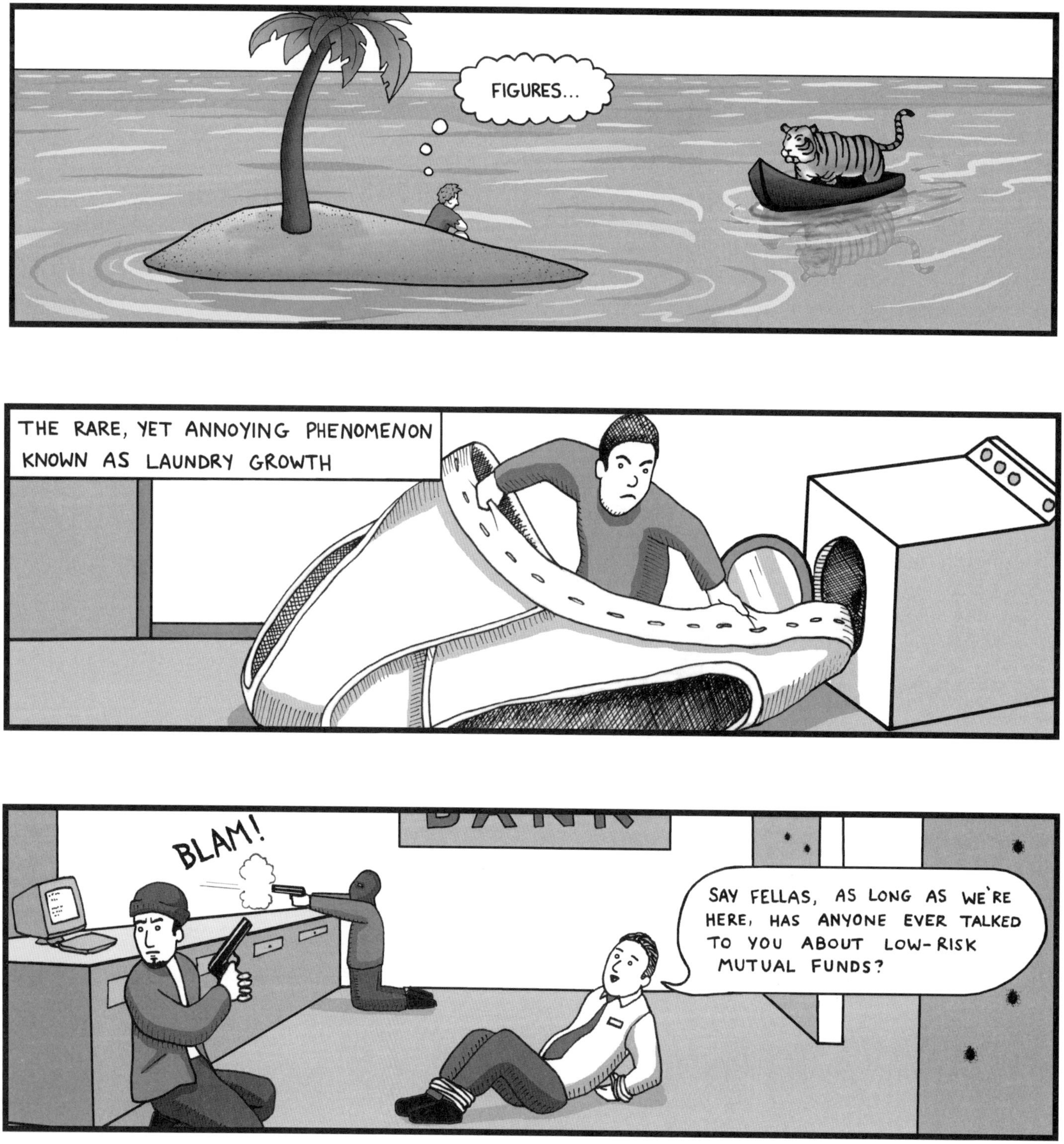
FIGURES...
THE RARE, YET ANNOYING PHENOMENON KNOWN AS LAUNDRY GROWTH
BLAM!
SAY FELLAS, AS LONG AS WE'RE HERE, HAS ANYONE EVER TALKED TO YOU ABOUT LOW-RISK MUTUAL FUNDS?

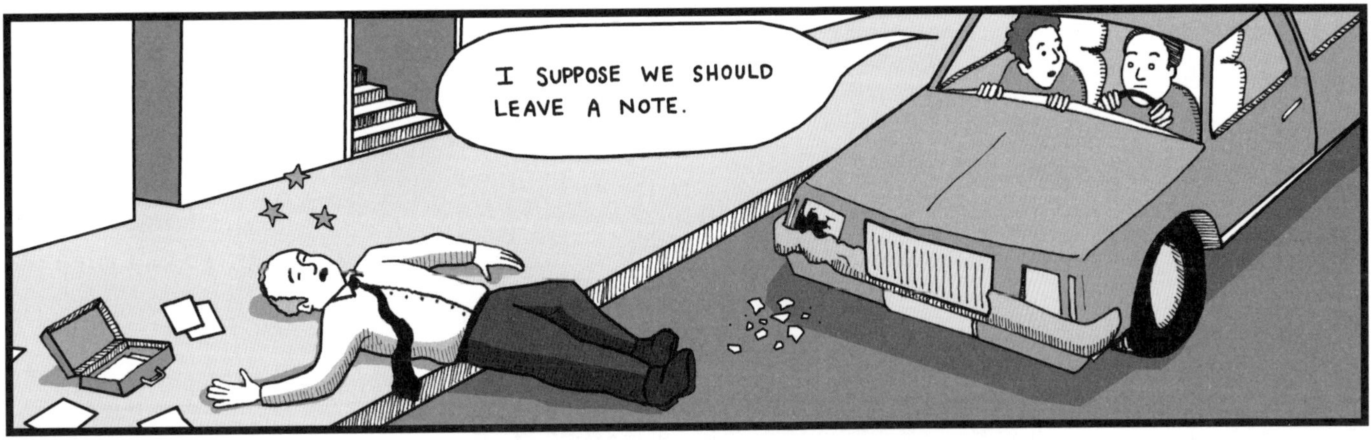
I SUPPOSE WE SHOULD LEAVE A NOTE.

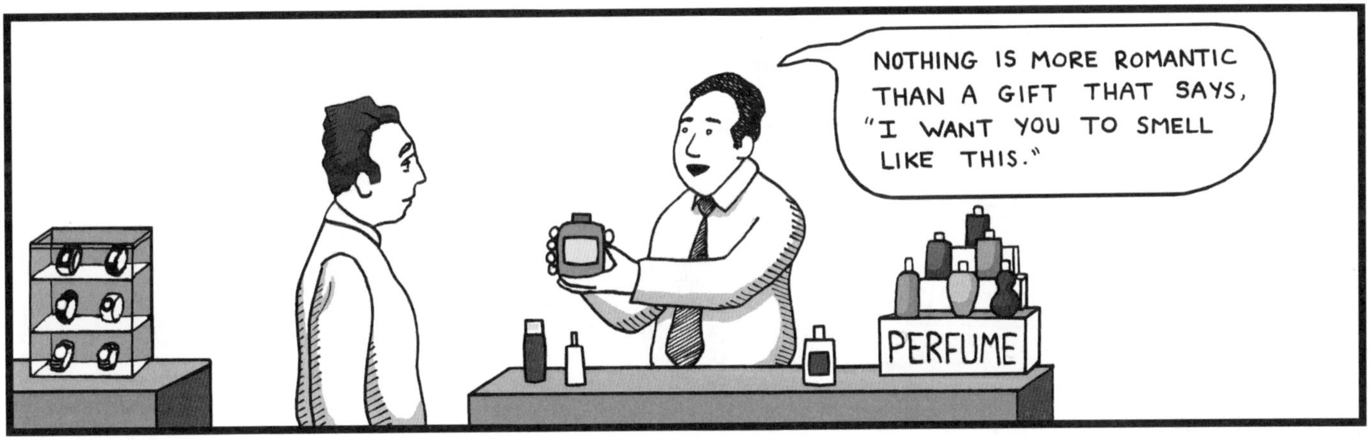
NOTHING IS MORE ROMANTIC THAN A GIFT THAT SAYS, "I WANT YOU TO SMELL LIKE THIS."
PERFUME

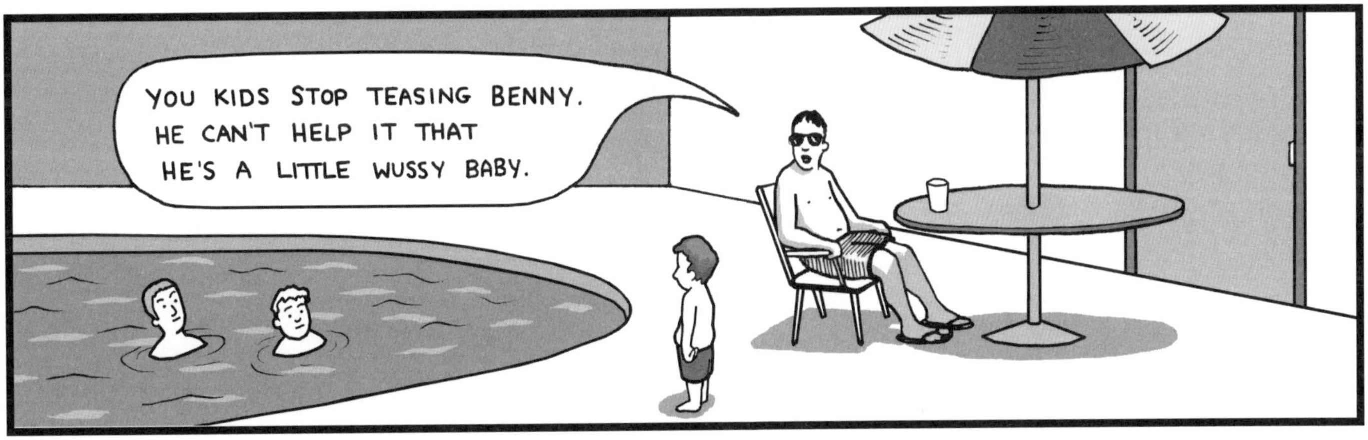
YOU KIDS STOP TEASING BENNY. HE CAN'T HELP IT THAT HE'S A LITTLE WUSSY BABY.

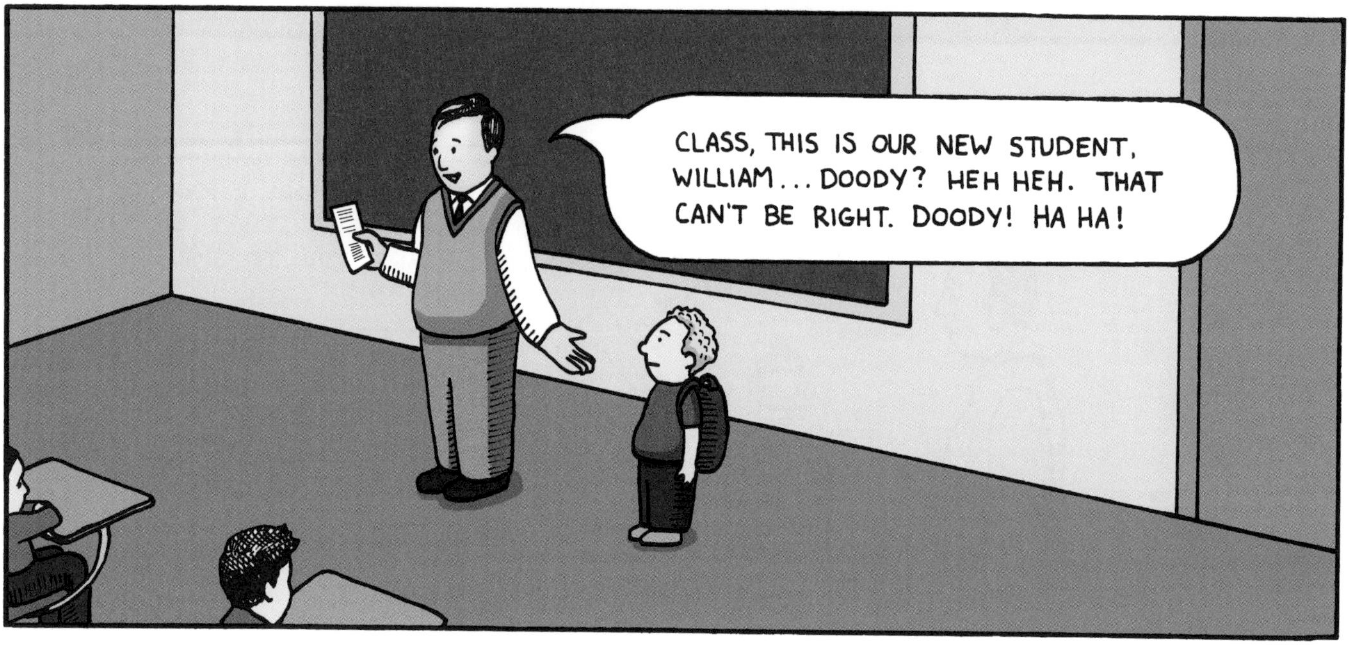
CLASS, THIS IS OUR NEW STUDENT, WILLIAM... DOODY? HEH HEH. THAT CAN'T BE RIGHT. DOODY! HA HA!

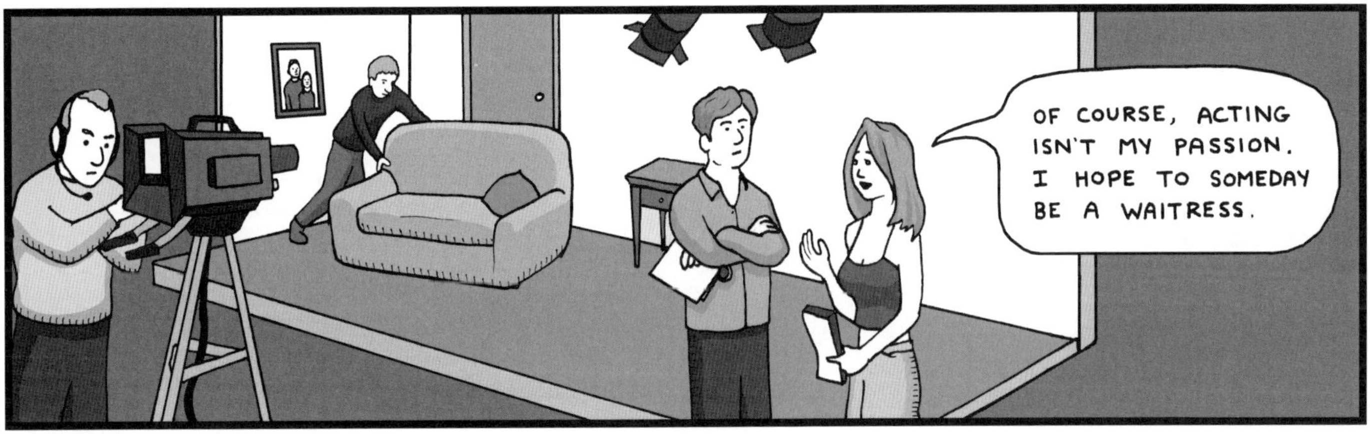
OF COURSE, ACTING ISN'T MY PASSION. I HOPE TO SOMEDAY BE A WAITRESS.

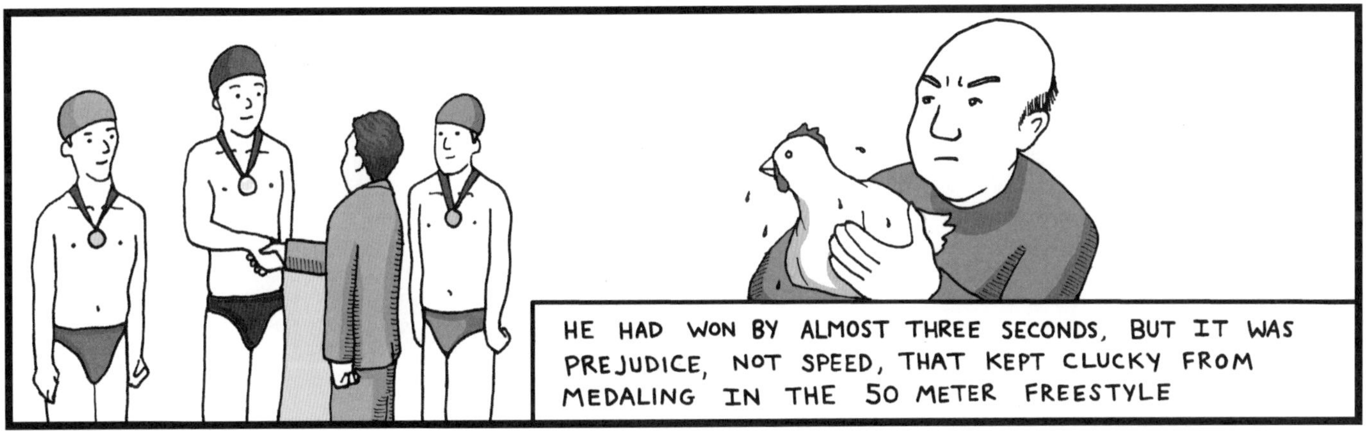
HE HAD WON BY ALMOST THREE SECONDS, BUT IT WAS PREJUDICE, NOT SPEED, THAT KEPT CLUCKY FROM MEDALING IN THE 50 METER FREESTYLE

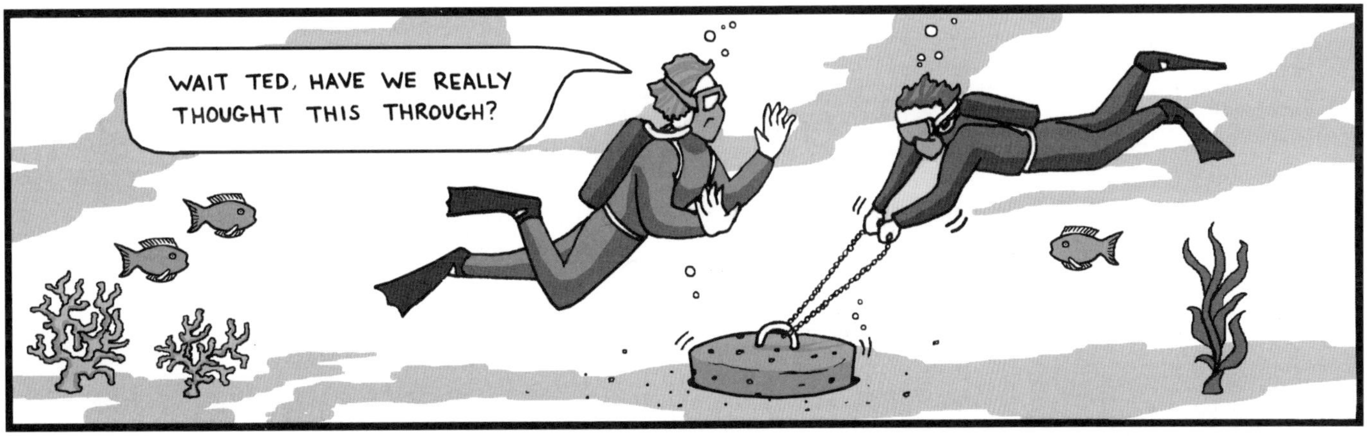
WAIT TED, HAVE WE REALLY THOUGHT THIS THROUGH?

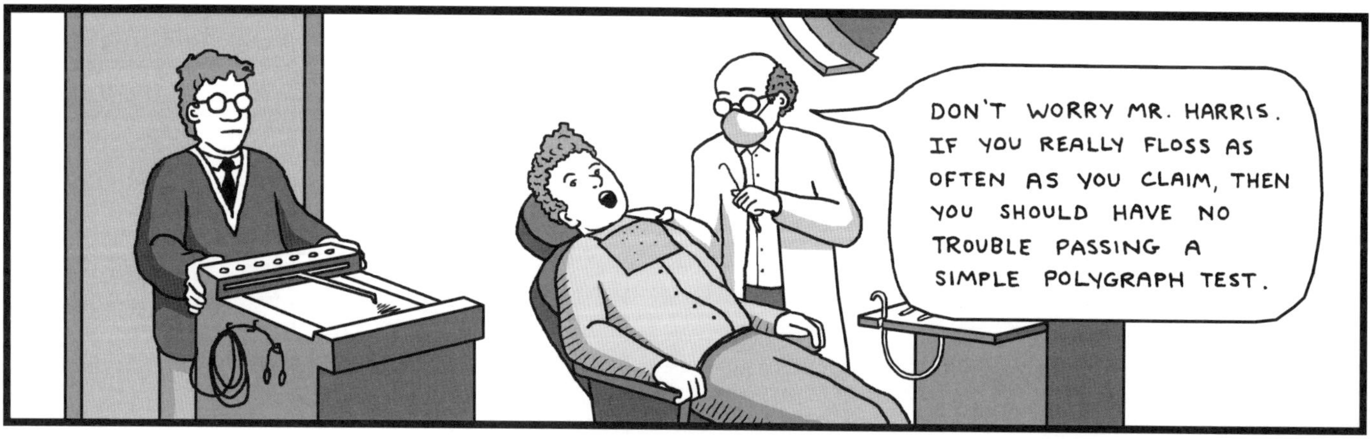
DON'T WORRY MR. HARRIS. IF YOU REALLY FLOSS AS OFTEN AS YOU CLAIM, THEN YOU SHOULD HAVE NO TROUBLE PASSING A SIMPLE POLYGRAPH TEST.

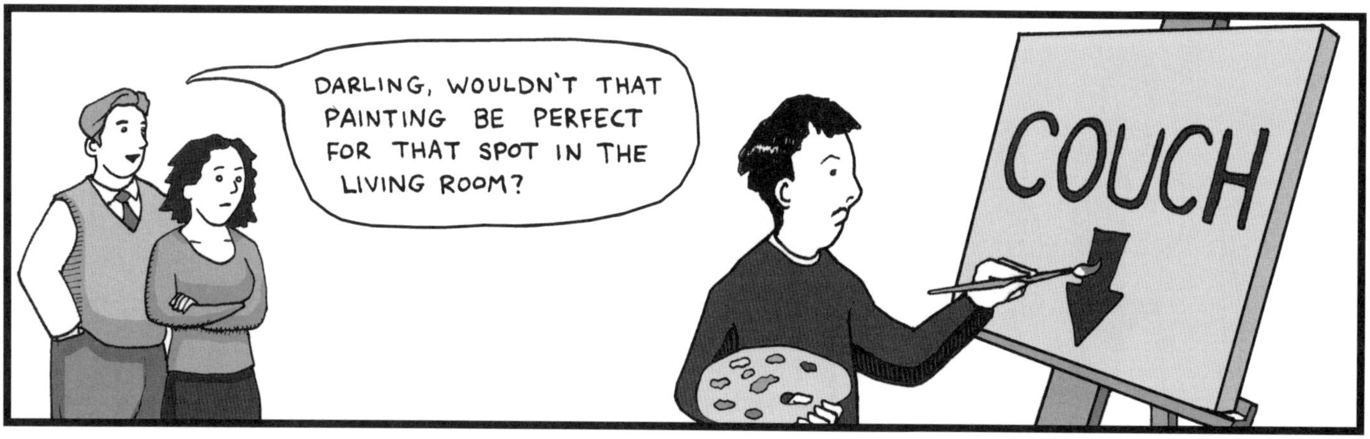
DARLING, WOULDN'T THAT PAINTING BE PERFECT FOR THAT SPOT IN THE LIVING ROOM?
COUCH

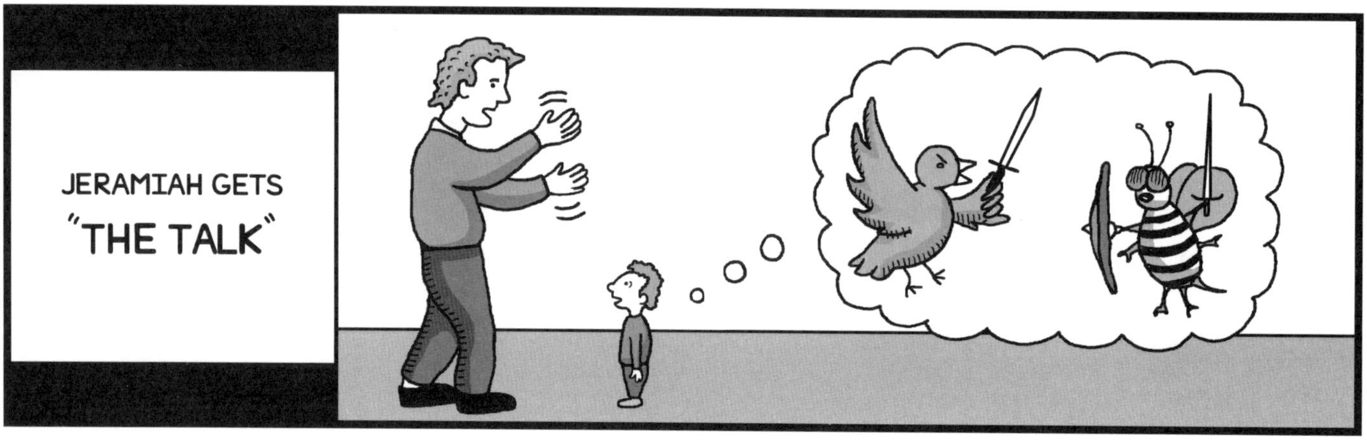
JERAMIAH GETS "THE TALK"

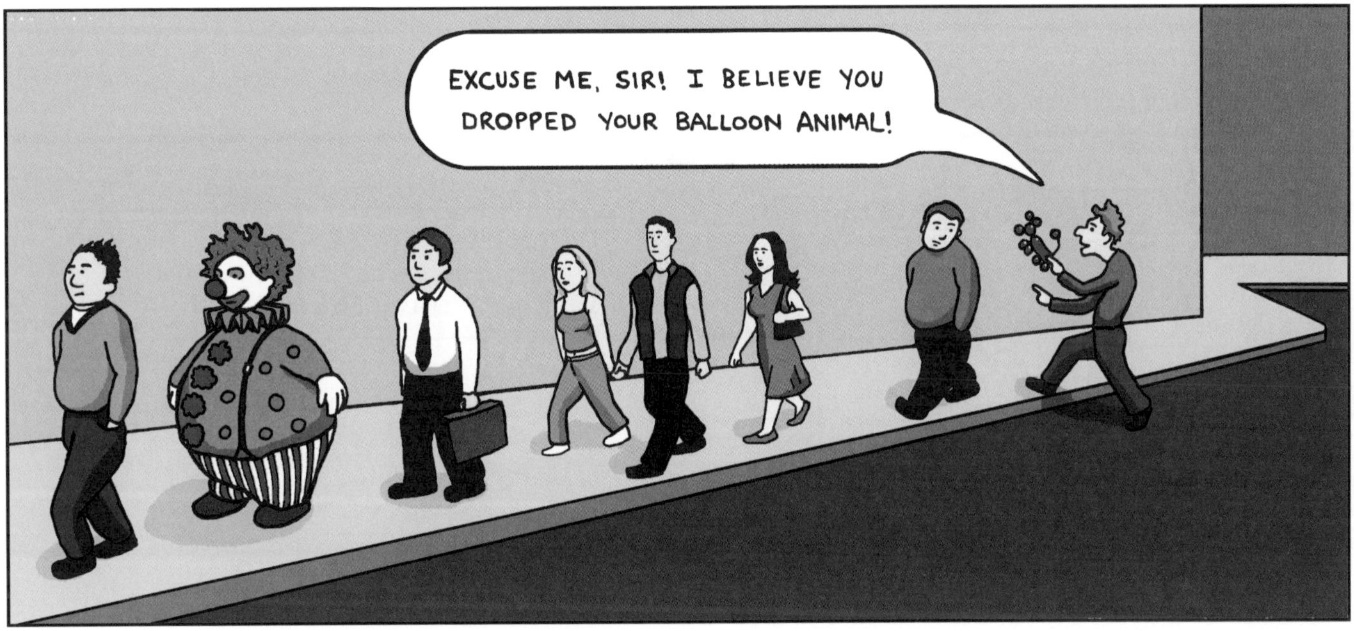
EXCUSE ME, SIR! I BELIEVE YOU DROPPED YOUR BALLOON ANIMAL!

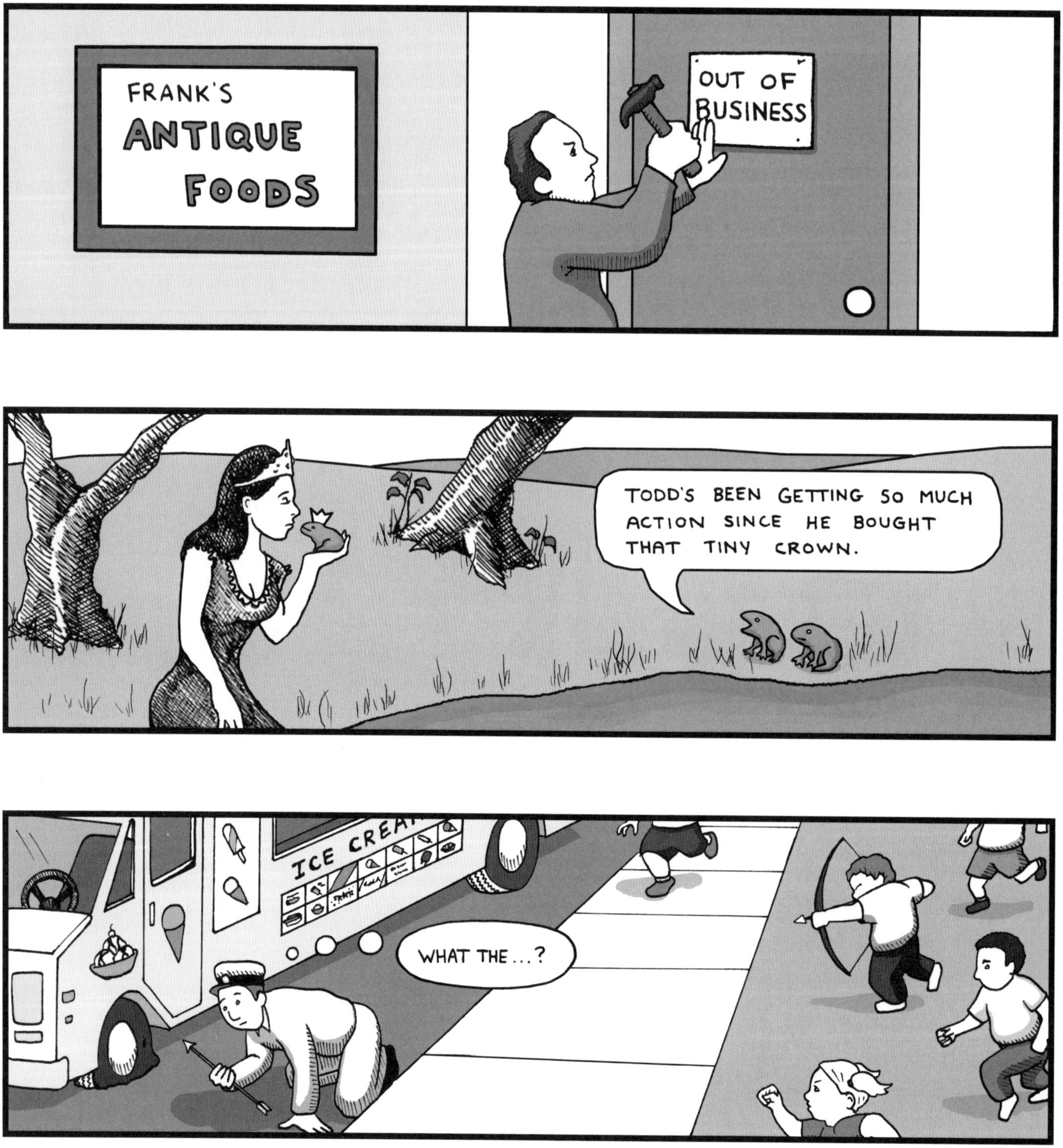
FRANK'S
ANTIQUE
FOODS
OUT OF
BUSINESS
TODD'S BEEN GETTING SO MUCH ACTION SINCE HE BOUGHT THAT TINY CROWN.
ICE CREA
WHAT THE . . . ?

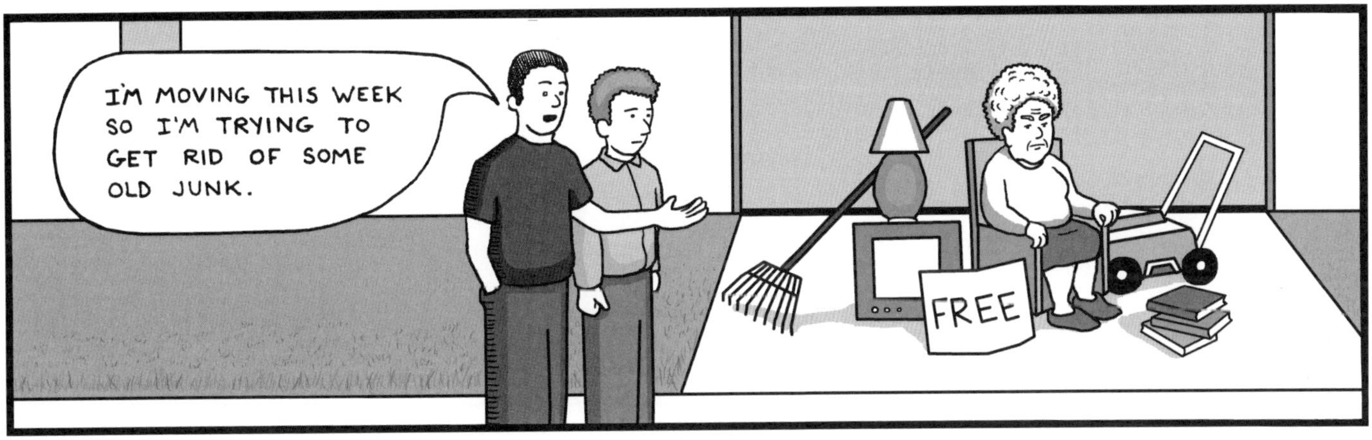
I'M MOVING THIS WEEK SO I'M TRYING TO GET RID OF SOME OLD JUNK.
FREE

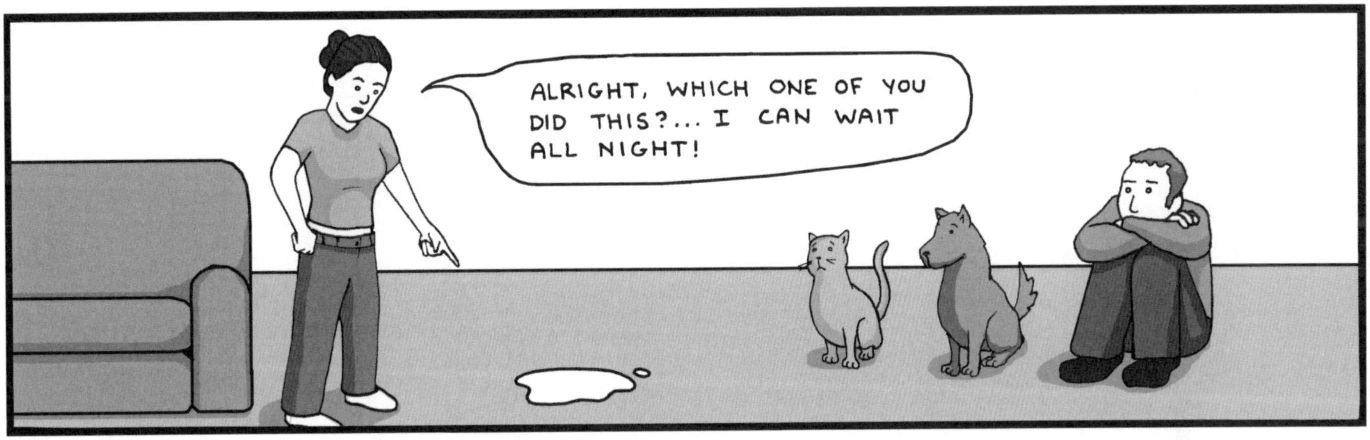
ALRIGHT, WHICH ONE OF YOU DID THIS?... I CAN WAIT ALL NIGHT!

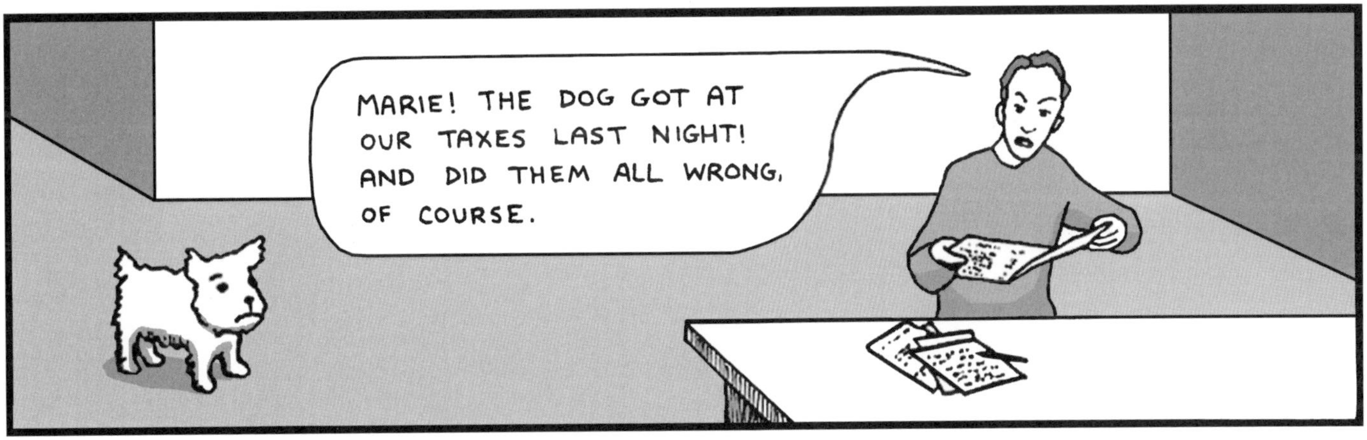
MARIE! THE DOG GOT AT OUR TAXES LAST NIGHT! AND DID THEM ALL WRONG, OF COURSE.

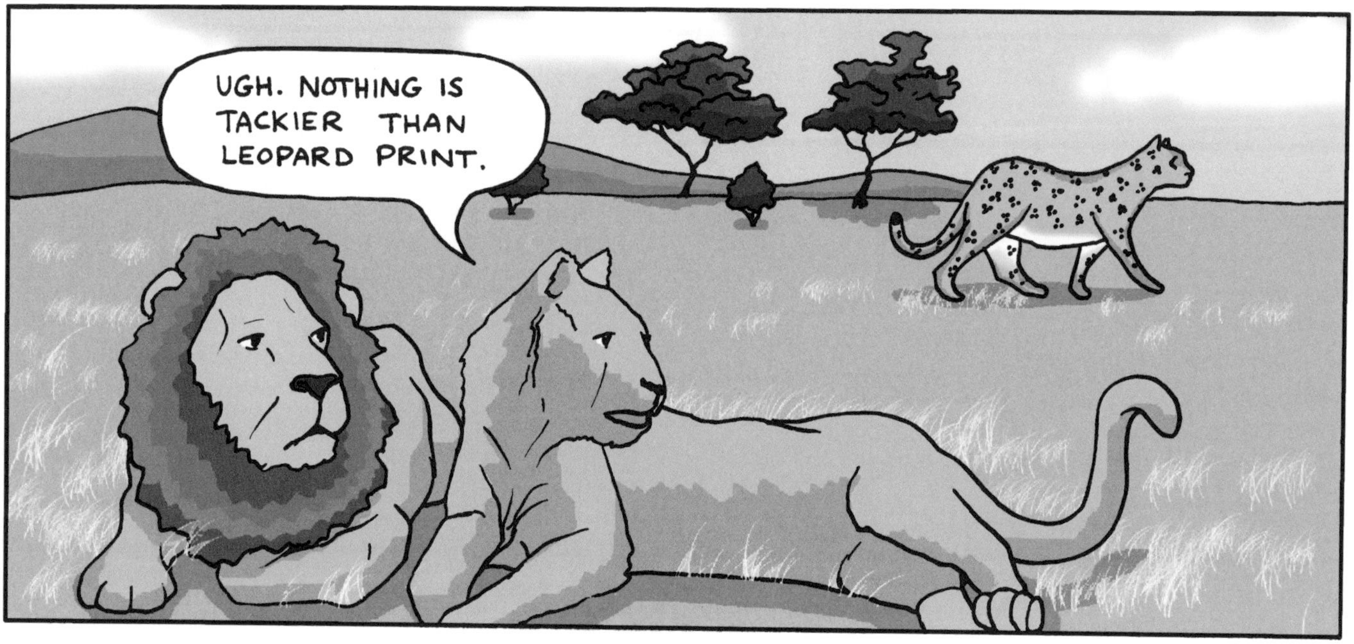
UGH. NOTHING IS TACKIER THAN LEOPARD PRINT.

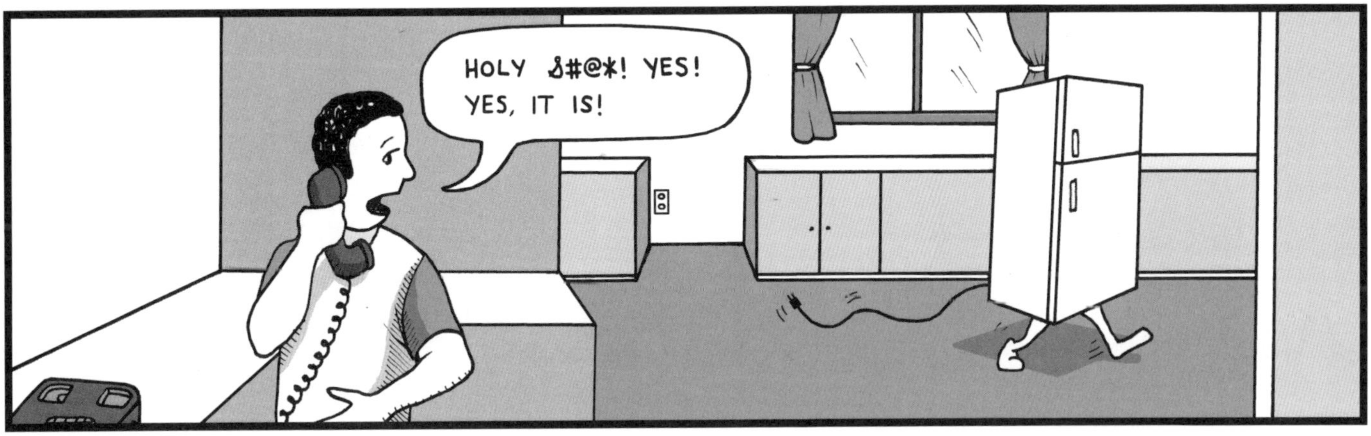
HOLY $#@*! YES! YES, IT IS!

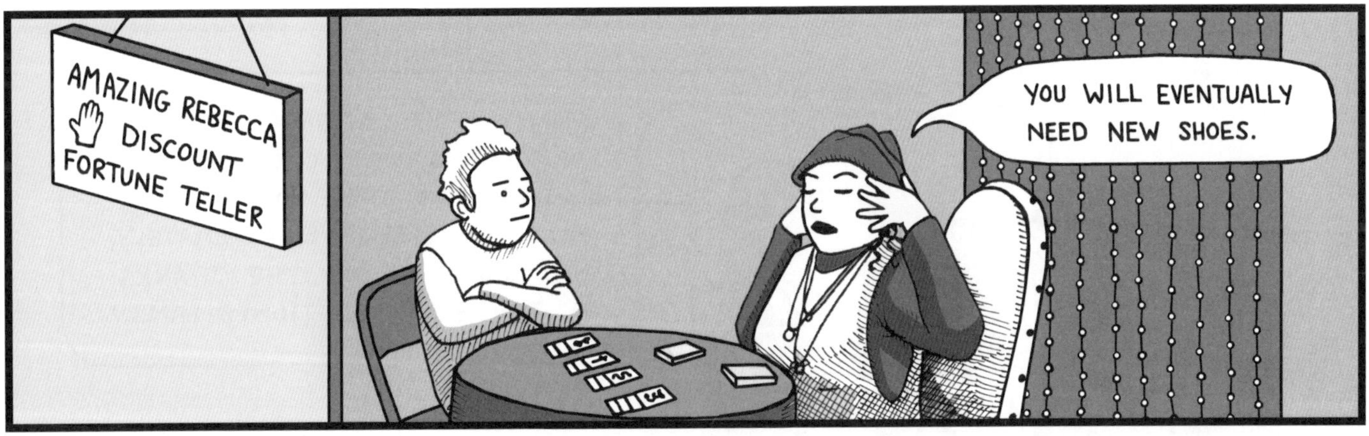
AMAZING REBECCA DISCOUNT FORTUNE TELLER
YOU WILL EVENTUALLY NEED NEW SHOES.

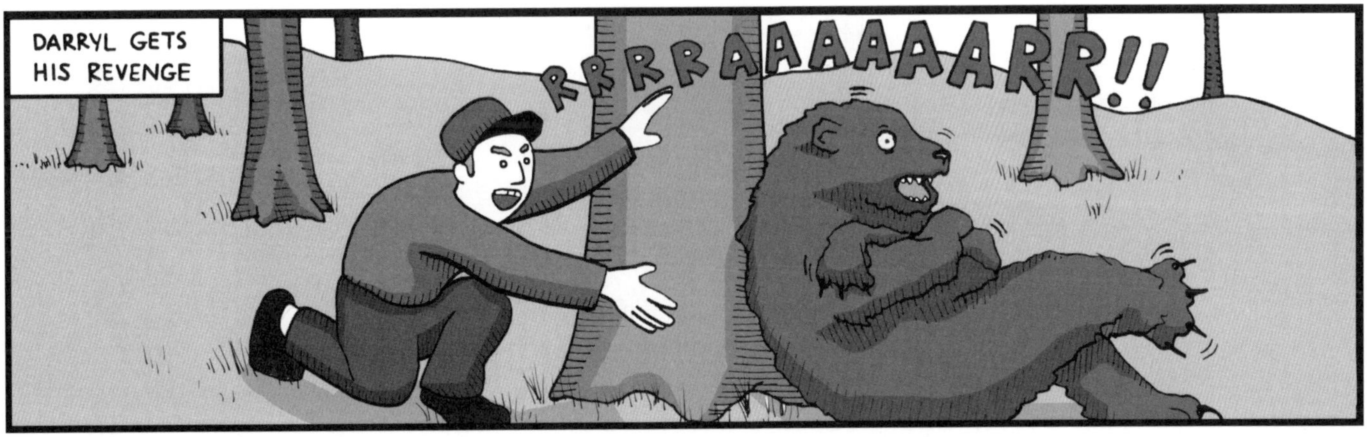
DARRYL GETS HIS REVENGE
RRRRAAAAAAARR!!

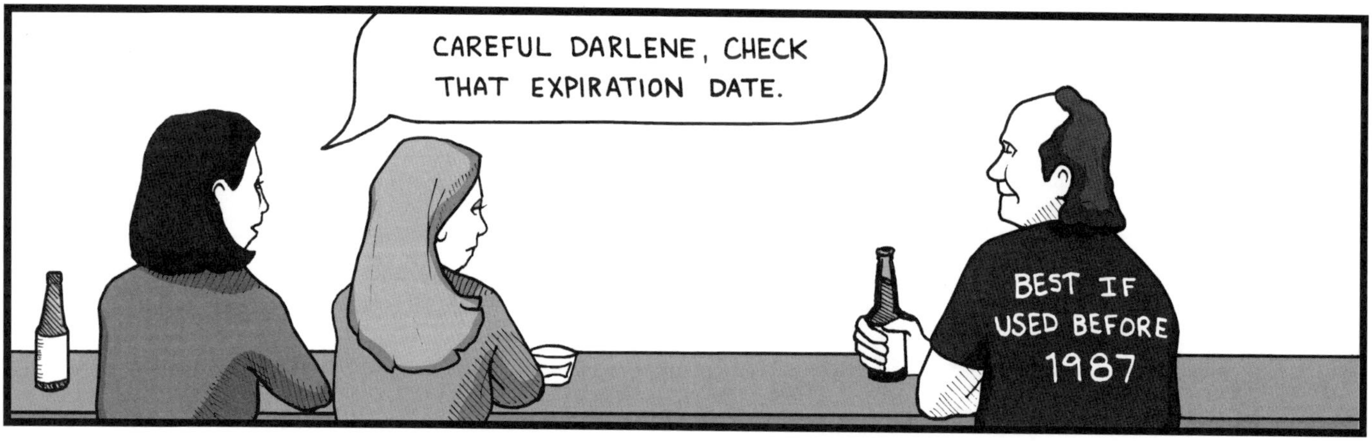
CAREFUL DARLENE, CHECK THAT EXPIRATION DATE.
BEST IF USED BEFORE 1987

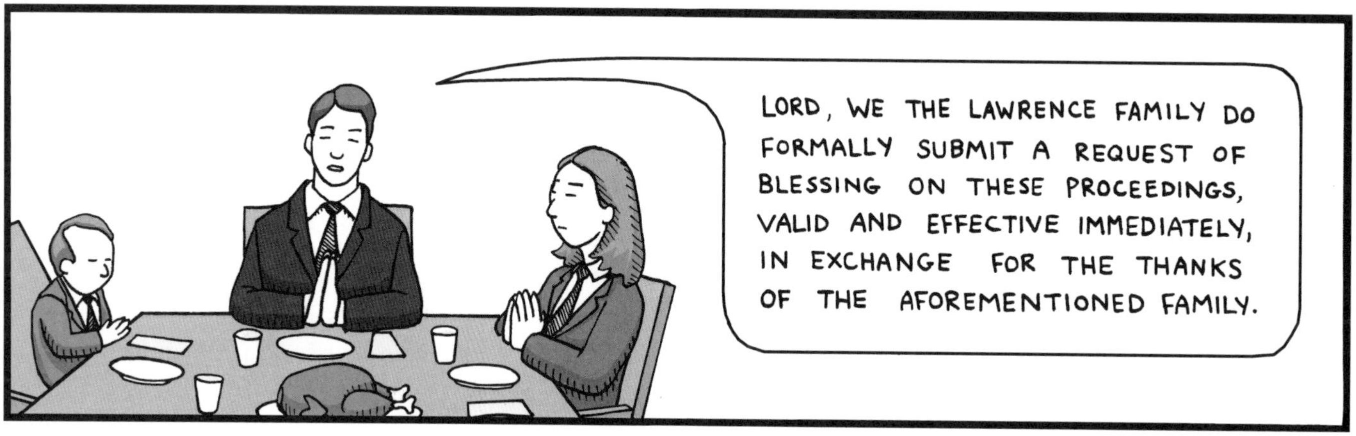
LORD, WE THE LAWRENCE FAMILY DO FORMALLY SUBMIT A REQUEST OF BLESSING ON THESE PROCEEDINGS, VALID AND EFFECTIVE IMMEDIATELY, IN EXCHANGE FOR THE THANKS OF THE AFOREMENTIONED FAMILY.

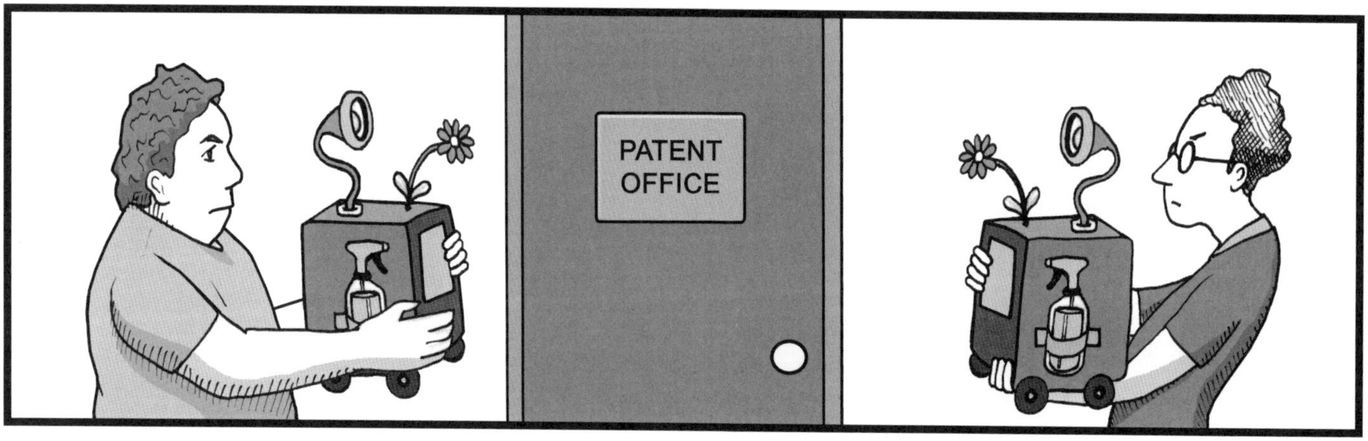
PATENT OFFICE

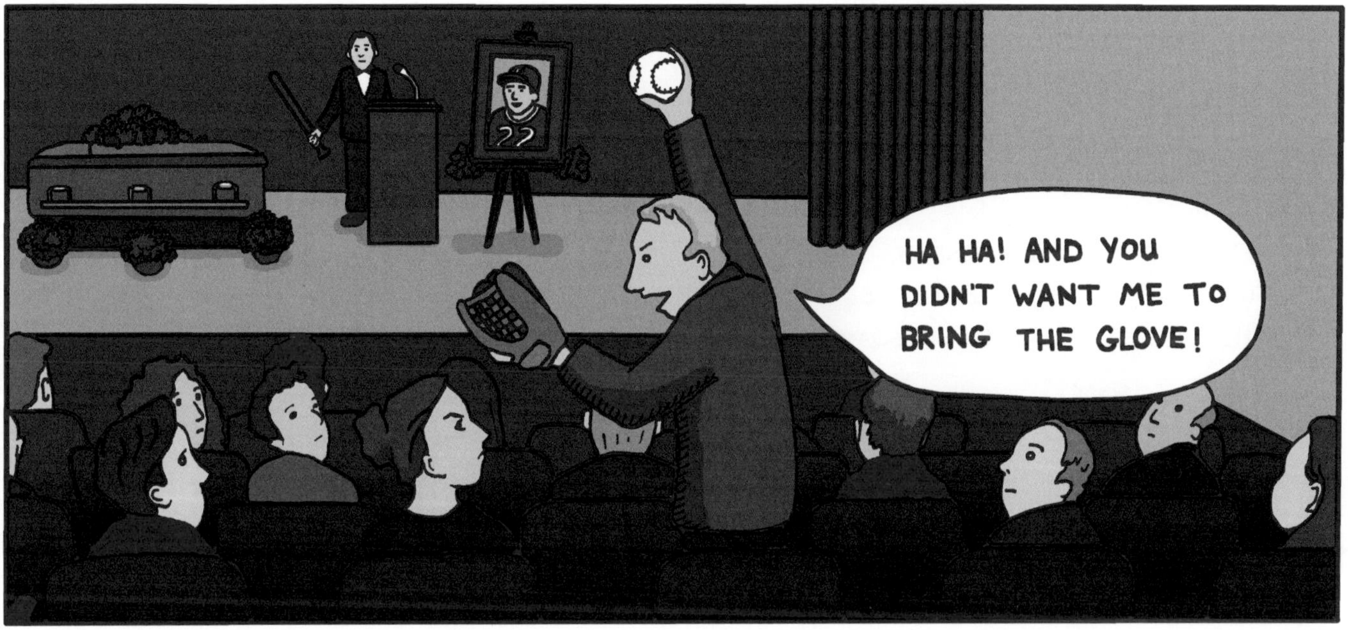
HA HA! AND YOU DIDN'T WANT ME TO BRING THE GLOVE!

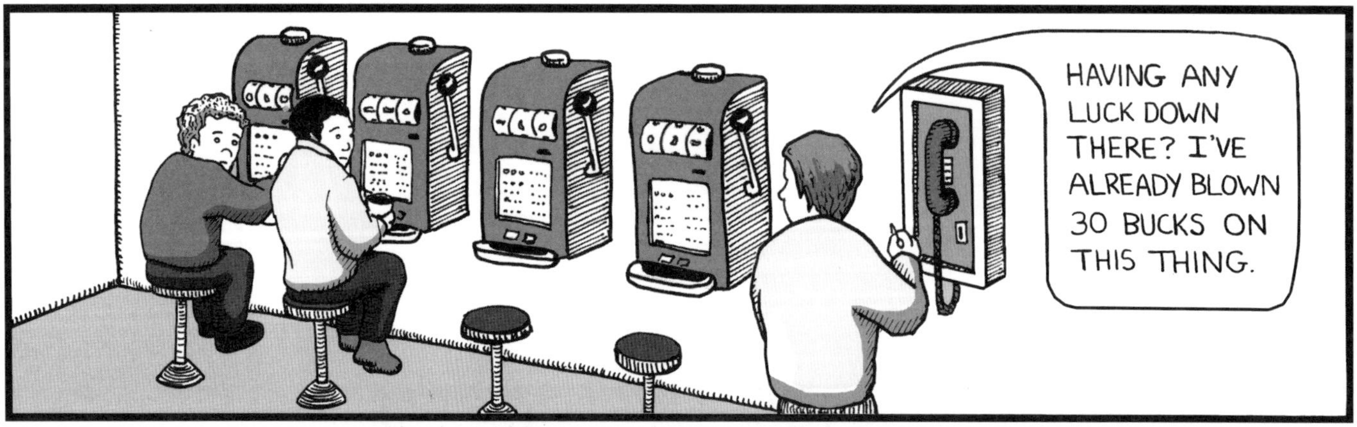
HAVING ANY LUCK DOWN THERE? I'VE ALREADY BLOWN 30 BUCKS ON THIS THING.

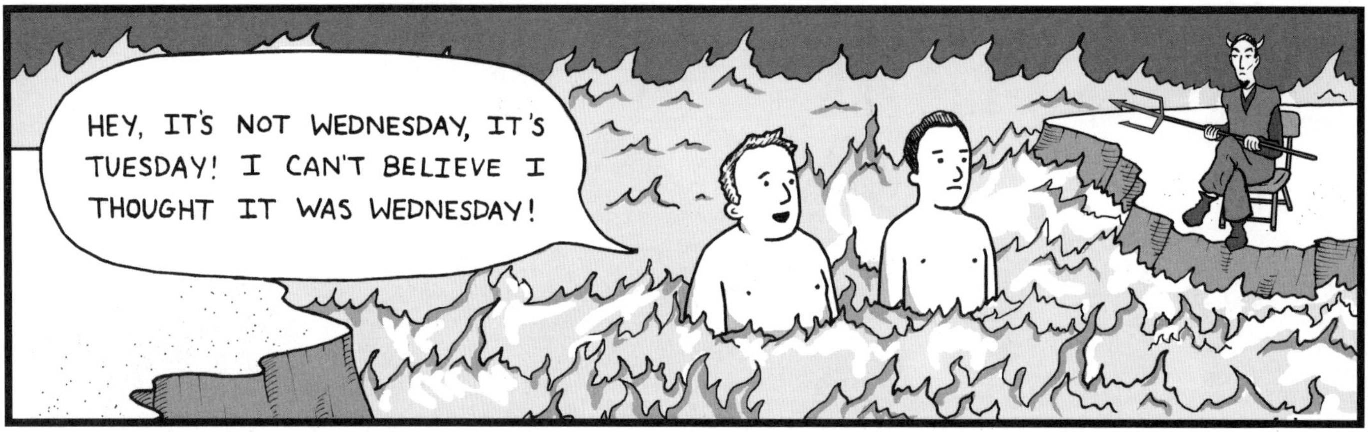
HEY, IT'S NOT WEDNESDAY, IT'S TUESDAY! I CAN'T BELIEVE I THOUGHT IT WAS WEDNESDAY!

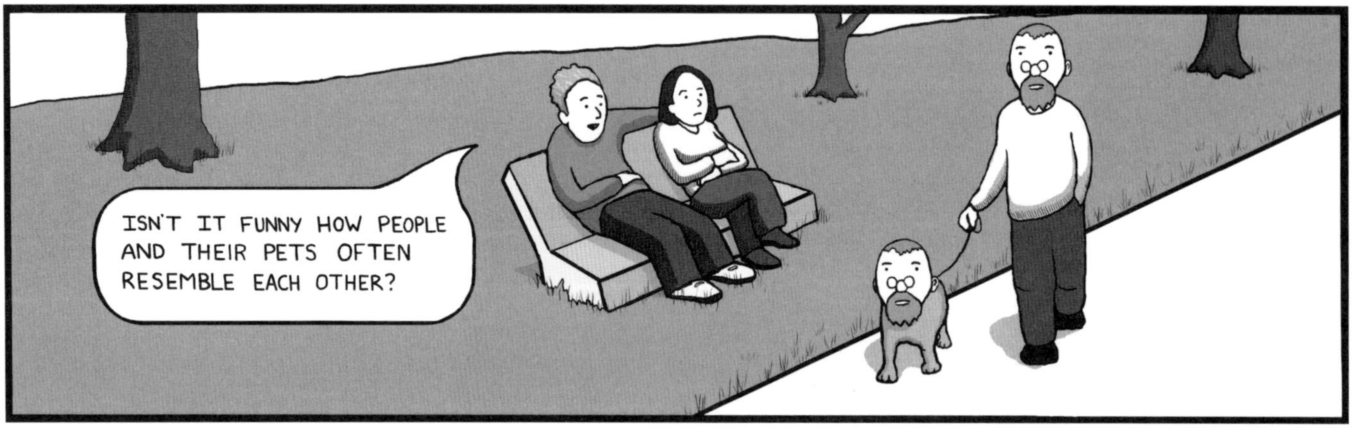
ISN'T IT FUNNY HOW PEOPLE AND THEIR PETS OFTEN RESEMBLE EACH OTHER?

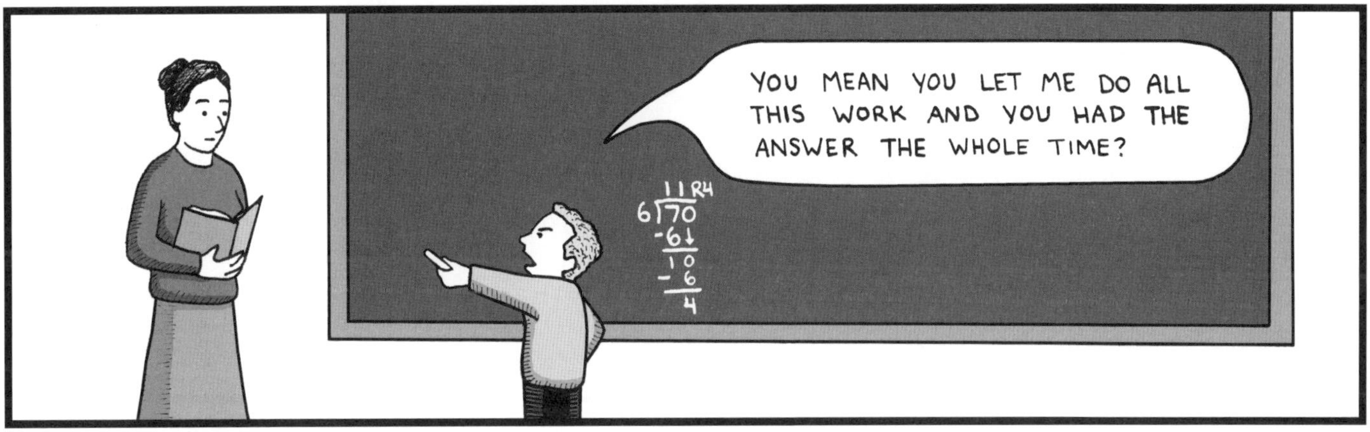
YOU MEAN YOU LET ME DO ALL THIS WORK AND YOU HAD THE ANSWER THE WHOLE TIME?
11 R4
6)70
-6
10
-6
4

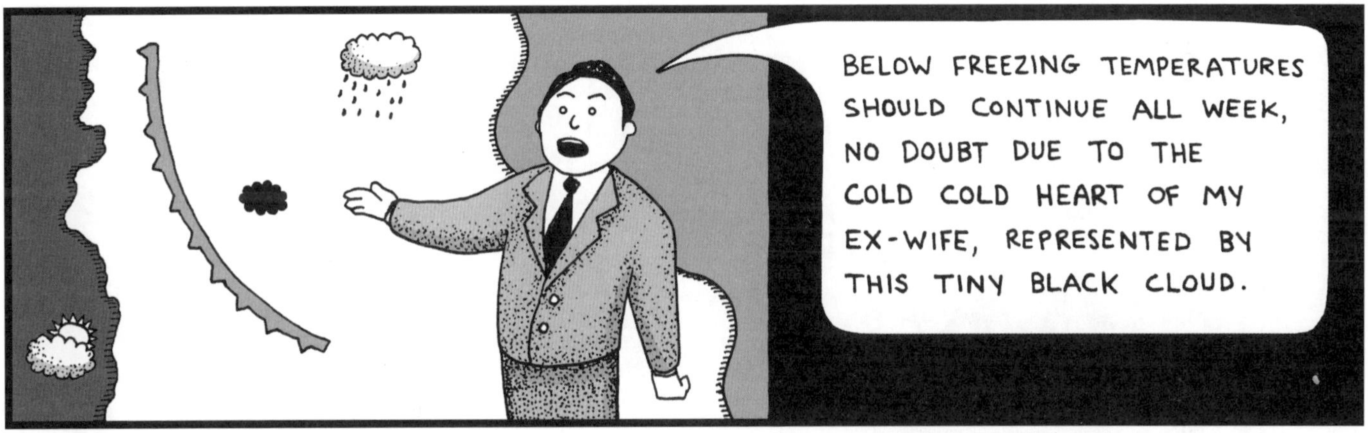
BELOW FREEZING TEMPERATURES SHOULD CONTINUE ALL WEEK, NO DOUBT DUE TO THE COLD COLD HEART OF MY EX-WIFE, REPRESENTED BY THIS TINY BLACK CLOUD.

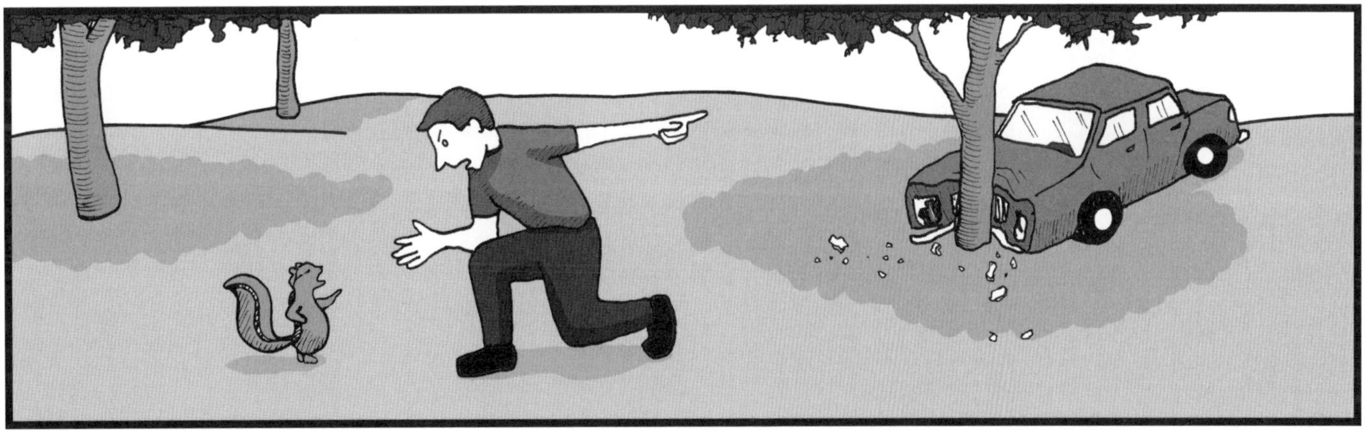

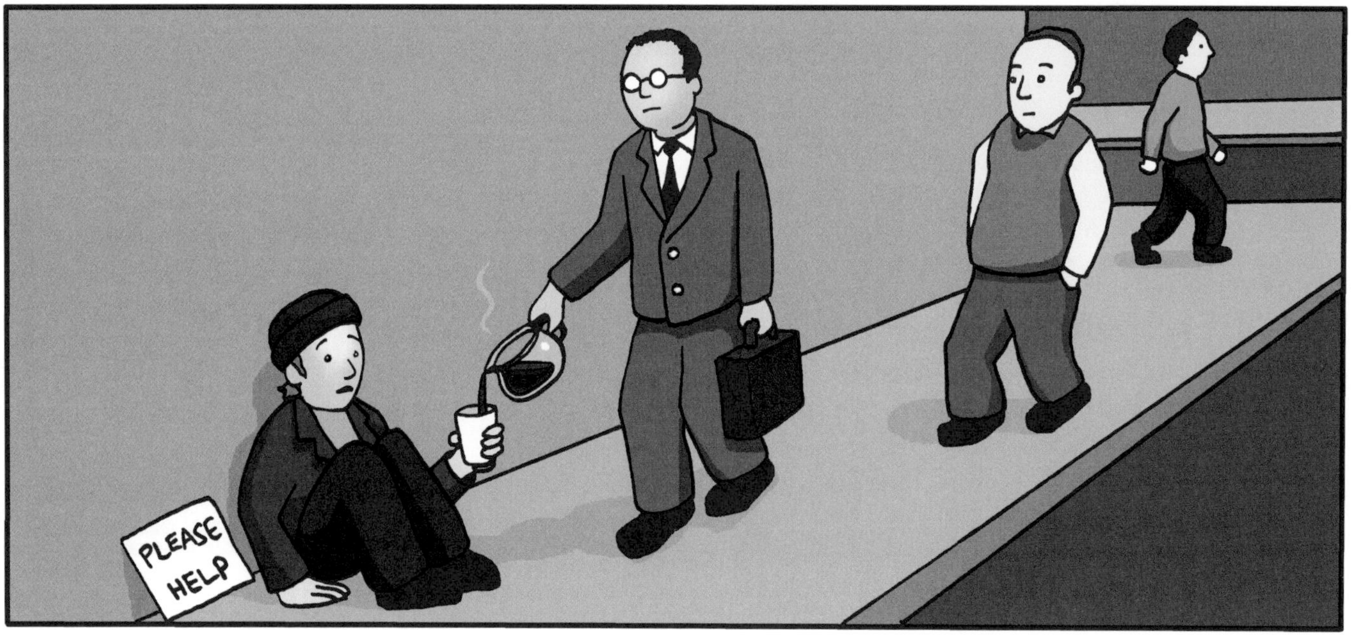
PLEASE
HELP

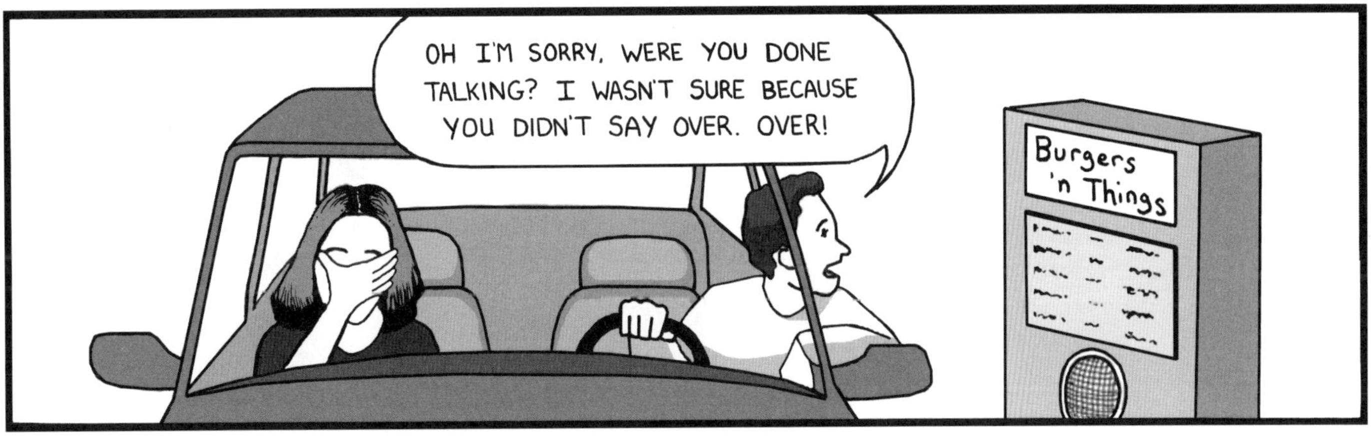
OH I'M SORRY, WERE YOU DONE TALKING? I WASN'T SURE BECAUSE YOU DIDN'T SAY OVER. OVER!
Burgers 'n Things

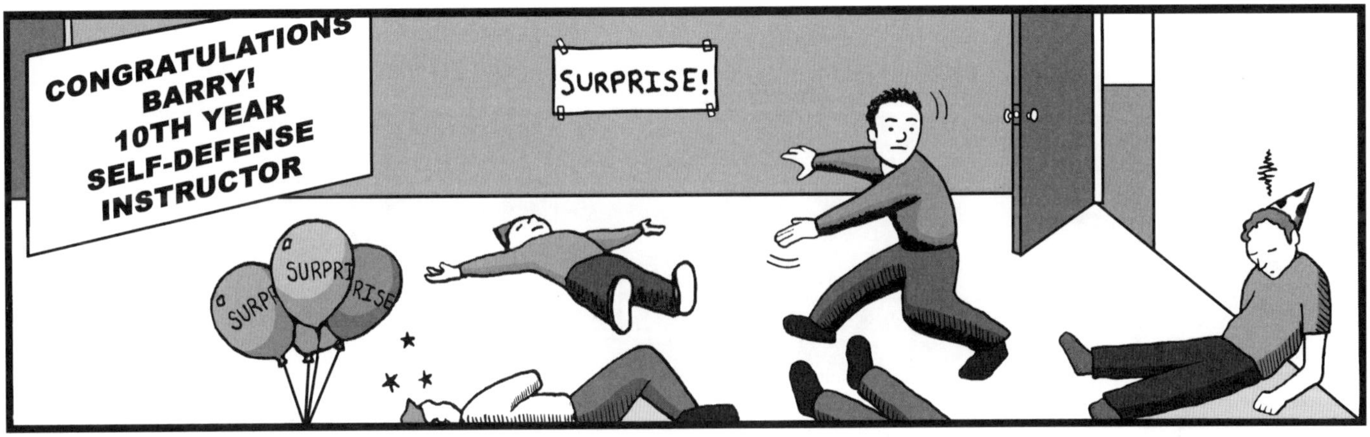
CONGRATULATIONS BARRY! 10TH YEAR SELF-DEFENSE INSTRUCTOR
SURPRISE!

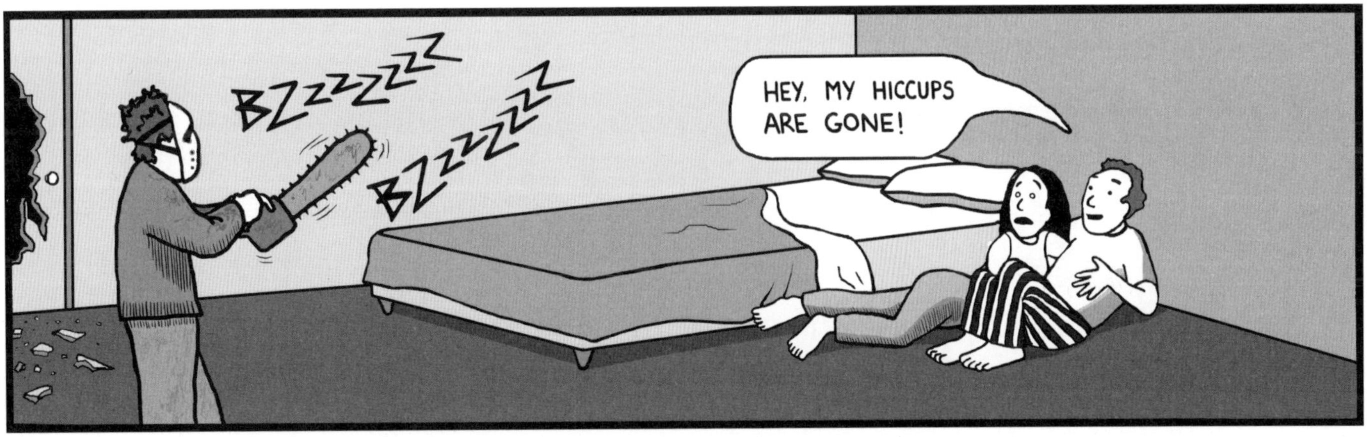
BZZZZZZZ
BZZZZZZZ
HEY, MY HICCUPS ARE GONE!

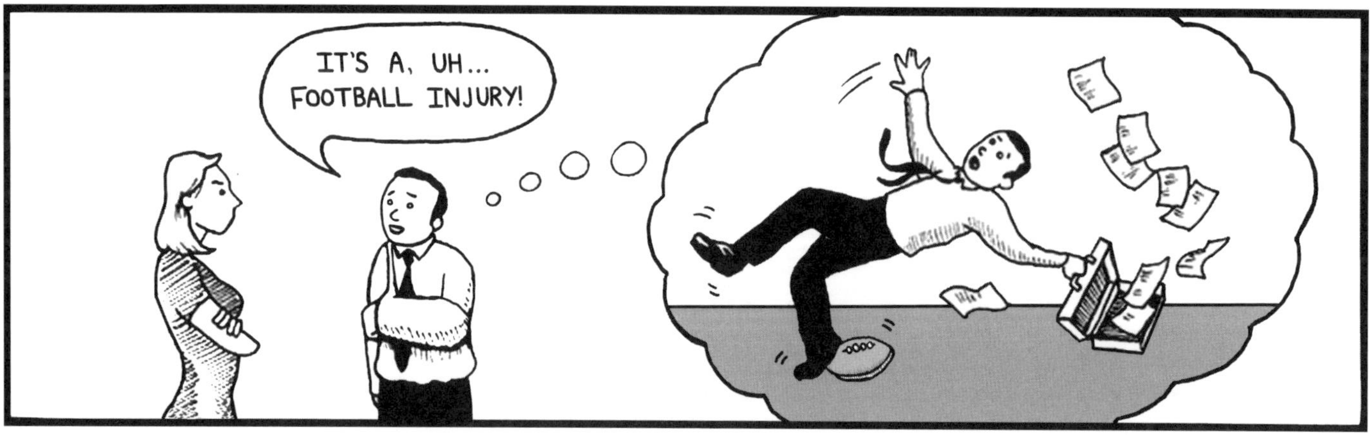
IT'S A, UH...
FOOTBALL INJURY!

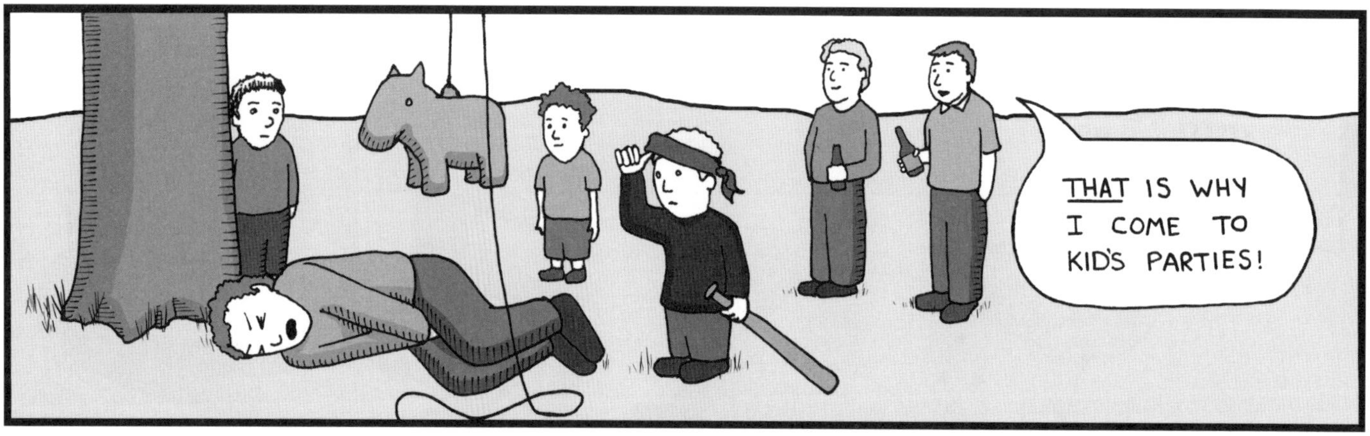
THAT IS WHY
I COME TO
KID'S PARTIES!

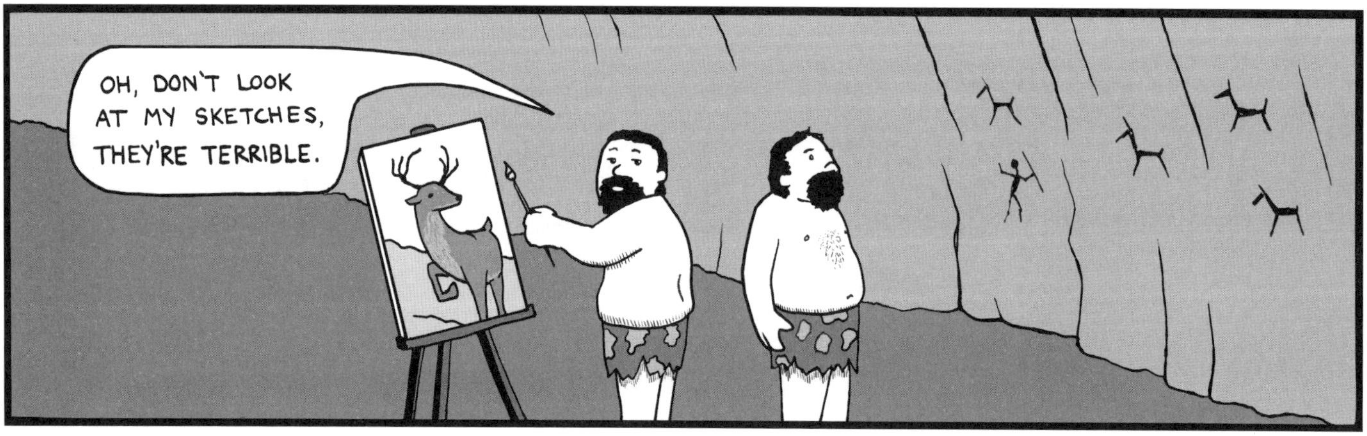
OH, DON'T LOOK
AT MY SKETCHES,
THEY'RE TERRIBLE.

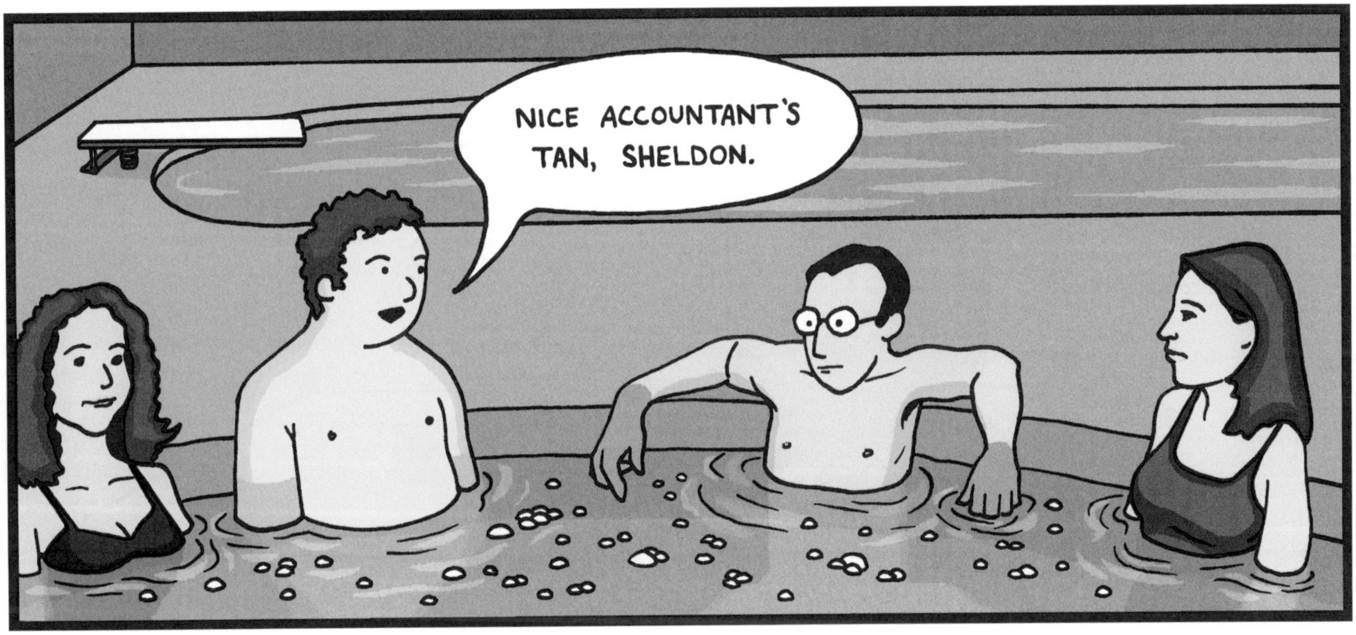
NICE ACCOUNTANT'S TAN, SHELDON.

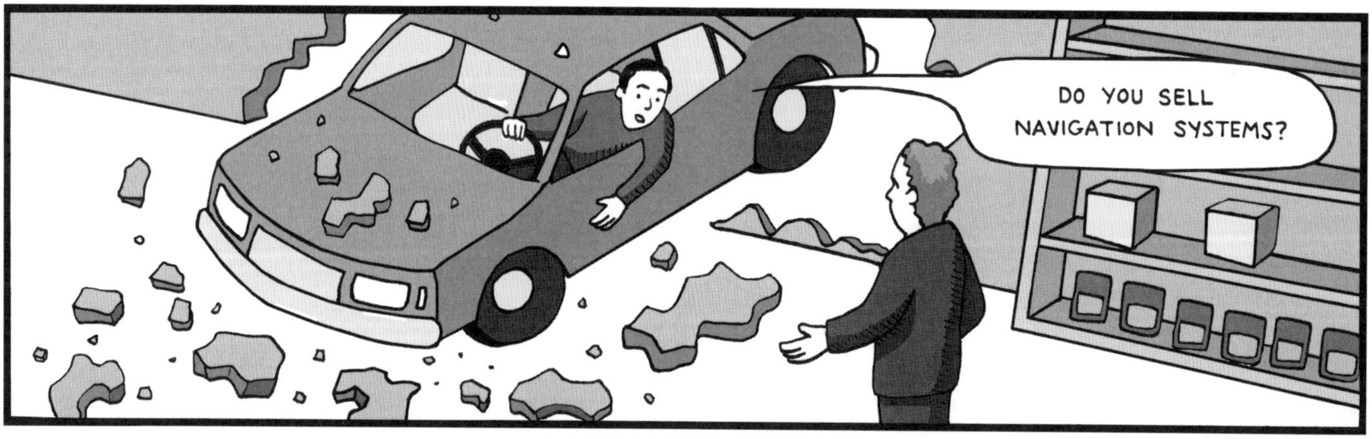
DO YOU SELL NAVIGATION SYSTEMS?

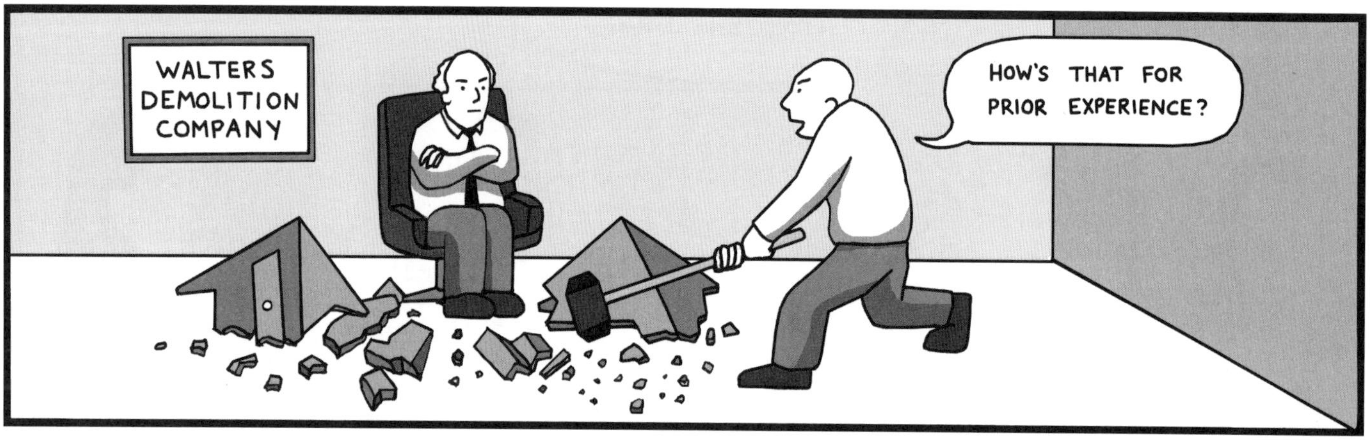
WALTERS DEMOLITION COMPANY
HOW'S THAT FOR PRIOR EXPERIENCE?

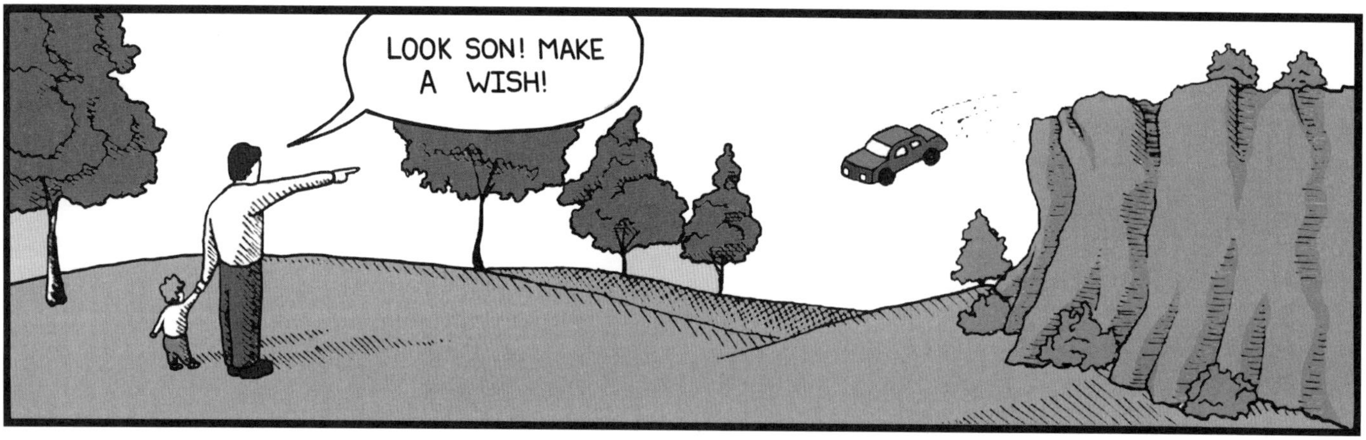
LOOK SON! MAKE A WISH!

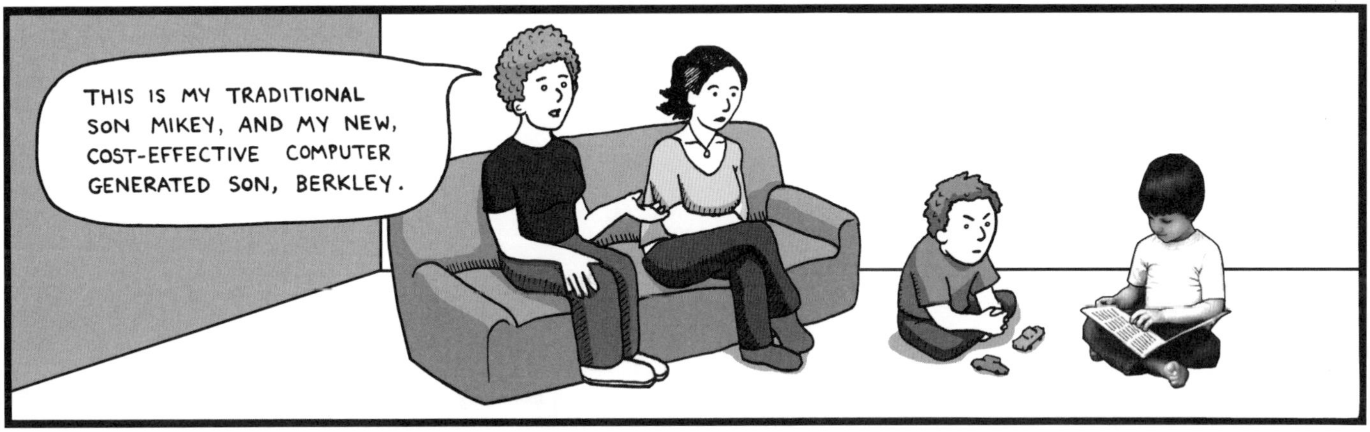
THIS IS MY TRADITIONAL SON MIKEY, AND MY NEW, COST-EFFECTIVE COMPUTER GENERATED SON, BERKLEY.

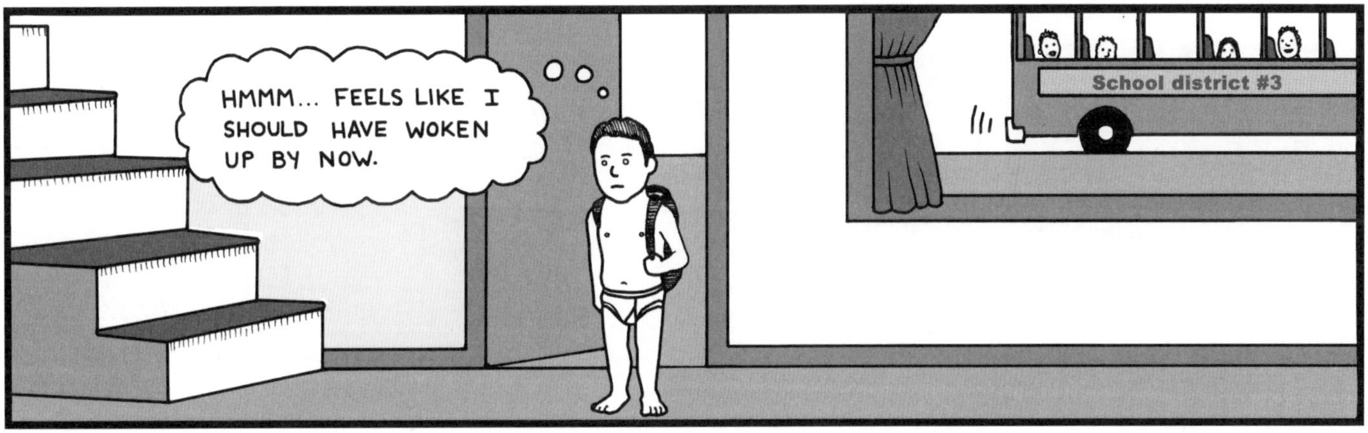
HMMM... FEELS LIKE I SHOULD HAVE WOKEN UP BY NOW.
School district #3

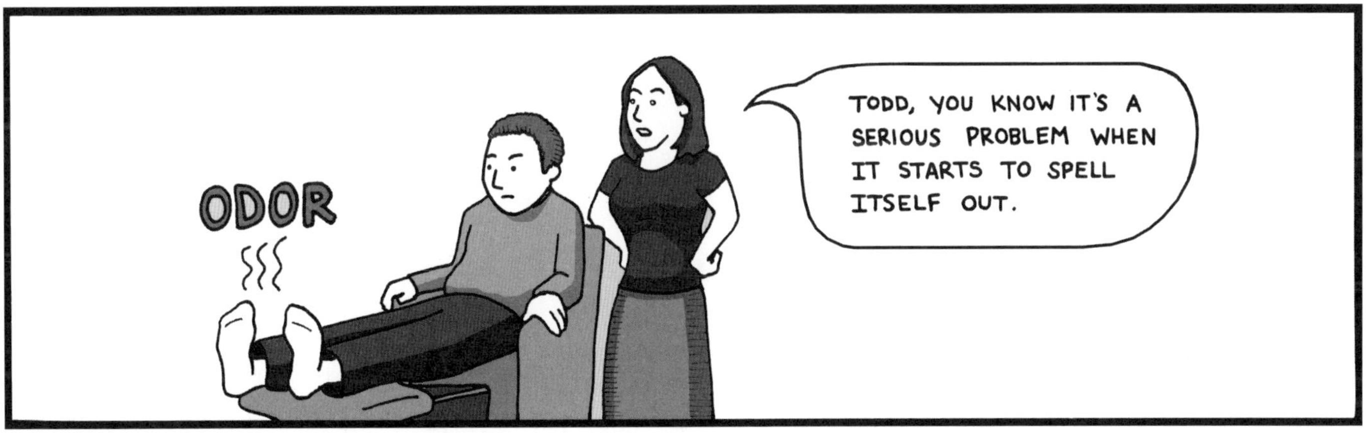
ODOR
TODD, YOU KNOW IT'S A SERIOUS PROBLEM WHEN IT STARTS TO SPELL ITSELF OUT.

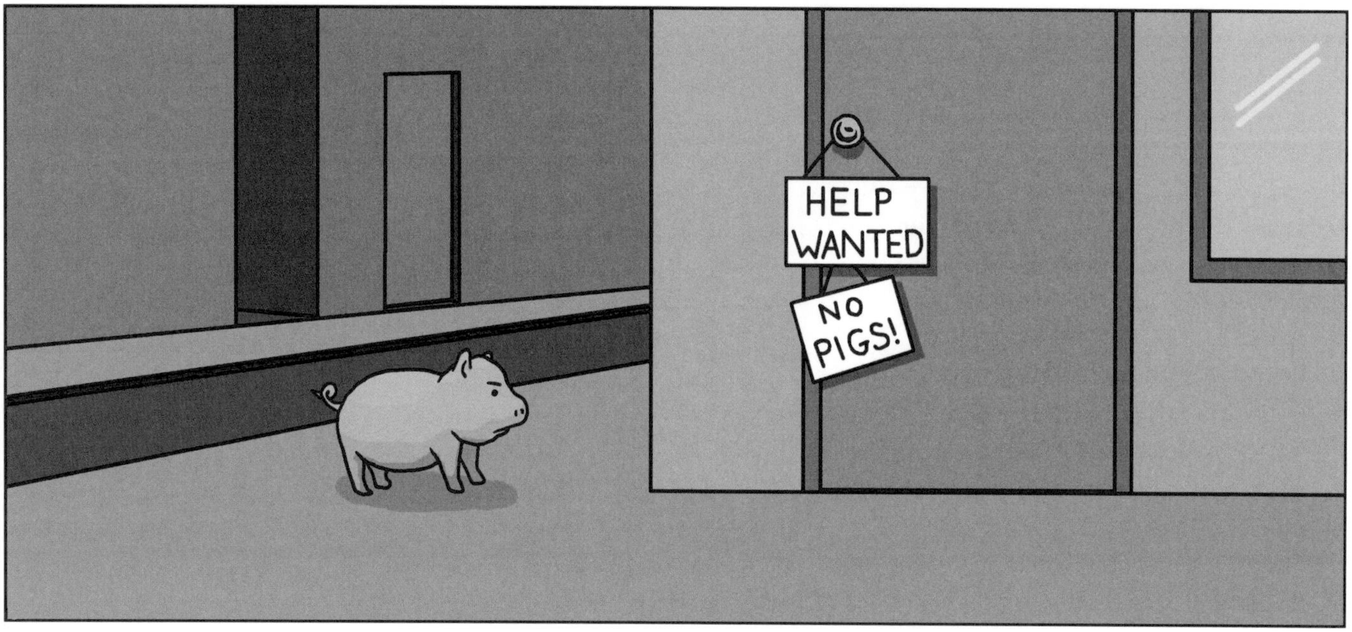
HELP
WANTED
NO
PIGS!

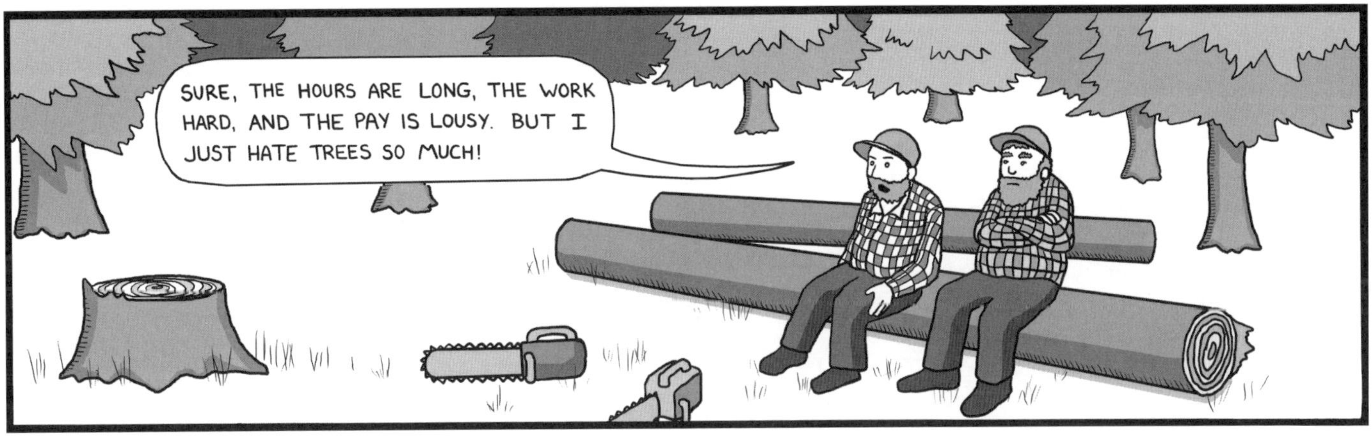
SURE, THE HOURS ARE LONG, THE WORK HARD, AND THE PAY IS LOUSY. BUT I JUST HATE TREES SO MUCH!

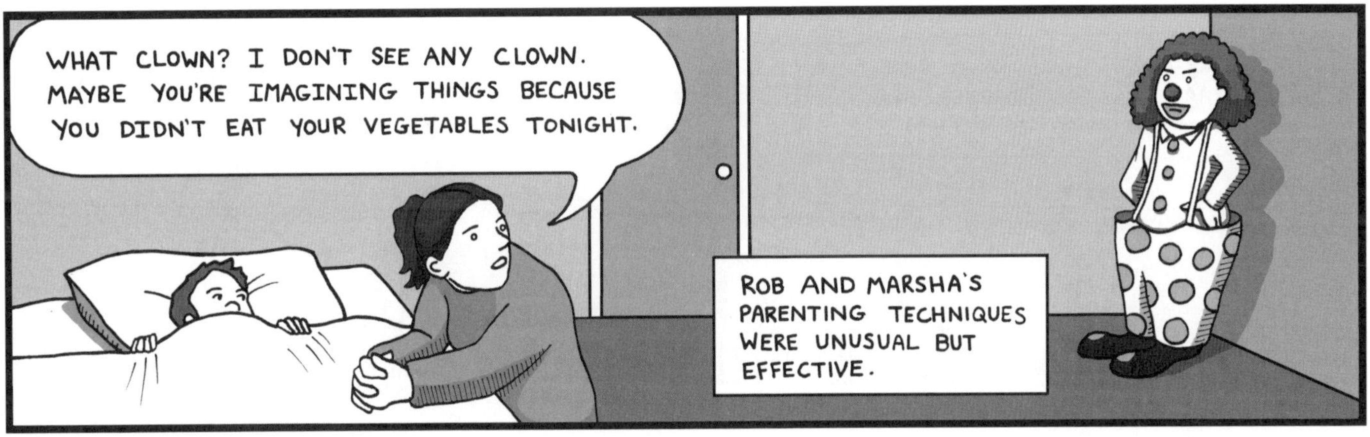
WHAT CLOWN? I DON'T SEE ANY CLOWN. MAYBE YOU'RE IMAGINING THINGS BECAUSE YOU DIDN'T EAT YOUR VEGETABLES TONIGHT.
ROB AND MARSHA'S PARENTING TECHNIQUES WERE UNUSUAL BUT EFFECTIVE.

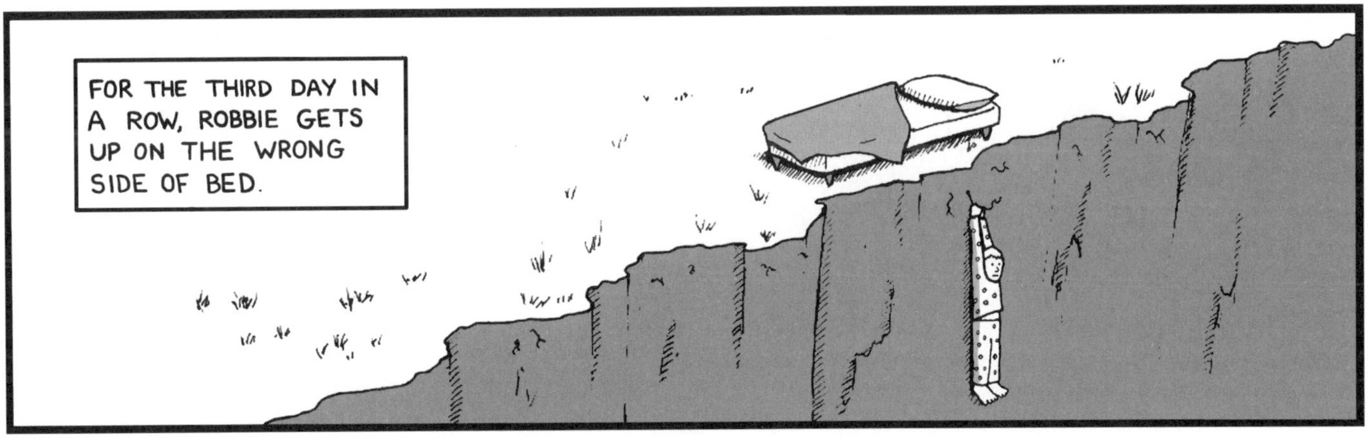
FOR THE THIRD DAY IN A ROW, ROBBIE GETS UP ON THE WRONG SIDE OF BED.

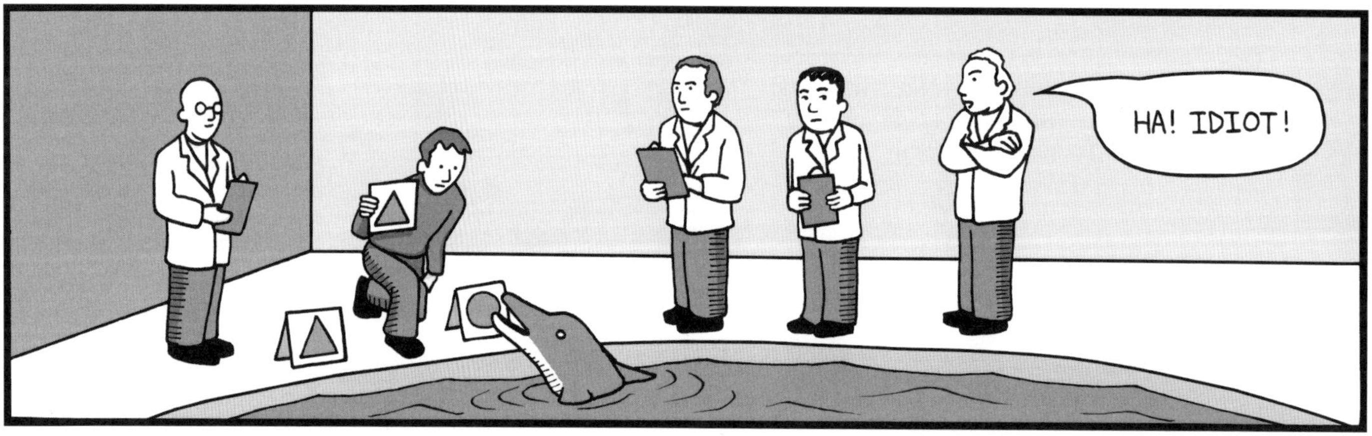
HA! IDIOT!

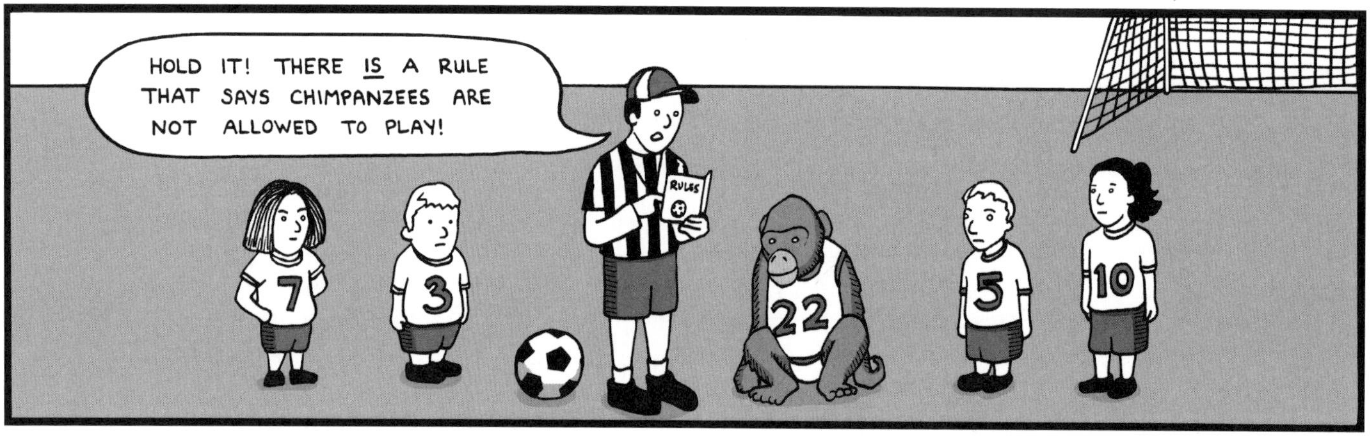
HOLD IT! THERE IS A RULE THAT SAYS CHIMPANZEES ARE NOT ALLOWED TO PLAY!
RULES
7
3
22
5
10

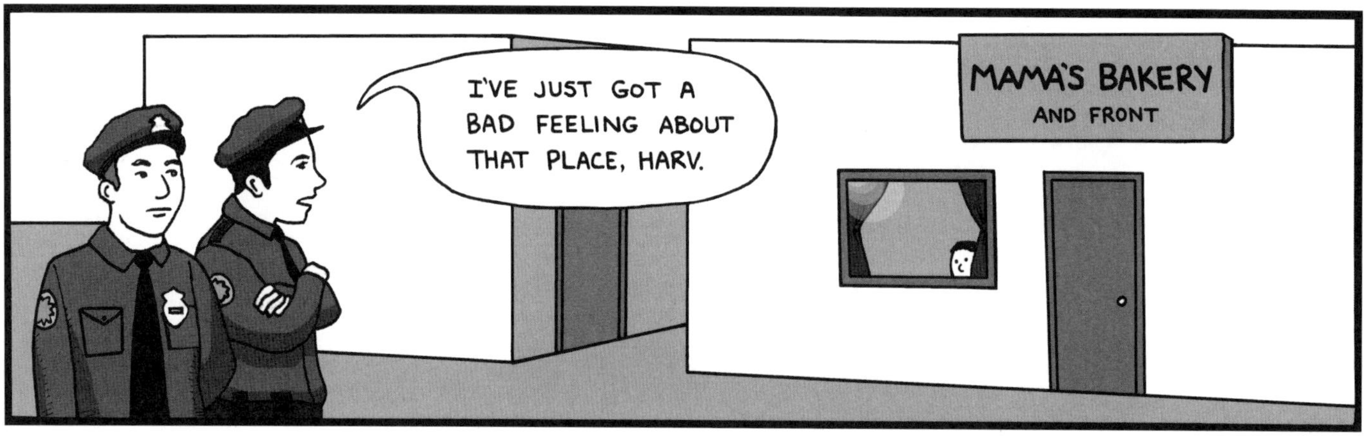
I'VE JUST GOT A BAD FEELING ABOUT THAT PLACE, HARV.
MAMA'S BAKERY
AND FRONT

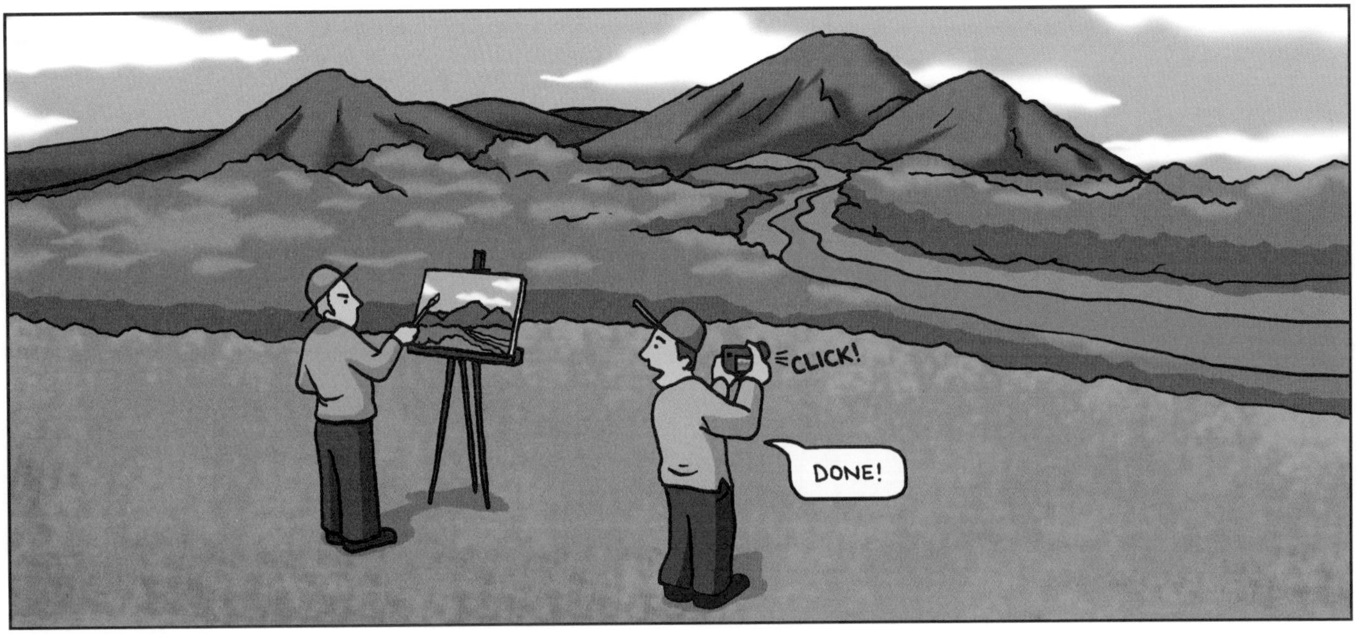
CLICK!
DONE!

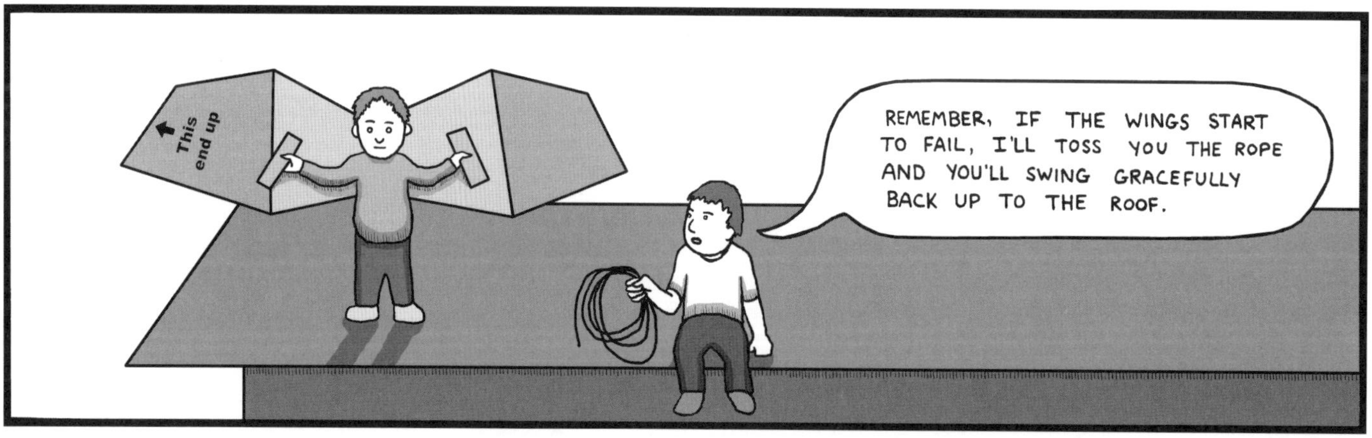
This end up
REMEMBER, IF THE WINGS START TO FAIL, I'LL TOSS YOU THE ROPE AND YOU'LL SWING GRACEFULLY BACK UP TO THE ROOF.

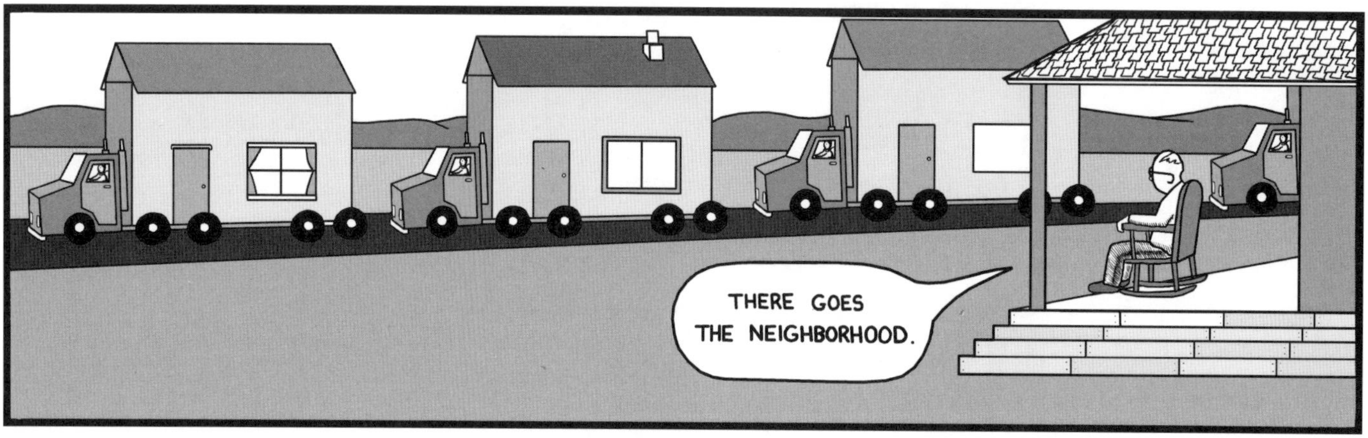
THERE GOES THE NEIGHBORHOOD.

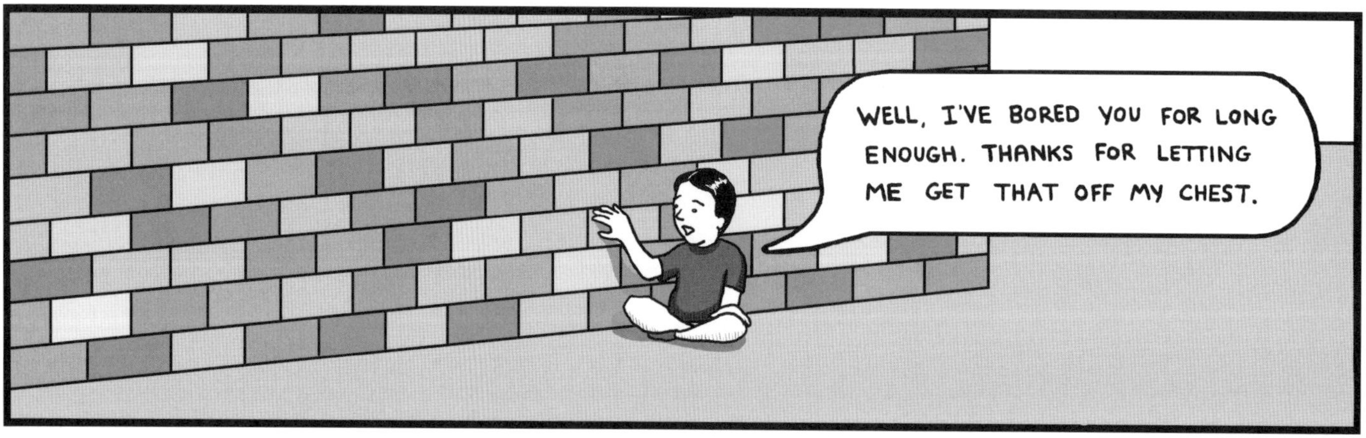
WELL, I'VE BORED YOU FOR LONG ENOUGH. THANKS FOR LETTING ME GET THAT OFF MY CHEST.

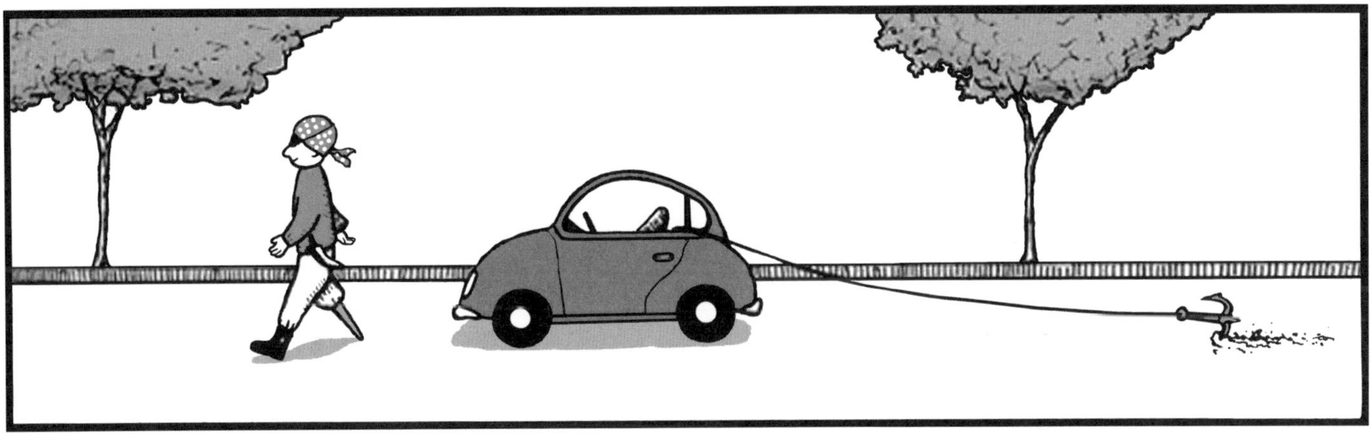

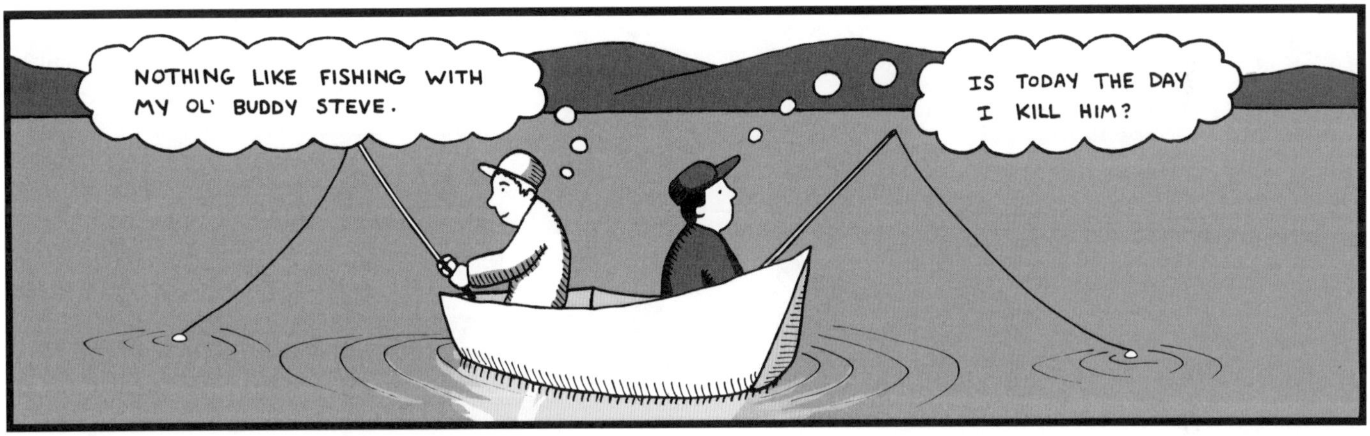
NOTHING LIKE FISHING WITH MY OL' BUDDY STEVE.
IS TODAY THE DAY I KILL HIM?

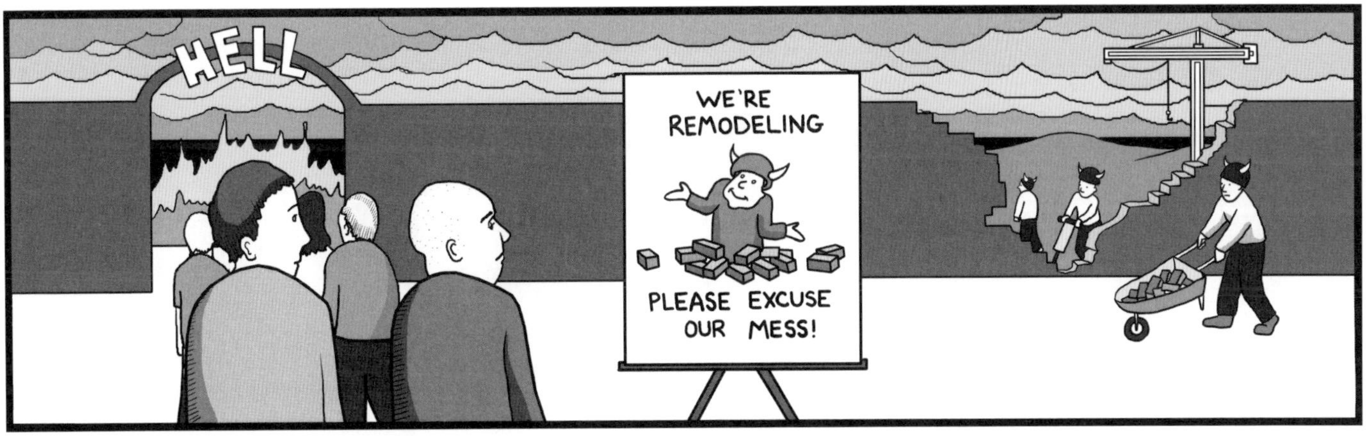
HELL
WE'RE REMODELING
PLEASE EXCUSE OUR MESS!

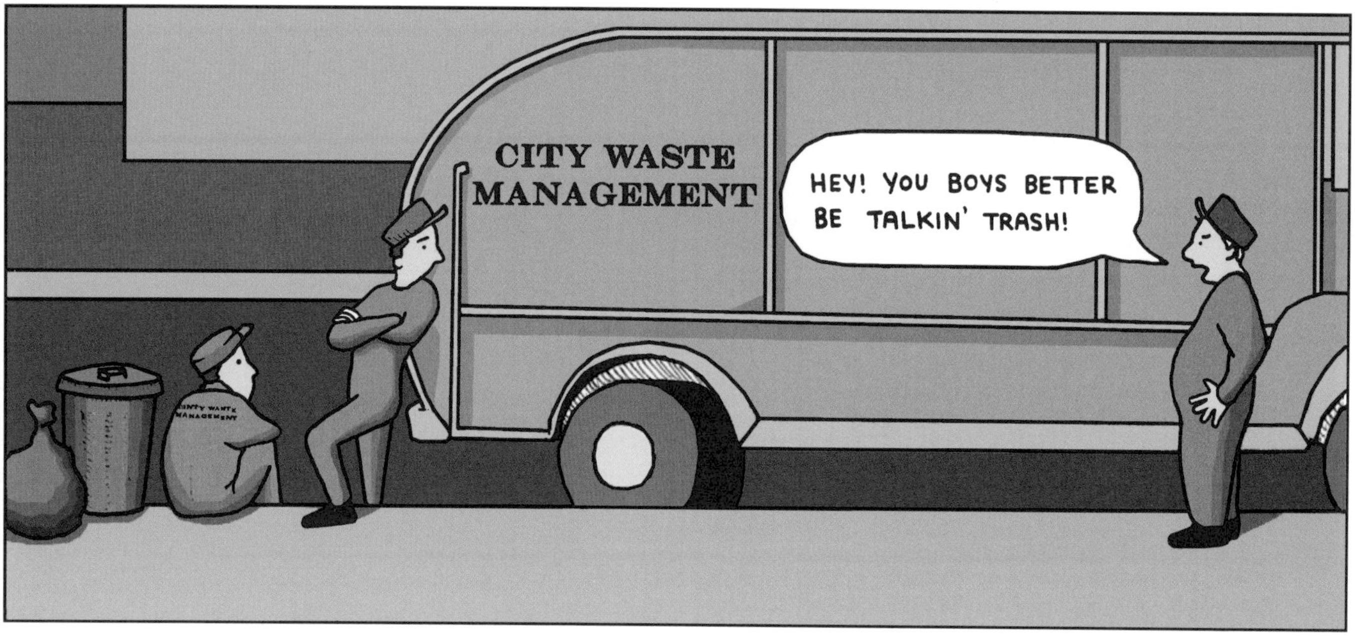
CITY WASTE
MANAGEMENT
HEY! YOU BOYS BETTER
BE TALKIN' TRASH!

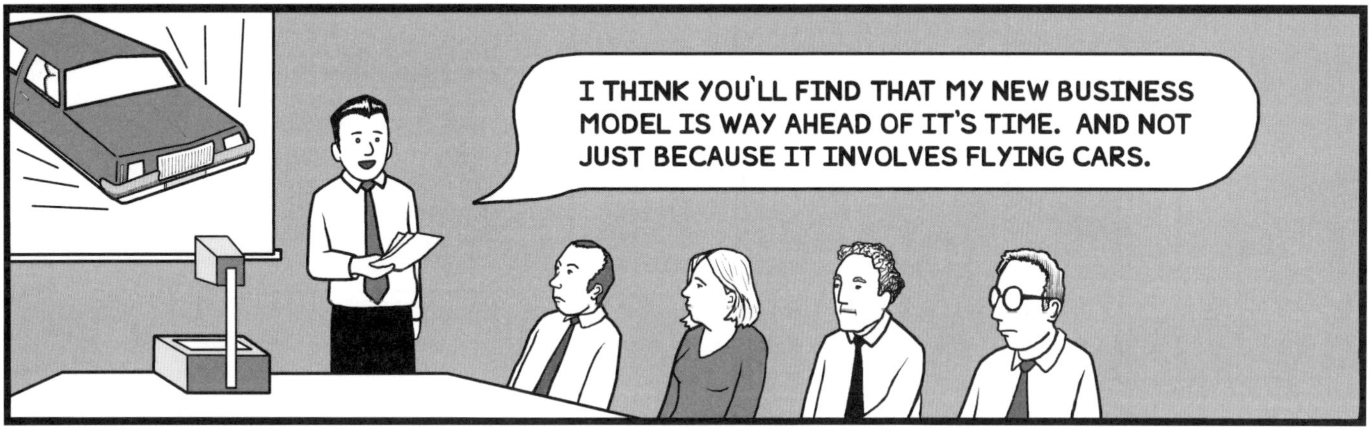
I THINK YOU'LL FIND THAT MY NEW BUSINESS MODEL IS WAY AHEAD OF IT'S TIME. AND NOT JUST BECAUSE IT INVOLVES FLYING CARS.

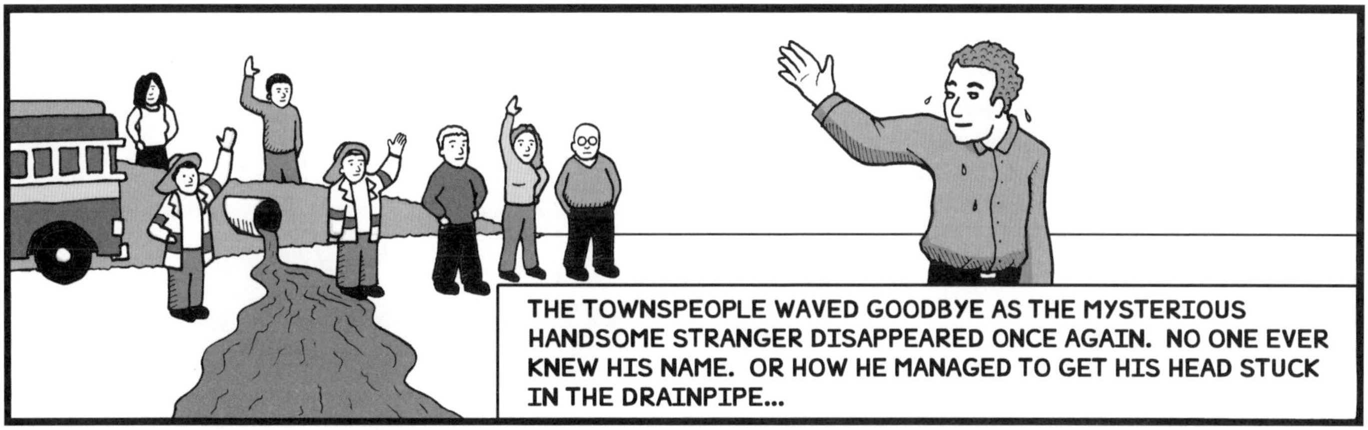
THE TOWNSPEOPLE WAVED GOODBYE AS THE MYSTERIOUS HANDSOME STRANGER DISAPPEARED ONCE AGAIN. NO ONE EVER KNEW HIS NAME. OR HOW HE MANAGED TO GET HIS HEAD STUCK IN THE DRAINPIPE...

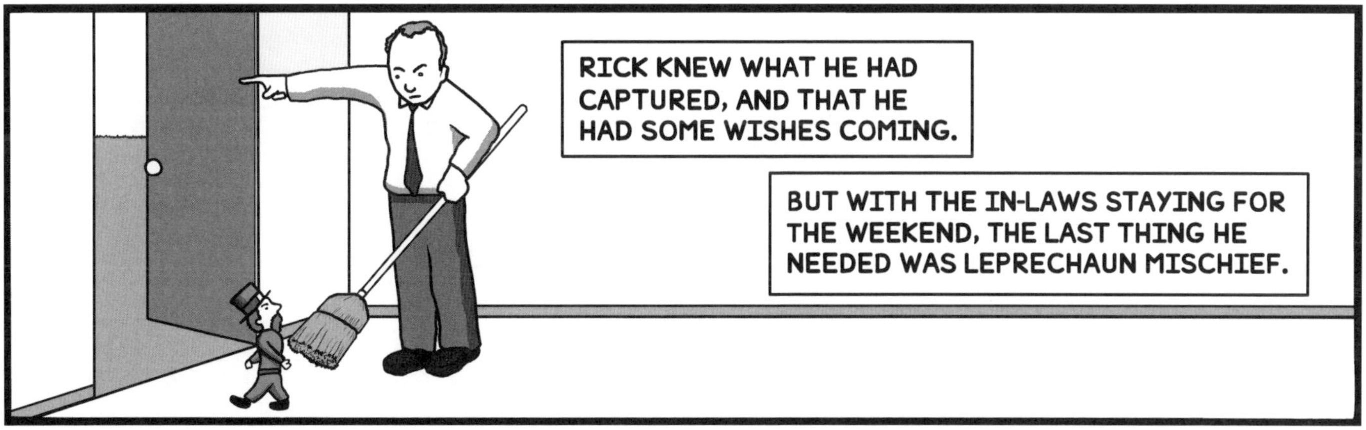
RICK KNEW WHAT HE HAD CAPTURED, AND THAT HE HAD SOME WISHES COMING.
BUT WITH THE IN-LAWS STAYING FOR THE WEEKEND, THE LAST THING HE NEEDED WAS LEPRECHAUN MISCHIEF.

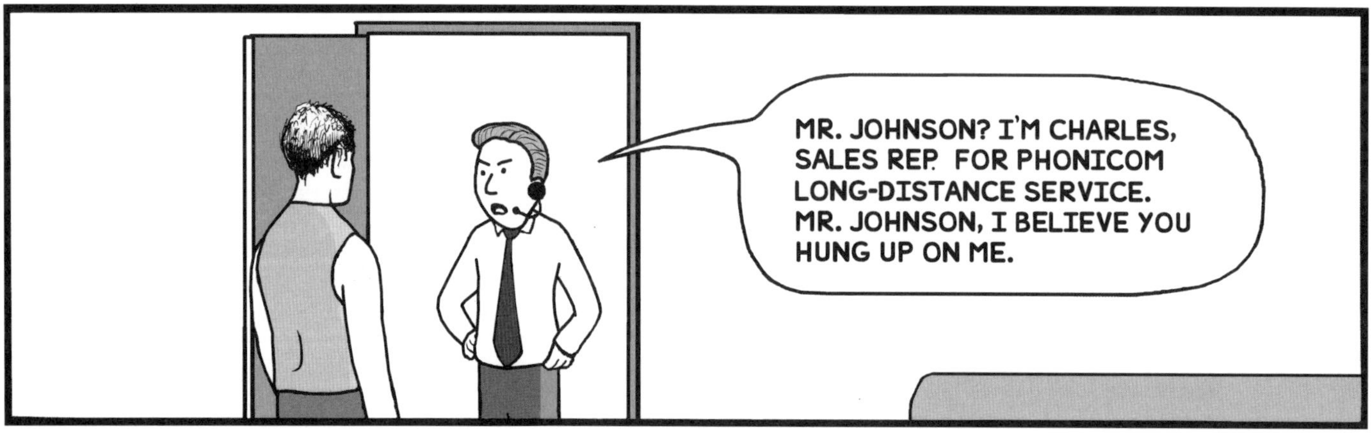
MR. JOHNSON? I'M CHARLES, SALES REP. FOR PHONICOM LONG-DISTANCE SERVICE. MR. JOHNSON, I BELIEVE YOU HUNG UP ON ME.

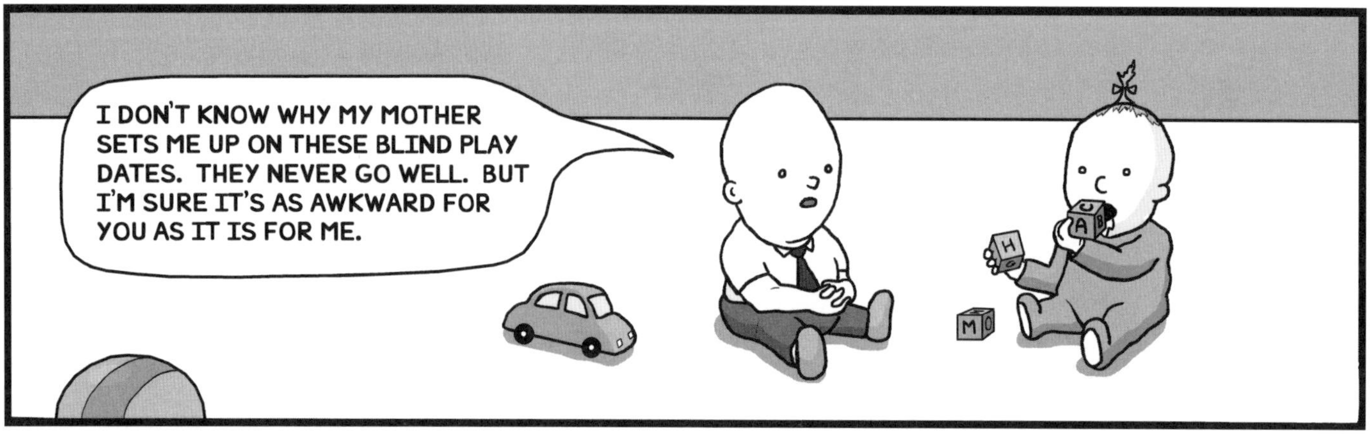
I DON'T KNOW WHY MY MOTHER SETS ME UP ON THESE BLIND PLAY DATES. THEY NEVER GO WELL. BUT I'M SURE IT'S AS AWKWARD FOR YOU AS IT IS FOR ME.

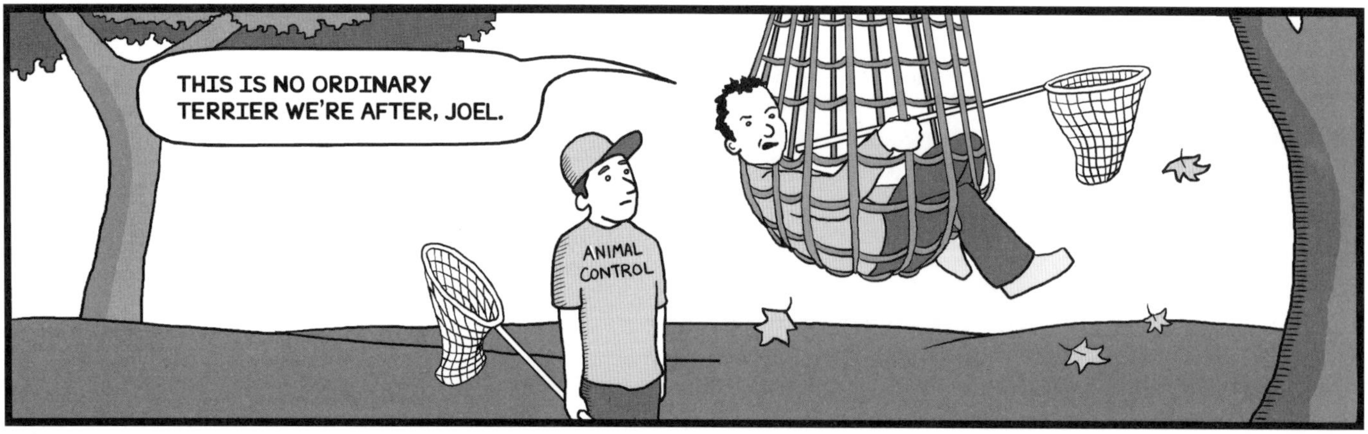
THIS IS NO ORDINARY TERRIER WE'RE AFTER, JOEL.
ANIMAL CONTROL

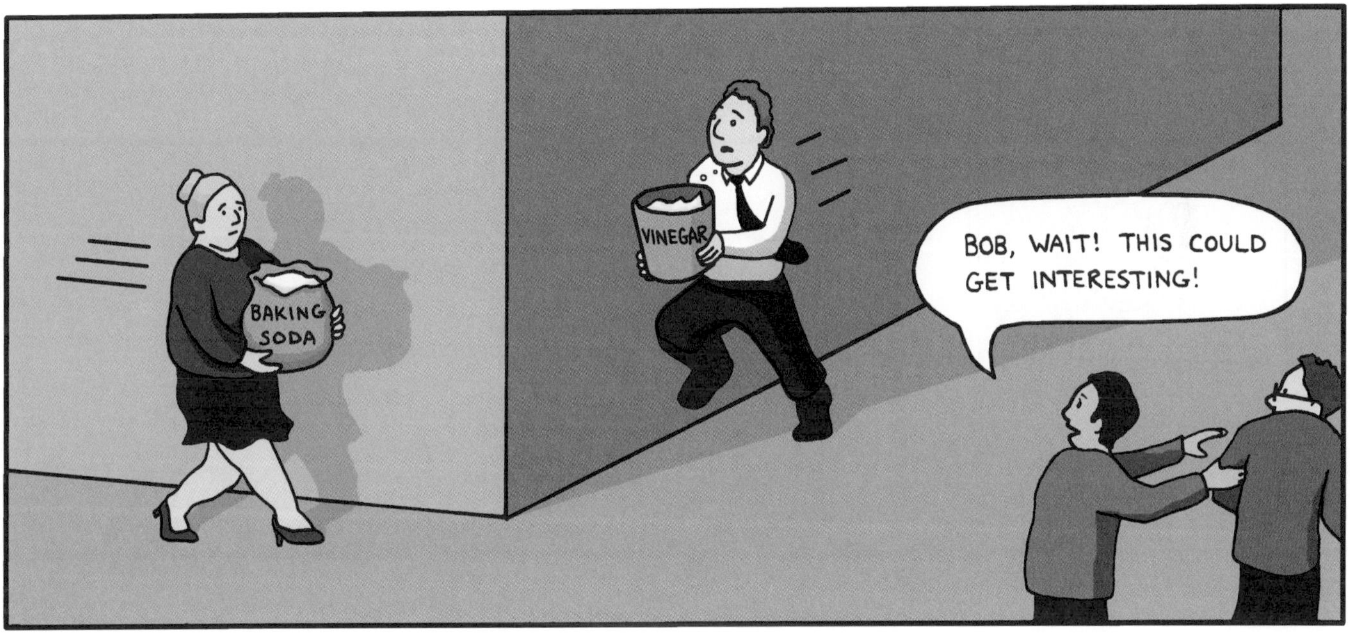
BAKING SODA
VINEGAR
BOB, WAIT! THIS COULD GET INTERESTING!

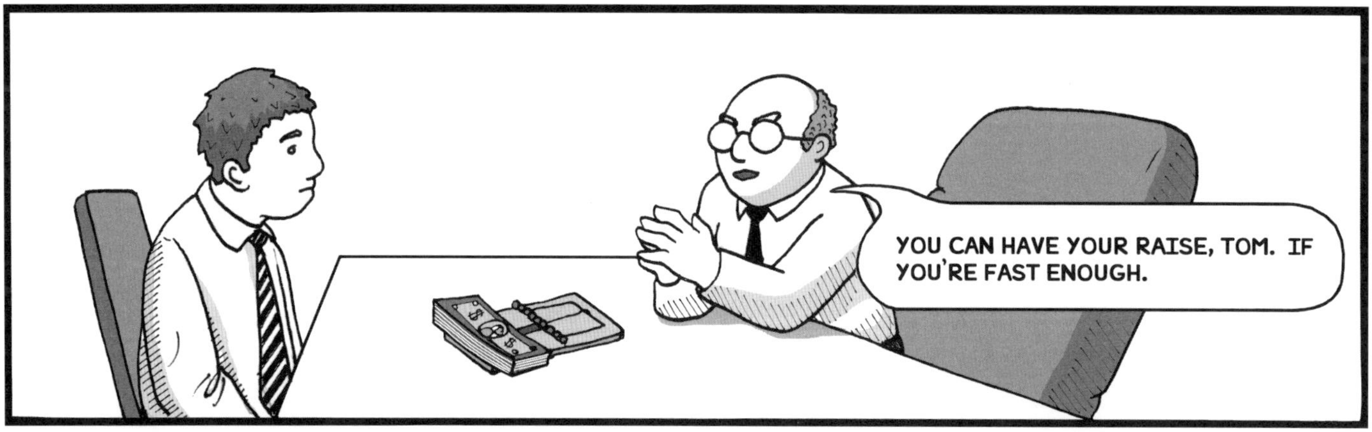
YOU CAN HAVE YOUR RAISE, TOM. IF YOU'RE FAST ENOUGH.

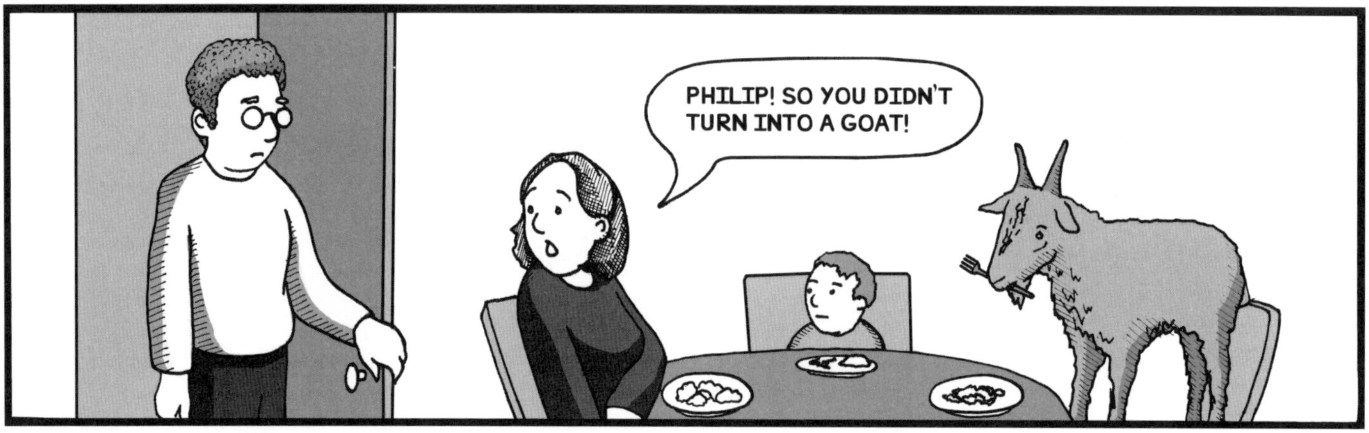
PHILIP! SO YOU DIDN'T TURN INTO A GOAT!

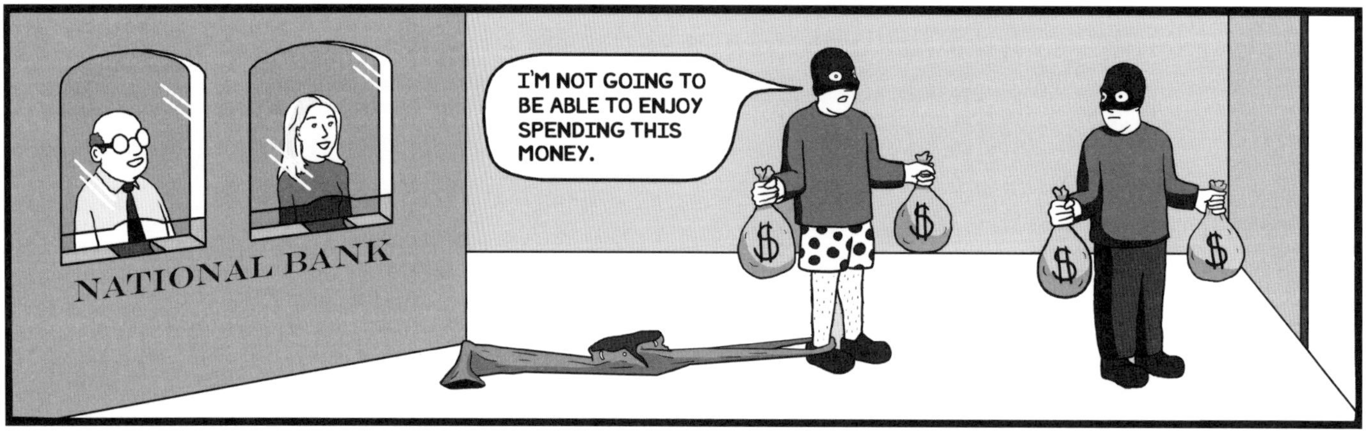
NATIONAL BANK
I'M NOT GOING TO BE ABLE TO ENJOY SPENDING THIS MONEY.

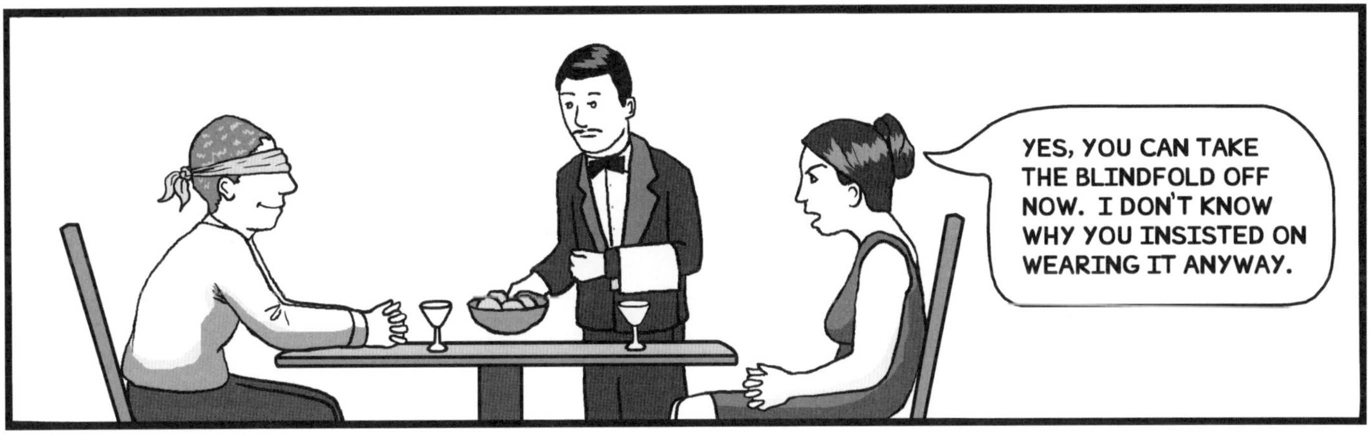
YES, YOU CAN TAKE THE BLINDFOLD OFF NOW. I DON'T KNOW WHY YOU INSISTED ON WEARING IT ANYWAY.

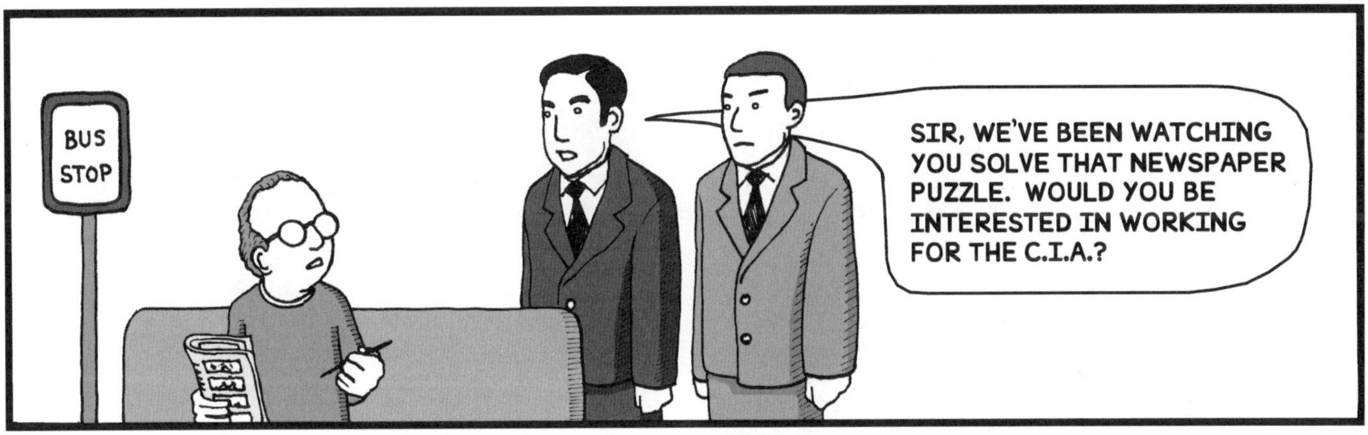
BUS STOP
SIR, WE'VE BEEN WATCHING YOU SOLVE THAT NEWSPAPER PUZZLE. WOULD YOU BE INTERESTED IN WORKING FOR THE C.I.A.?

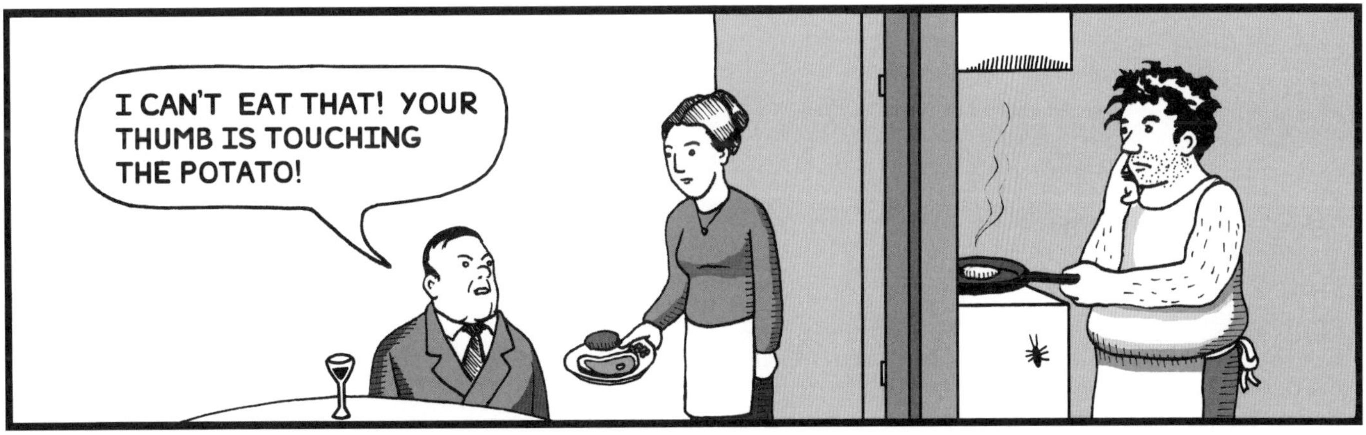
I CAN'T EAT THAT! YOUR THUMB IS TOUCHING THE POTATO!

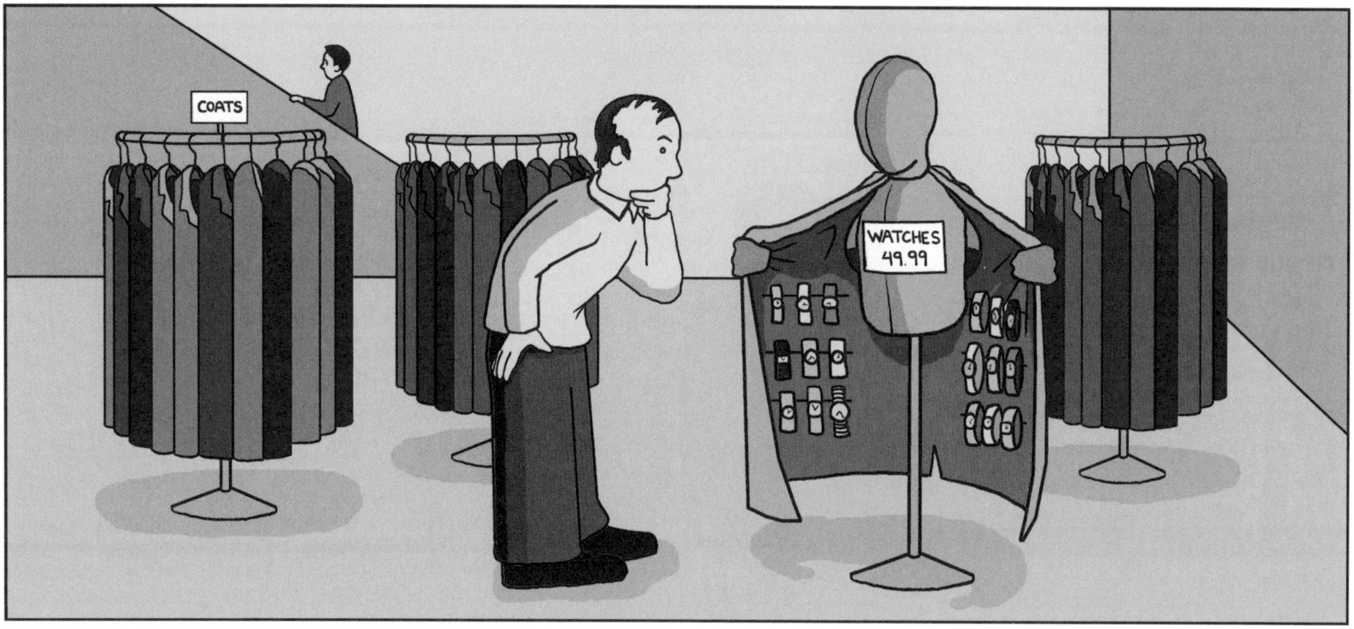
COATS
WATCHES
49.99

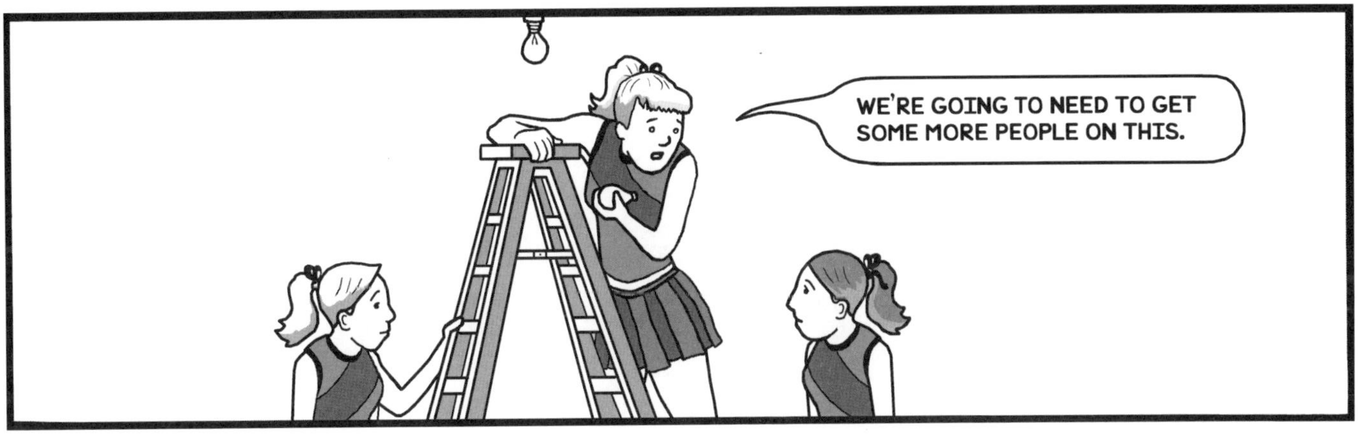
WE'RE GOING TO NEED TO GET SOME MORE PEOPLE ON THIS.

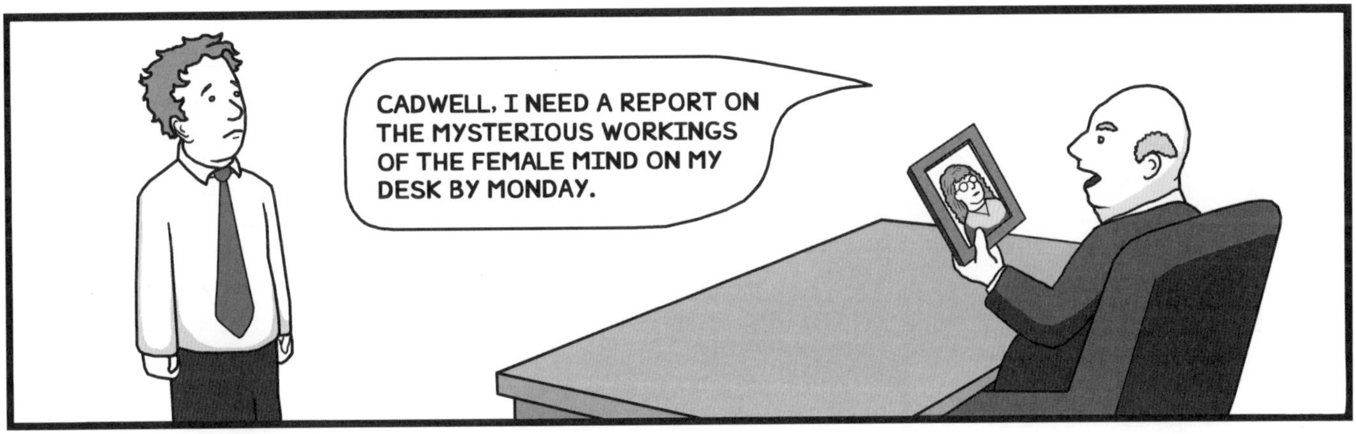
CADWELL, I NEED A REPORT ON THE MYSTERIOUS WORKINGS OF THE FEMALE MIND ON MY DESK BY MONDAY.

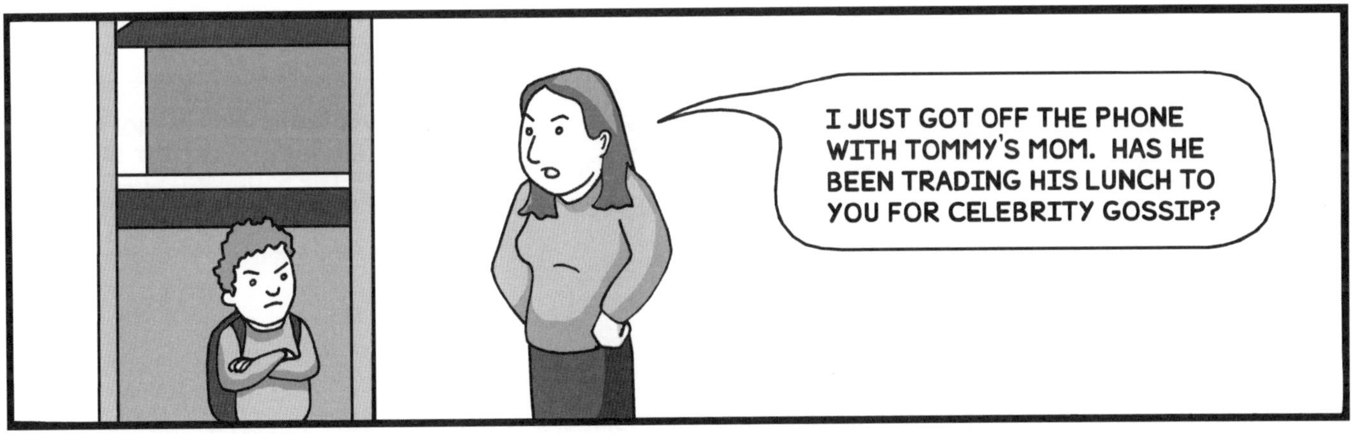
I JUST GOT OFF THE PHONE WITH TOMMY'S MOM. HAS HE BEEN TRADING HIS LUNCH TO YOU FOR CELEBRITY GOSSIP?

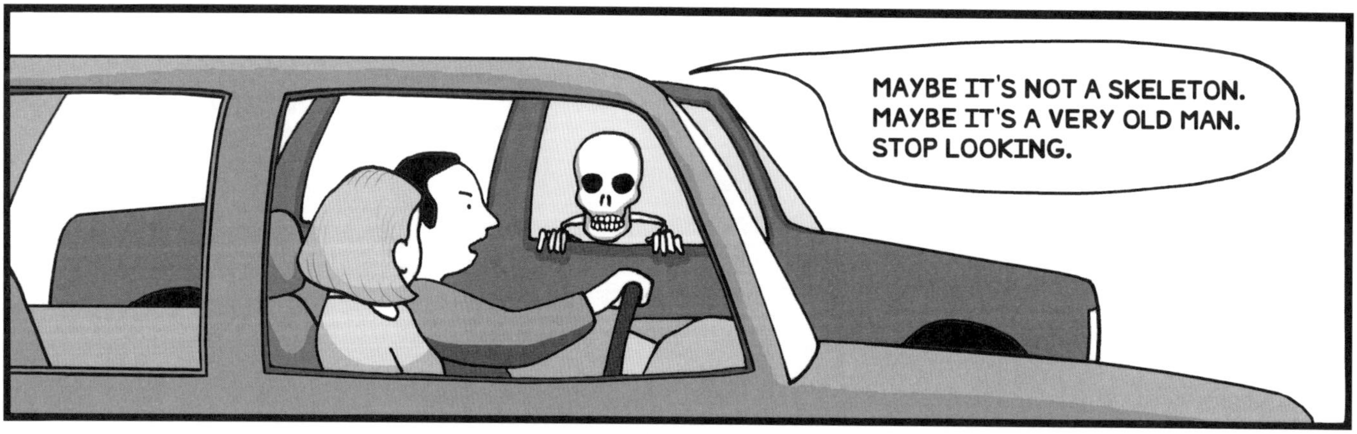
MAYBE IT'S NOT A SKELETON. MAYBE IT'S A VERY OLD MAN. STOP LOOKING.

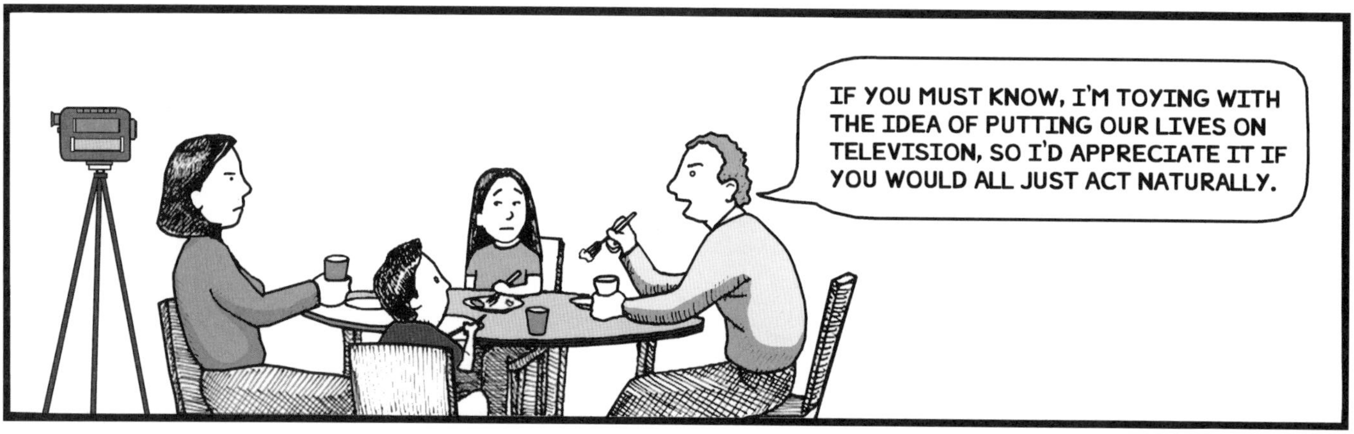
IF YOU MUST KNOW, I'M TOYING WITH THE IDEA OF PUTTING OUR LIVES ON TELEVISION, SO I'D APPRECIATE IT IF YOU WOULD ALL JUST ACT NATURALLY.

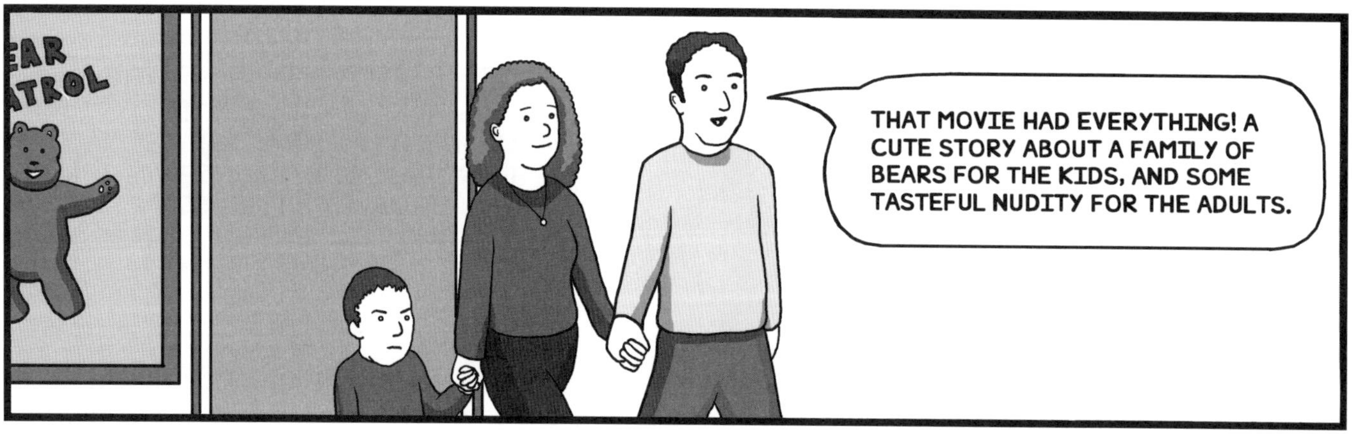
THAT MOVIE HAD EVERYTHING! A CUTE STORY ABOUT A FAMILY OF BEARS FOR THE KIDS, AND SOME TASTEFUL NUDITY FOR THE ADULTS.

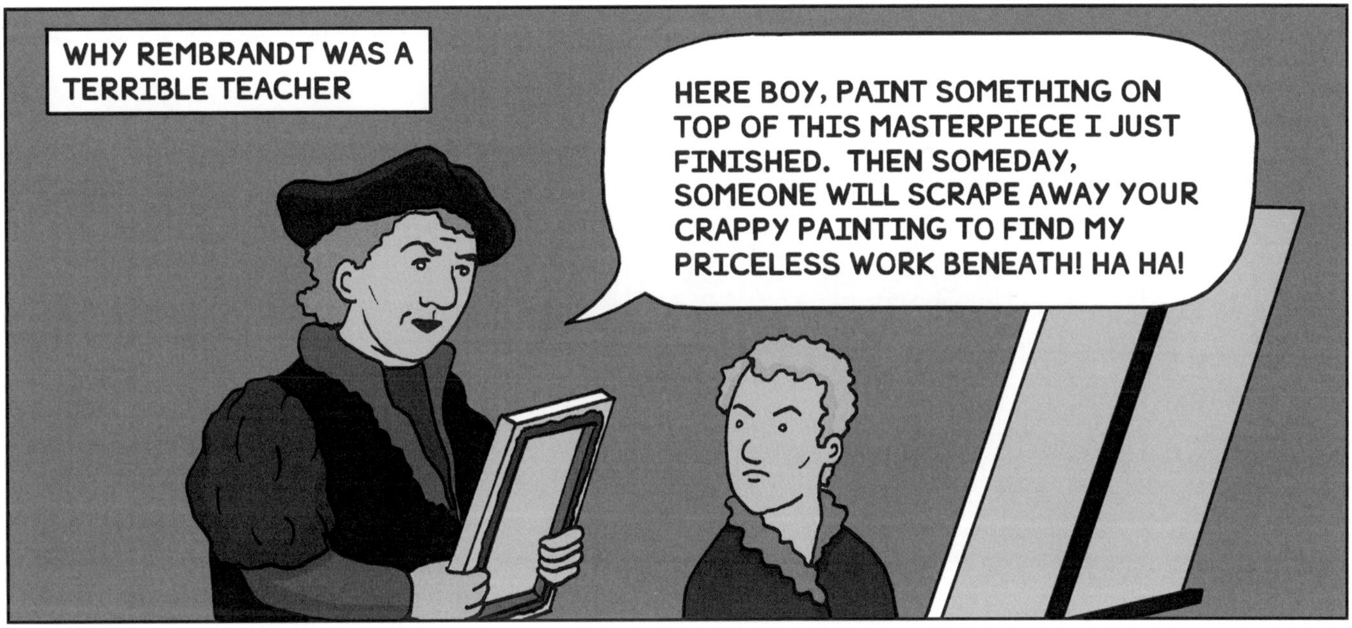
WHY REMBRANDT WAS A TERRIBLE TEACHER
HERE BOY, PAINT SOMETHING ON TOP OF THIS MASTERPIECE I JUST FINISHED. THEN SOMEDAY, SOMEONE WILL SCRAPE AWAY YOUR CRAPPY PAINTING TO FIND MY PRICELESS WORK BENEATH! HA HA!

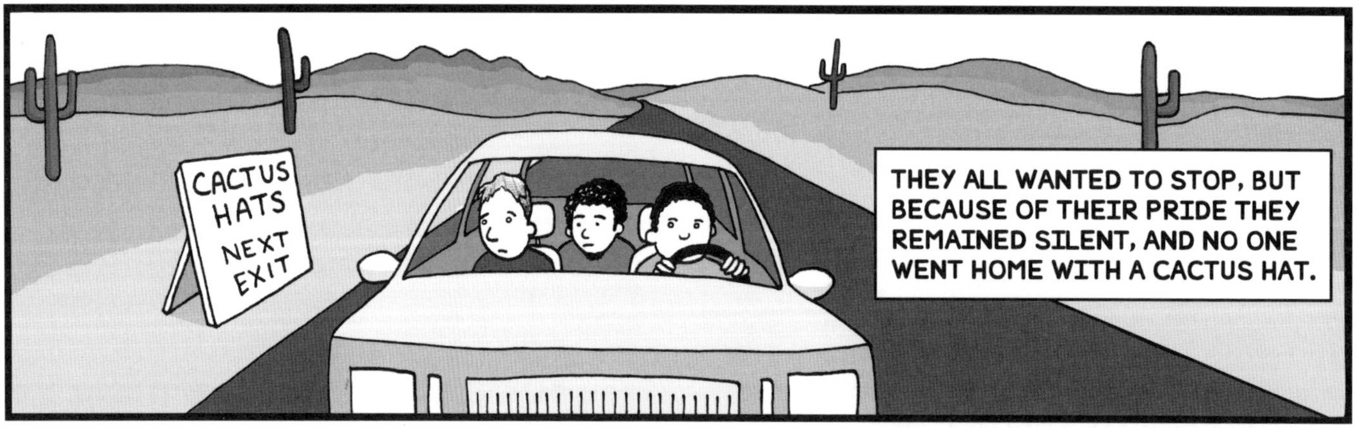
CACTUS HATS NEXT EXIT
THEY ALL WANTED TO STOP, BUT BECAUSE OF THEIR PRIDE THEY REMAINED SILENT, AND NO ONE WENT HOME WITH A CACTUS HAT.

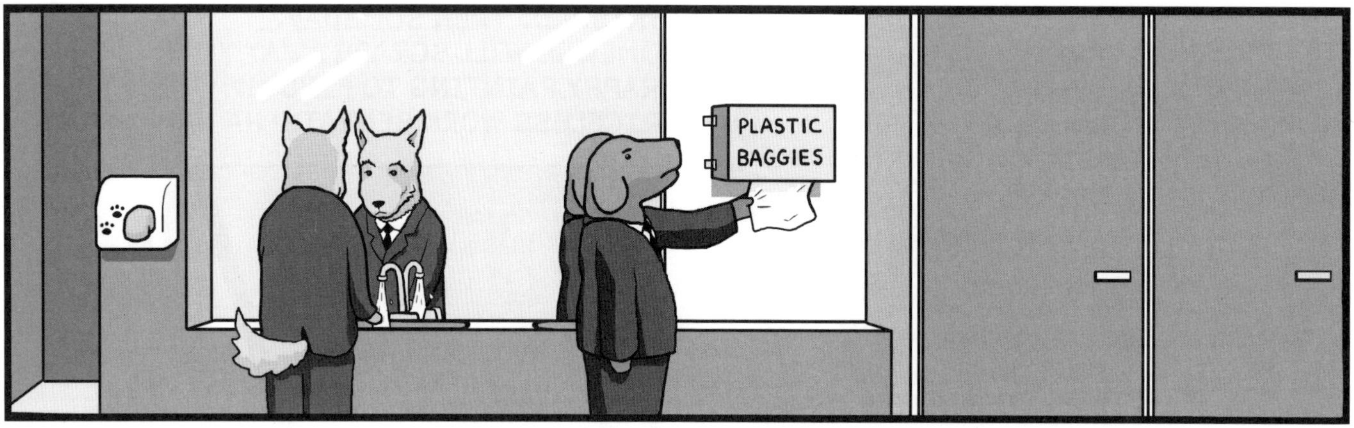
PLASTIC BAGGIES

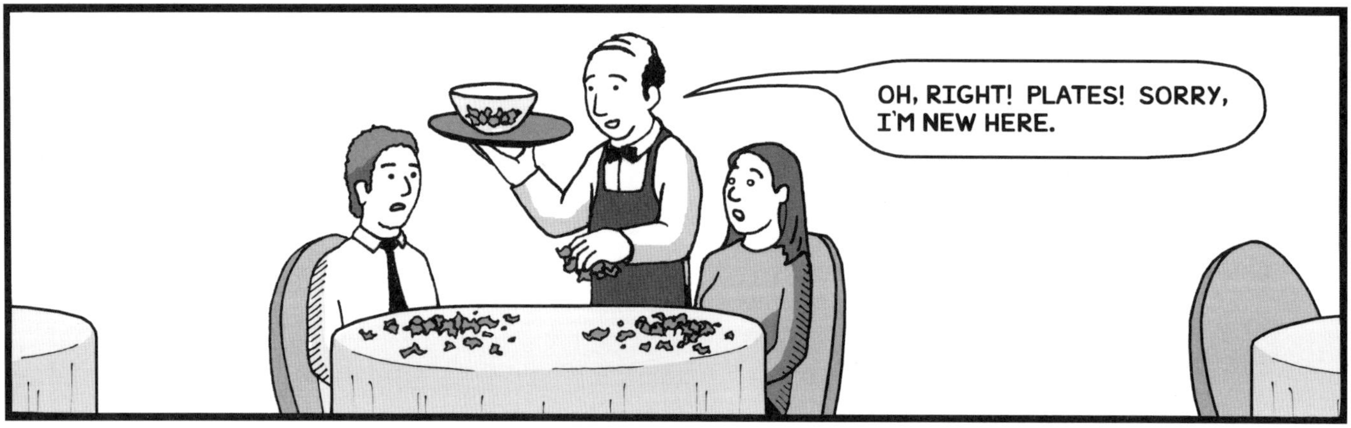
OH, RIGHT! PLATES! SORRY, I'M NEW HERE.

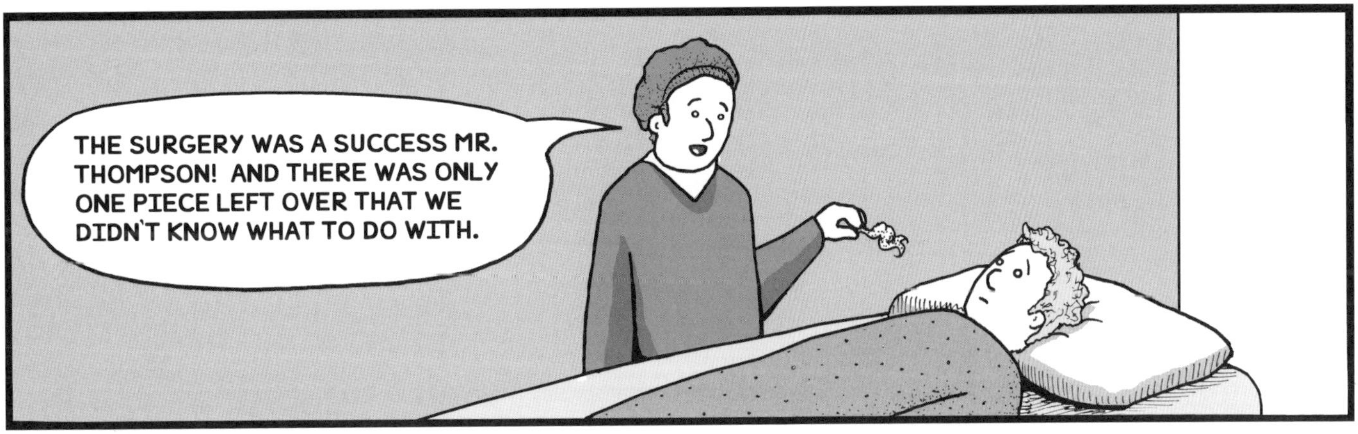
THE SURGERY WAS A SUCCESS MR. THOMPSON! AND THERE WAS ONLY ONE PIECE LEFT OVER THAT WE DIDN'T KNOW WHAT TO DO WITH.

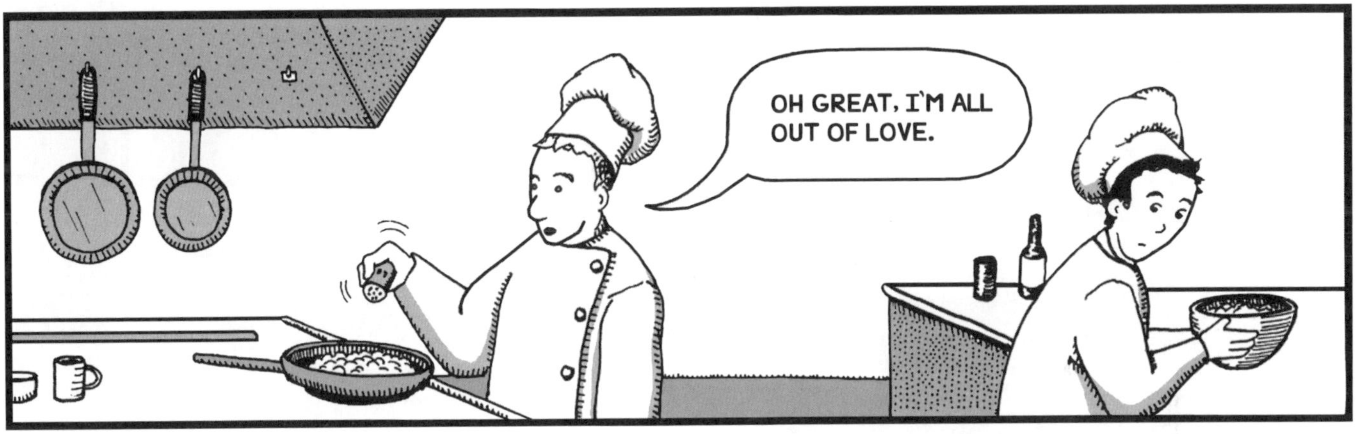
OH GREAT, I'M ALL OUT OF LOVE.

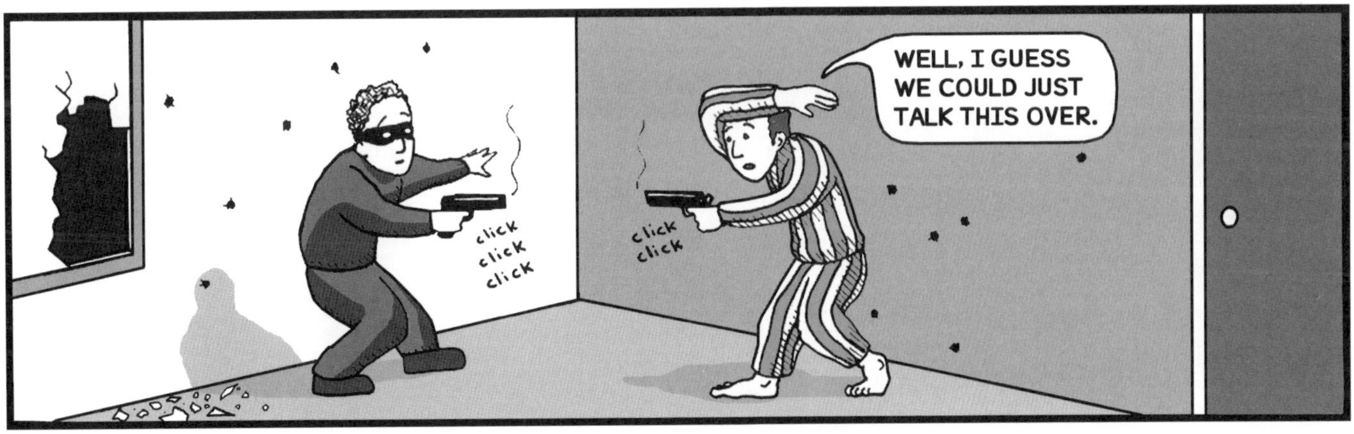
click
click
click
click
click
WELL, I GUESS WE COULD JUST TALK THIS OVER.

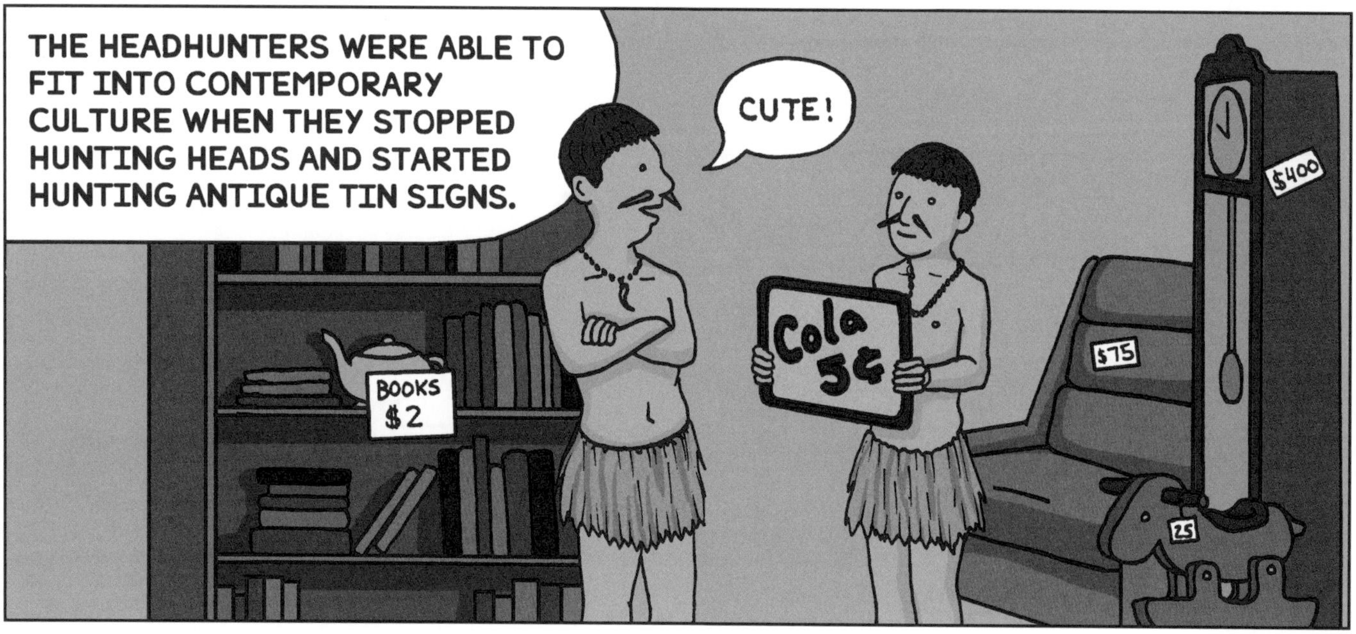
THE HEADHUNTERS WERE ABLE TO FIT INTO CONTEMPORARY CULTURE WHEN THEY STOPPED HUNTING HEADS AND STARTED HUNTING ANTIQUE TIN SIGNS.
CUTE!
BOOKS $2
Cola 5¢
$75
$400
25

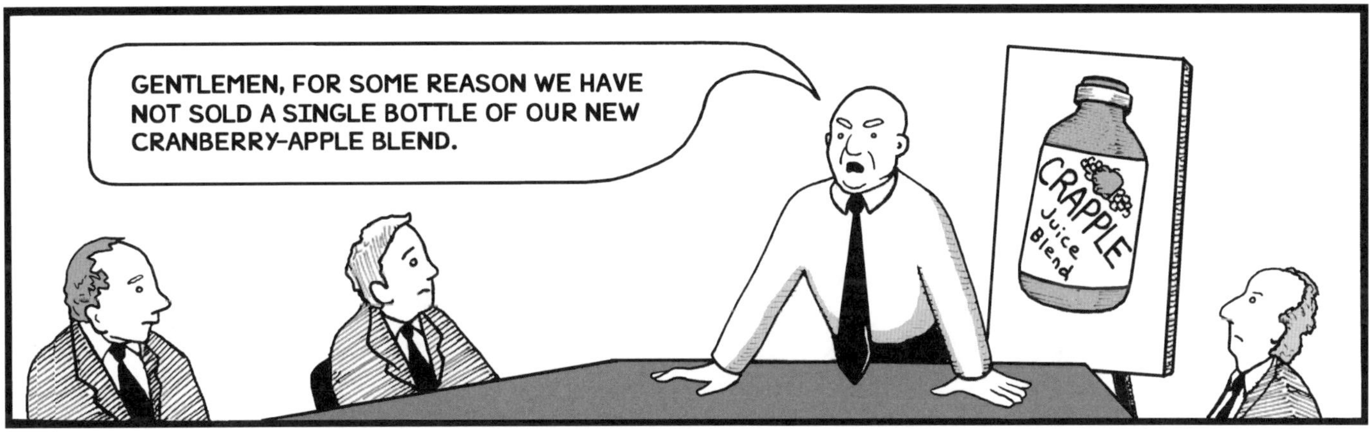
GENTLEMEN, FOR SOME REASON WE HAVE NOT SOLD A SINGLE BOTTLE OF OUR NEW CRANBERRY-APPLE BLEND.
CRAPPLE
Juice Blend

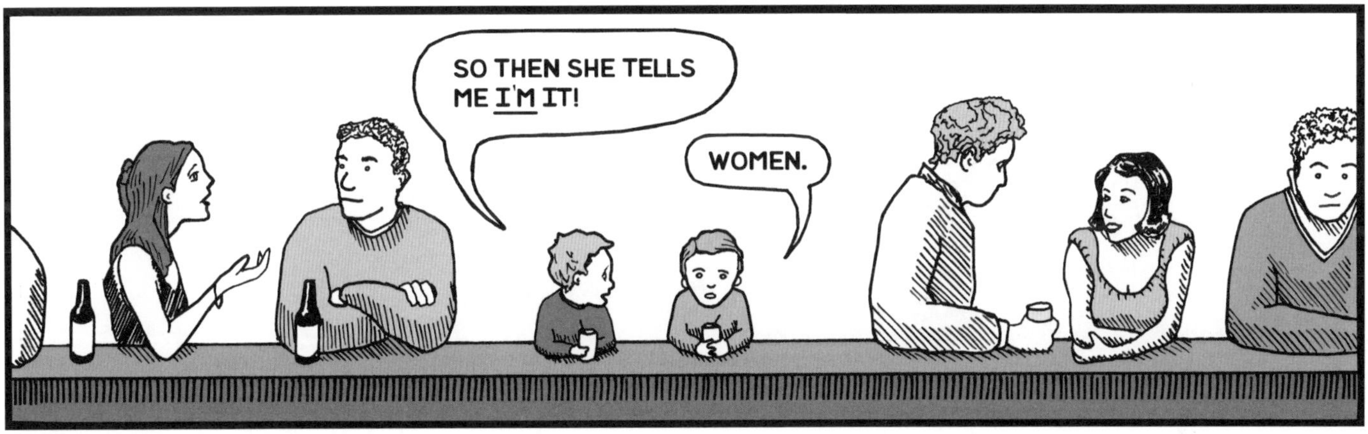
SO THEN SHE TELLS ME I'M IT!
WOMEN.

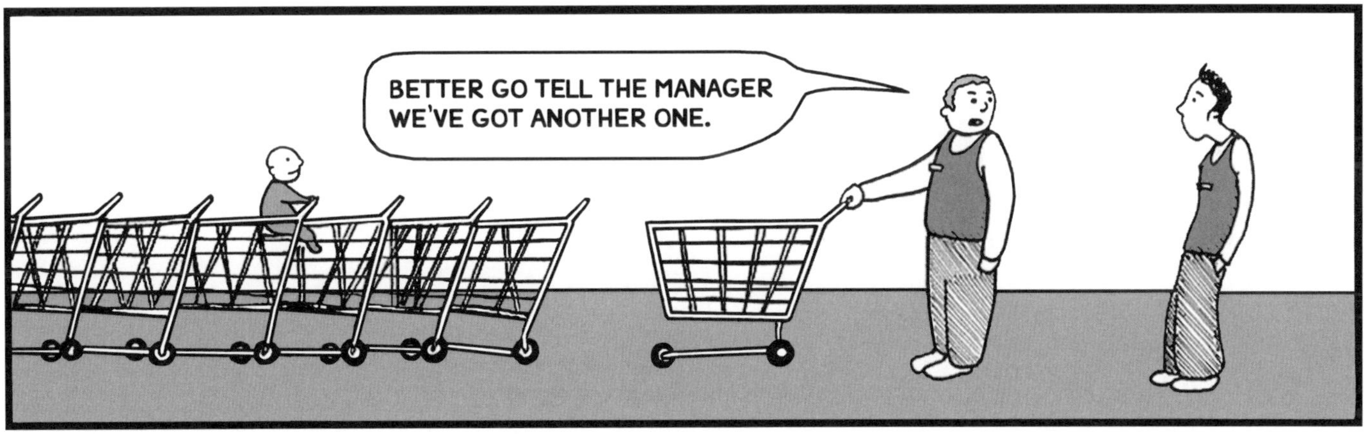
BETTER GO TELL THE MANAGER WE'VE GOT ANOTHER ONE.

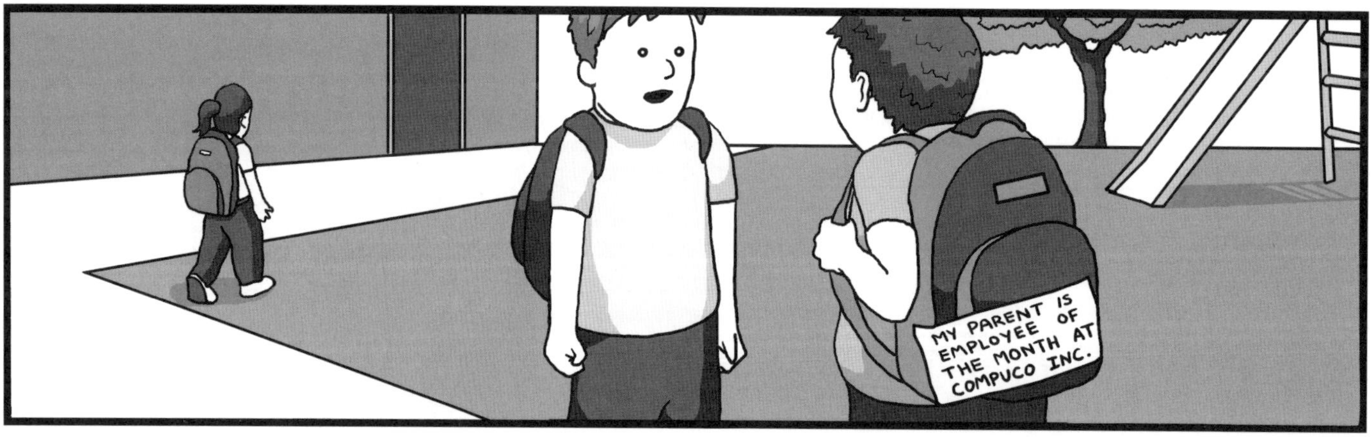
MY PARENT IS EMPLOYEE OF THE MONTH AT COMPUCO INC.

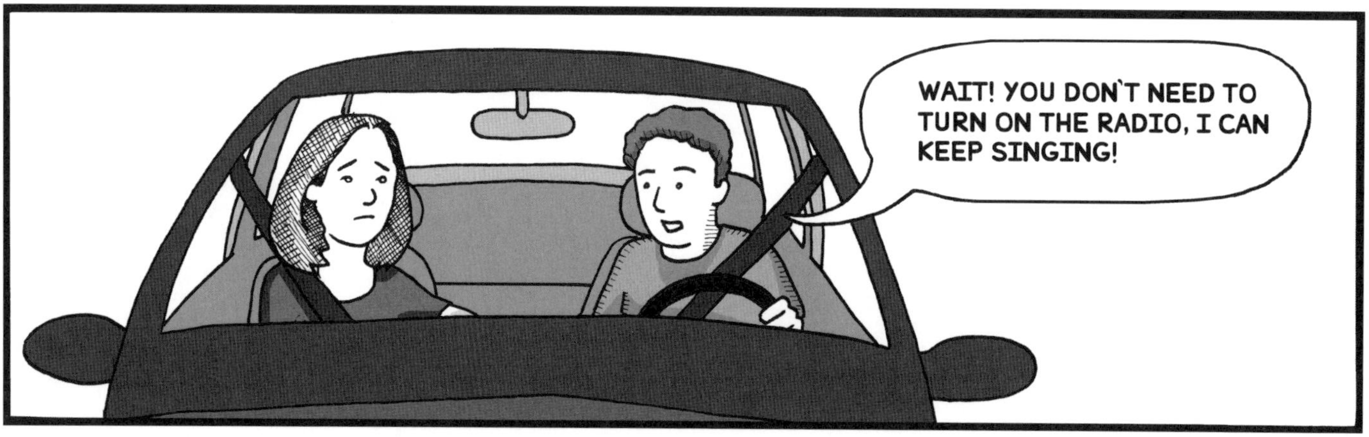
WAIT! YOU DON'T NEED TO TURN ON THE RADIO, I CAN KEEP SINGING!

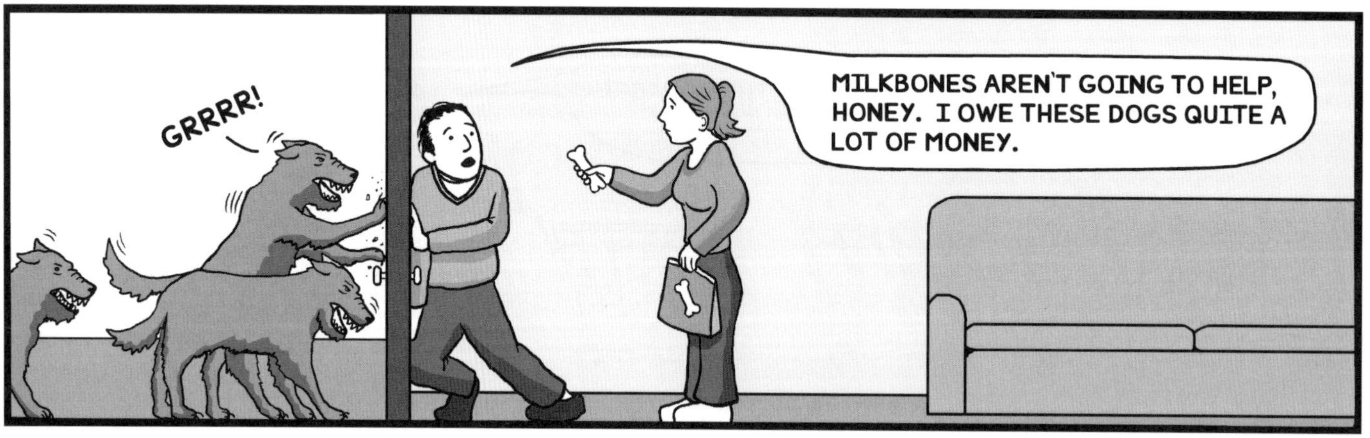
GRRRR!
MILKBONES AREN'T GOING TO HELP, HONEY. I OWE THESE DOGS QUITE A LOT OF MONEY.

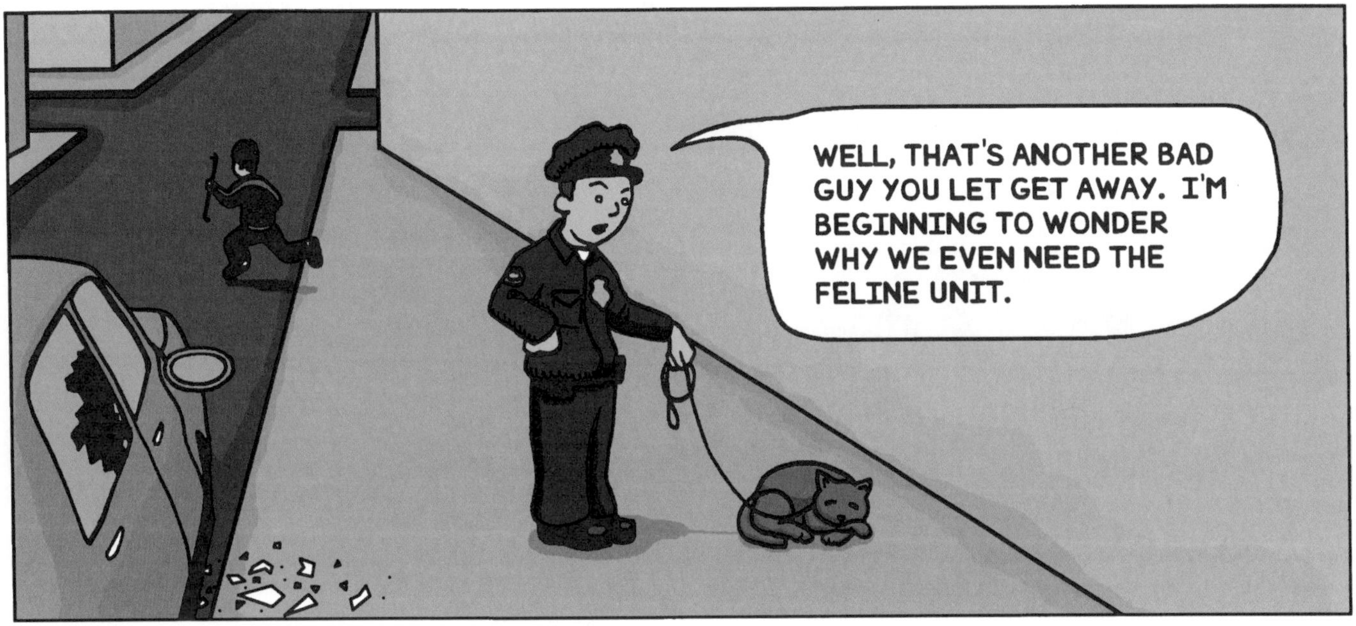
WELL, THAT'S ANOTHER BAD GUY YOU LET GET AWAY. I'M BEGINNING TO WONDER WHY WE EVEN NEED THE FELINE UNIT.

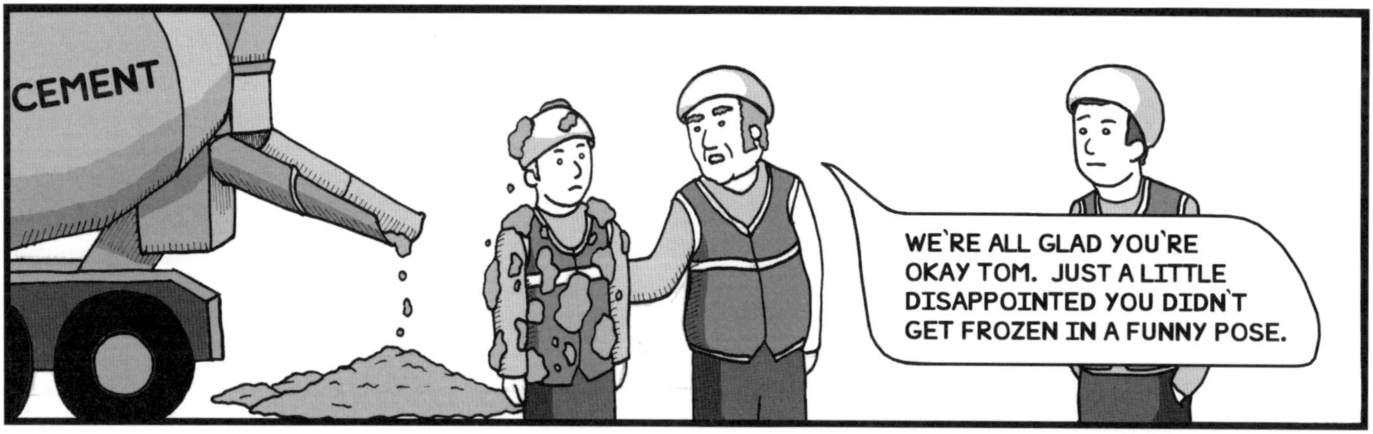
CEMENT
WE'RE ALL GLAD YOU'RE OKAY TOM. JUST A LITTLE DISAPPOINTED YOU DIDN'T GET FROZEN IN A FUNNY POSE.

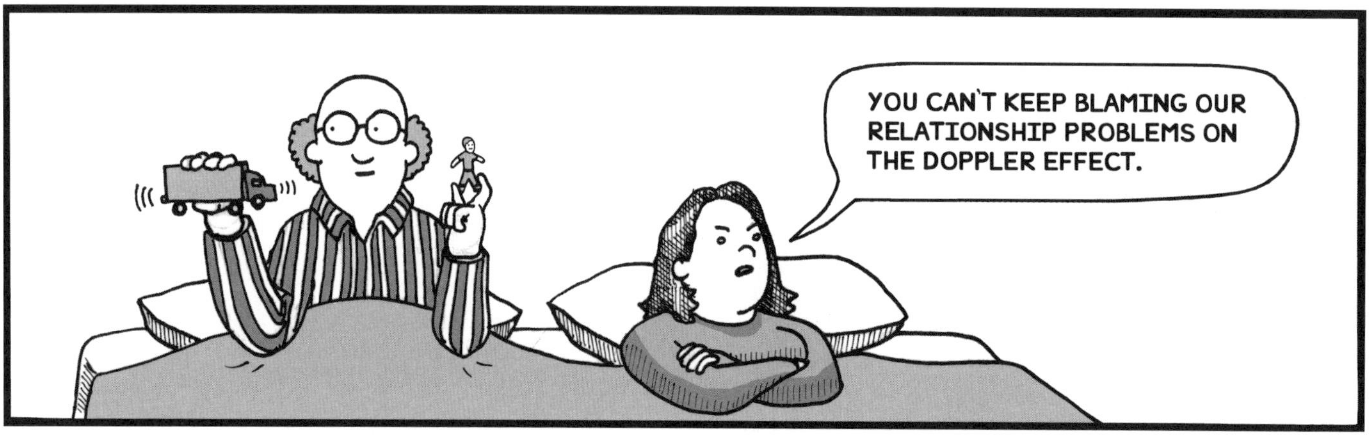
YOU CAN'T KEEP BLAMING OUR RELATIONSHIP PROBLEMS ON THE DOPPLER EFFECT.

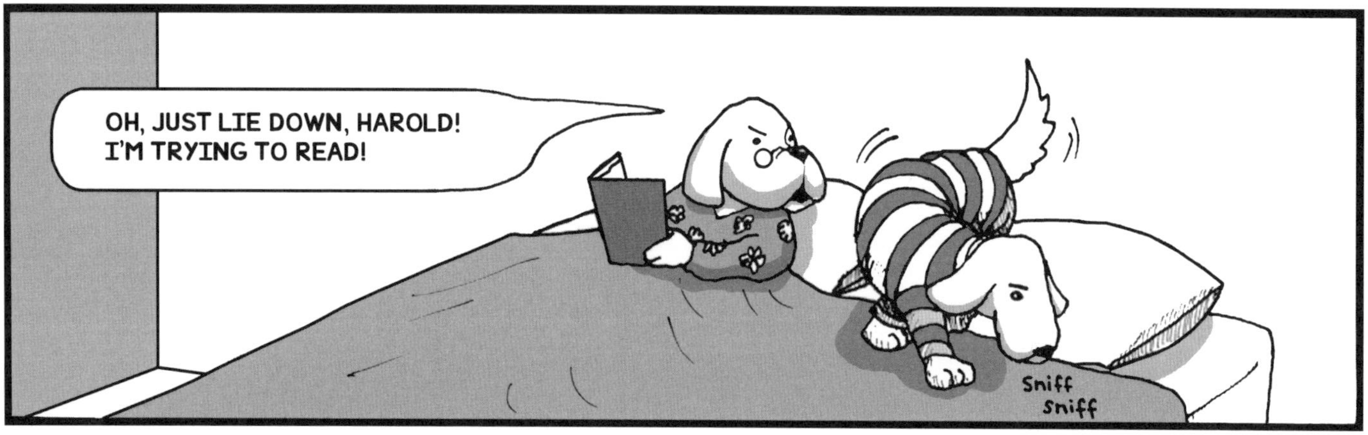
OH, JUST LIE DOWN, HAROLD! I'M TRYING TO READ!
Sniff sniff

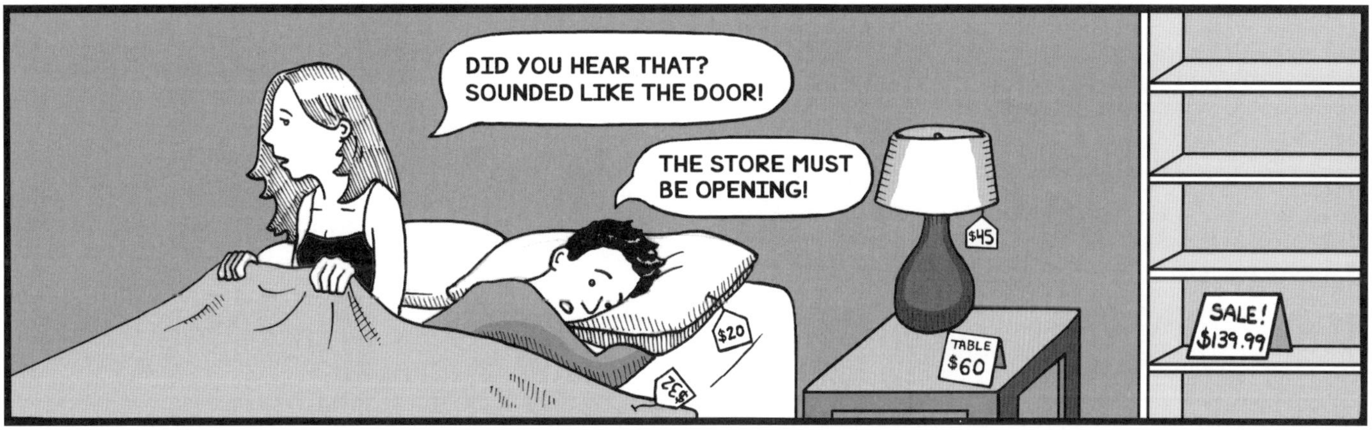
DID YOU HEAR THAT? SOUNDED LIKE THE DOOR!
THE STORE MUST BE OPENING!
$45
$20
$32
TABLE $60
SALE! $139.99

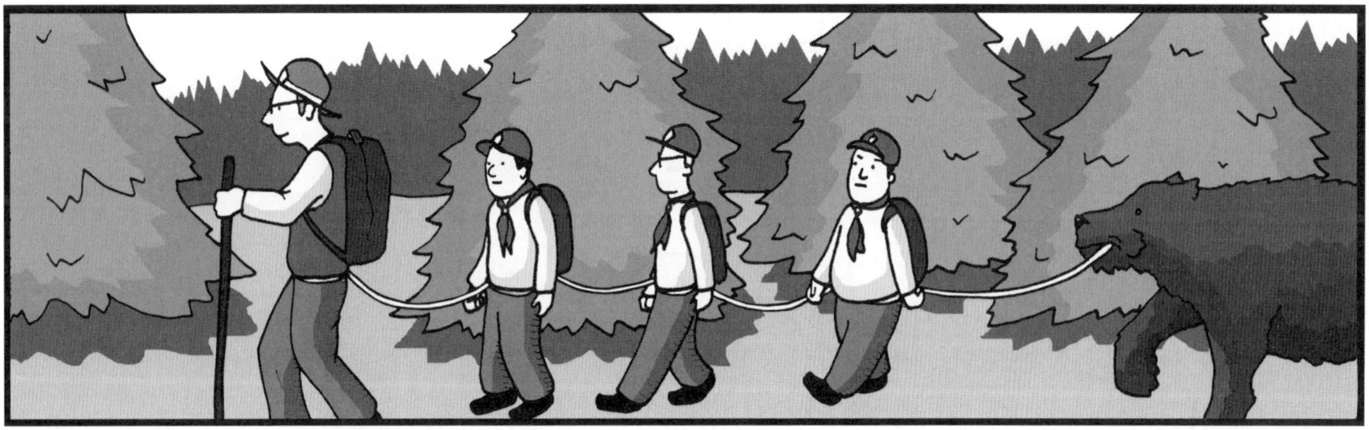

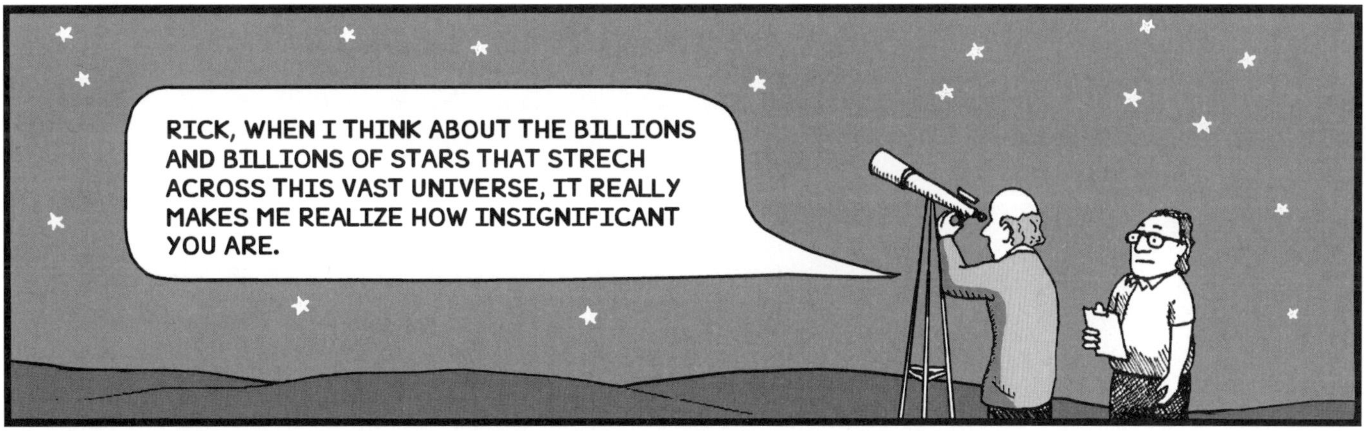
RICK, WHEN I THINK ABOUT THE BILLIONS AND BILLIONS OF STARS THAT STRECH ACROSS THIS VAST UNIVERSE, IT REALLY MAKES ME REALIZE HOW INSIGNIFICANT YOU ARE.

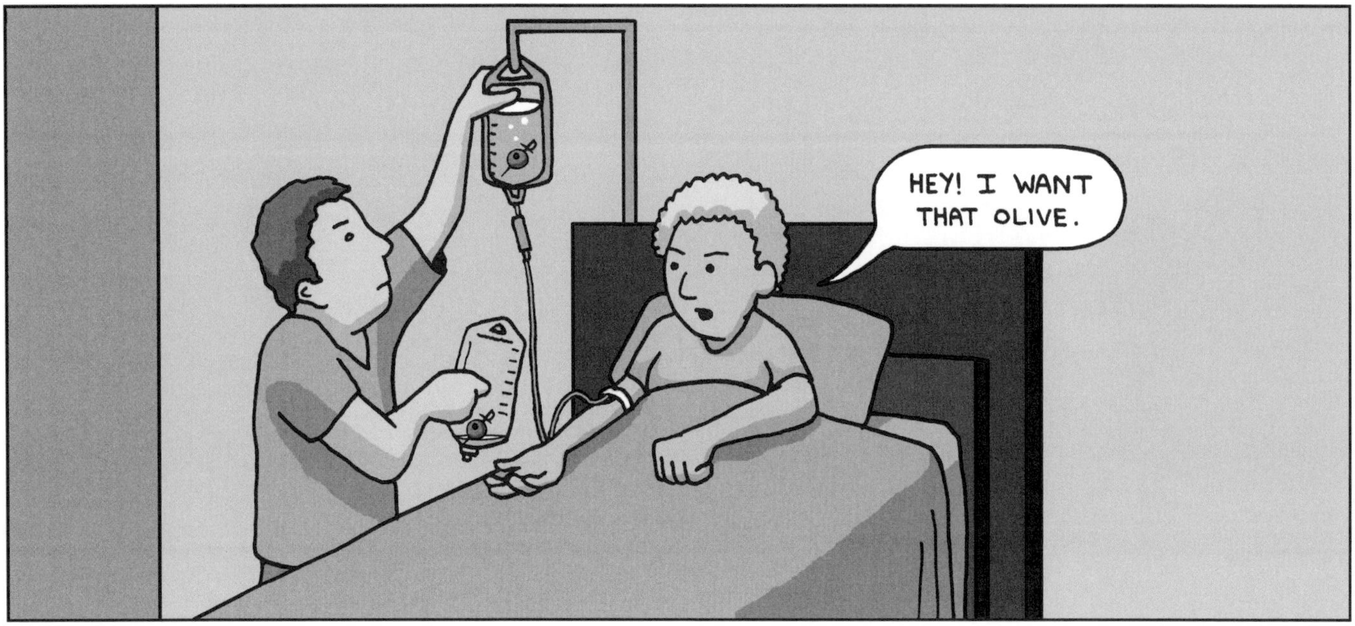
HEY! I WANT THAT OLIVE.

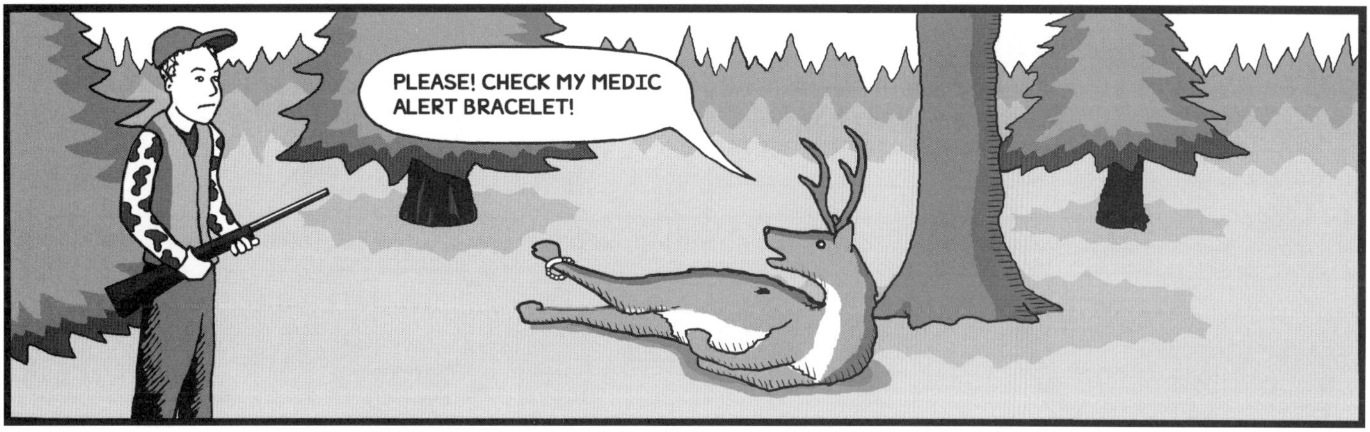
PLEASE! CHECK MY MEDIC ALERT BRACELET!

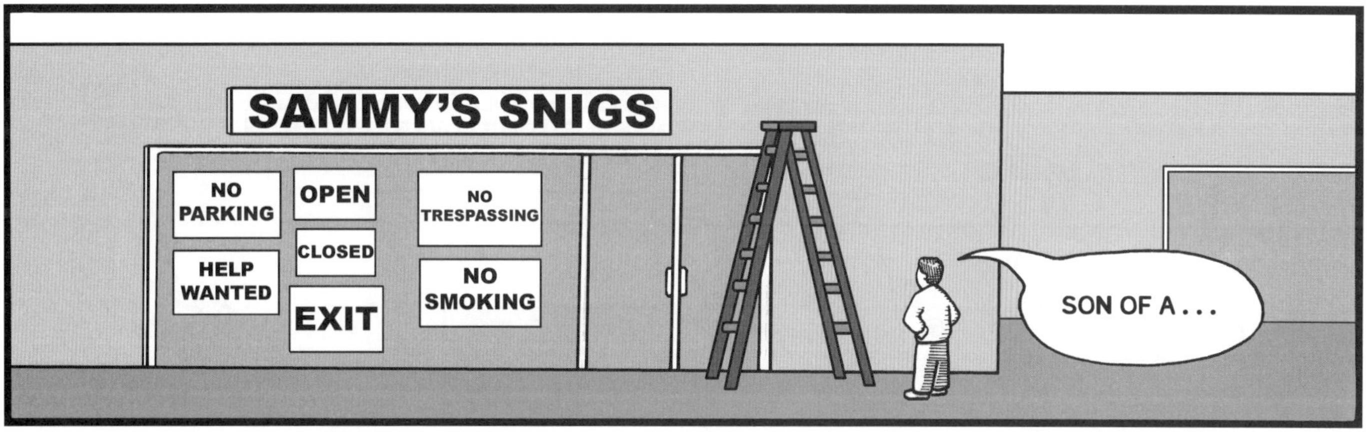
SAMMY'S SNIGS
NO PARKING
OPEN
NO TRESPASSING
HELP WANTED
CLOSED
NO SMOKING
EXIT
SON OF A . . .

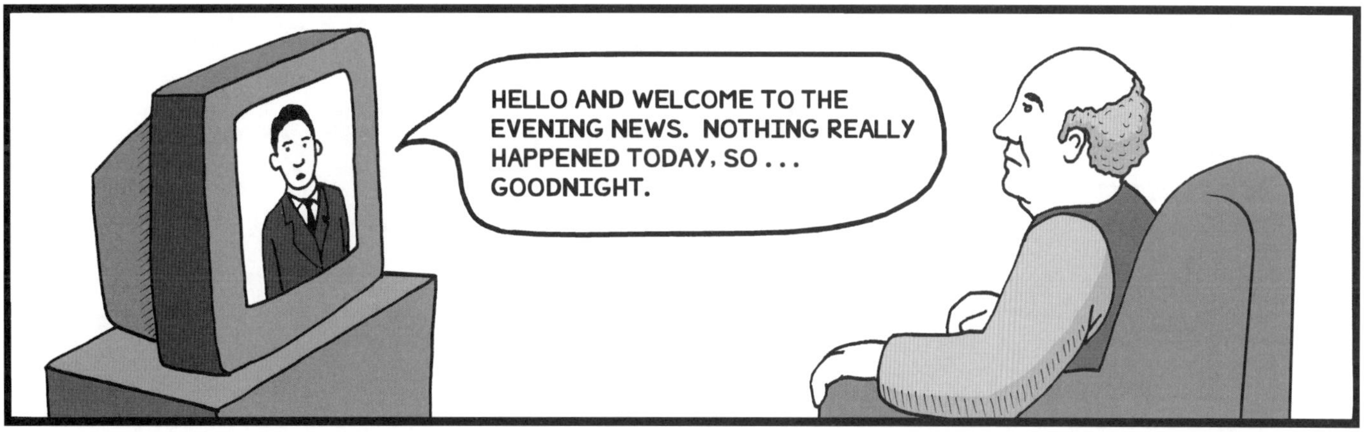
HELLO AND WELCOME TO THE EVENING NEWS. NOTHING REALLY HAPPENED TODAY, SO . . . GOODNIGHT.

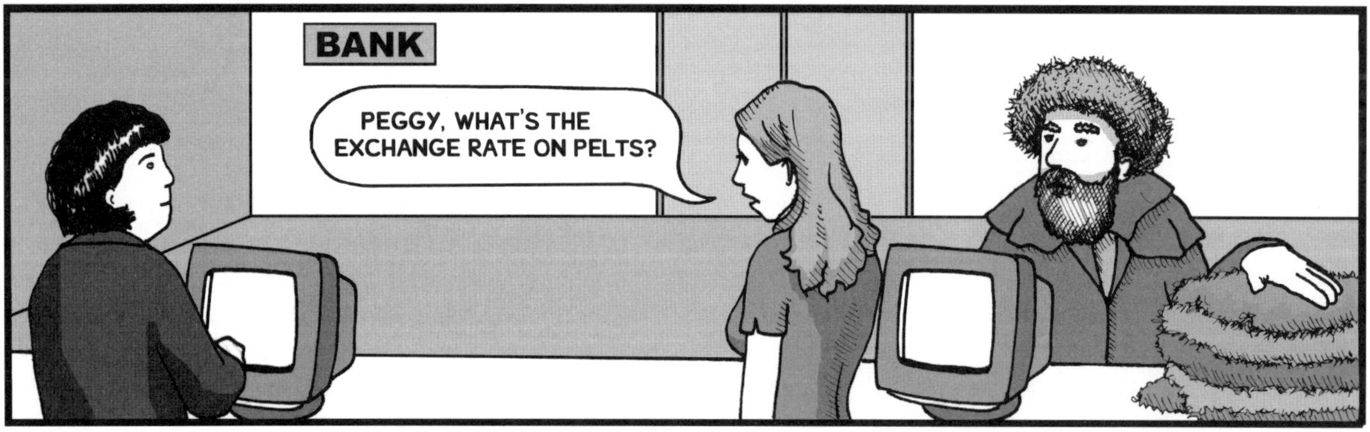
BANK
PEGGY, WHAT'S THE EXCHANGE RATE ON PELTS?

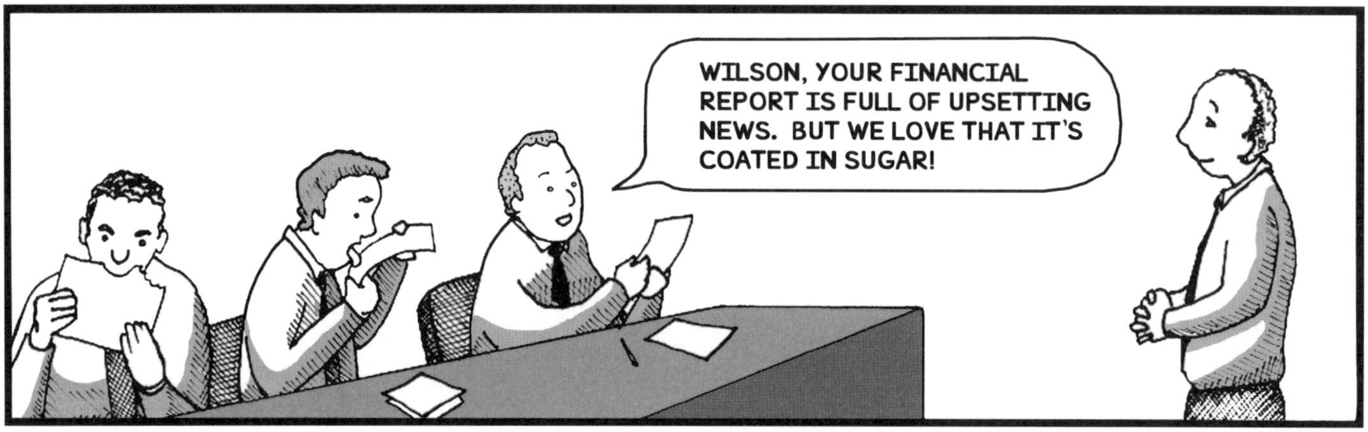
WILSON, YOUR FINANCIAL REPORT IS FULL OF UPSETTING NEWS. BUT WE LOVE THAT IT'S COATED IN SUGAR!

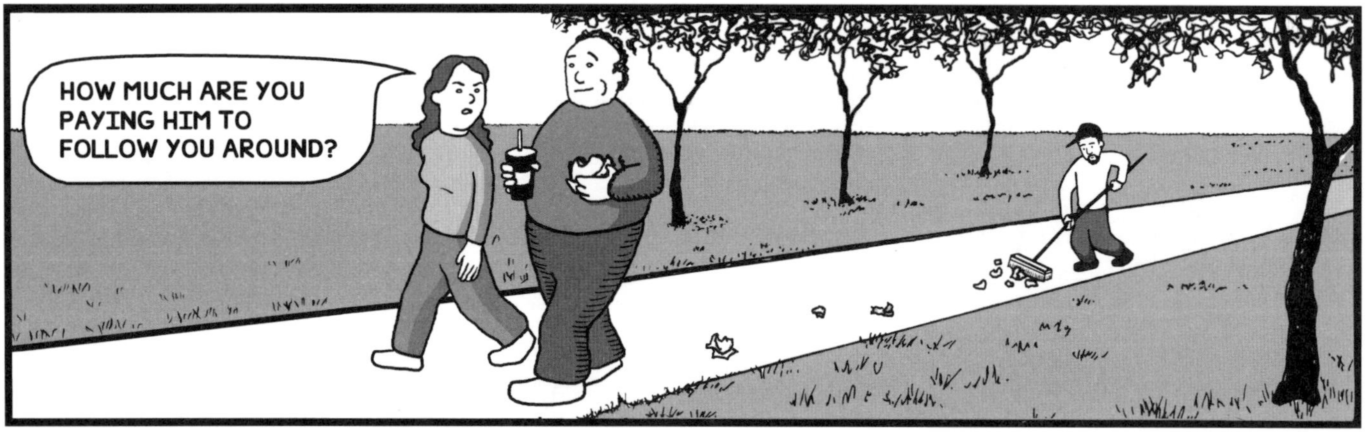
HOW MUCH ARE YOU PAYING HIM TO FOLLOW YOU AROUND?

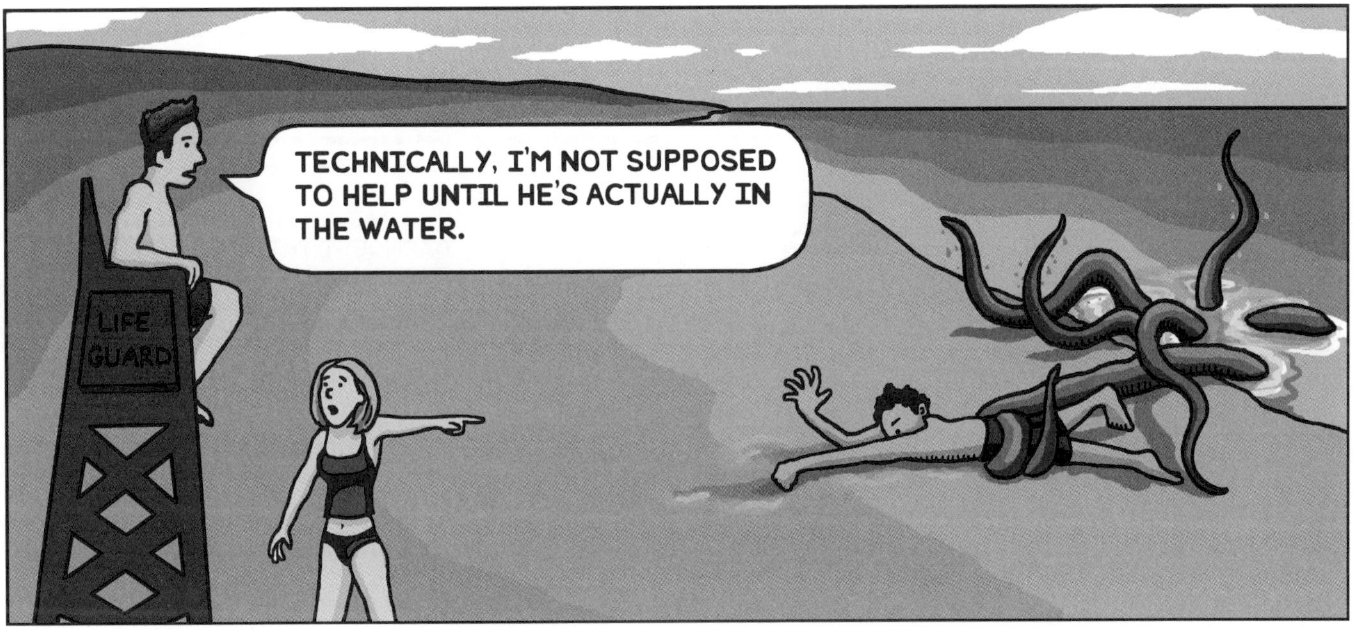
LIFE GUARD
TECHNICALLY, I'M NOT SUPPOSED TO HELP UNTIL HE'S ACTUALLY IN THE WATER.

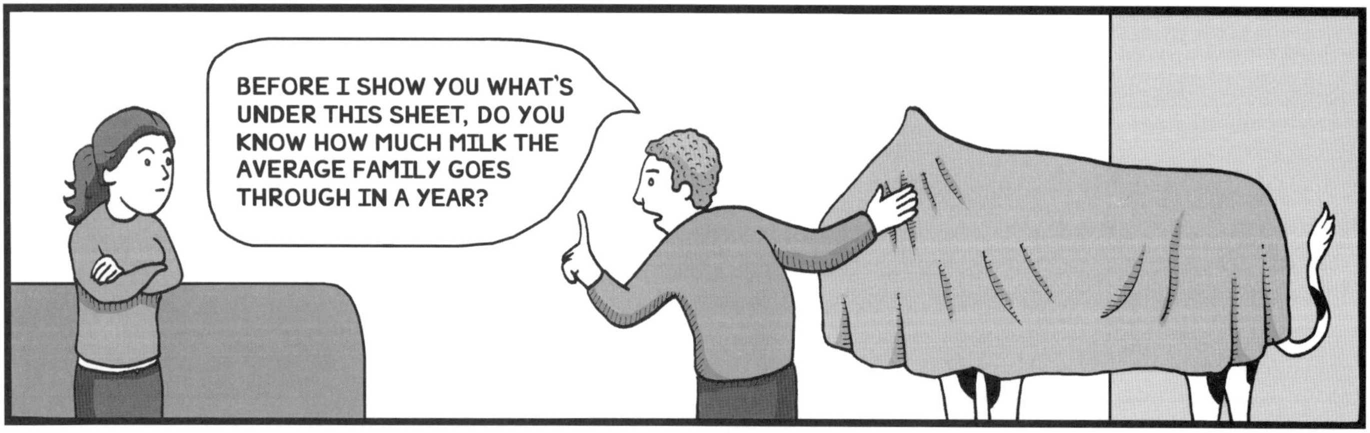
BEFORE I SHOW YOU WHAT'S UNDER THIS SHEET, DO YOU KNOW HOW MUCH MILK THE AVERAGE FAMILY GOES THROUGH IN A YEAR?

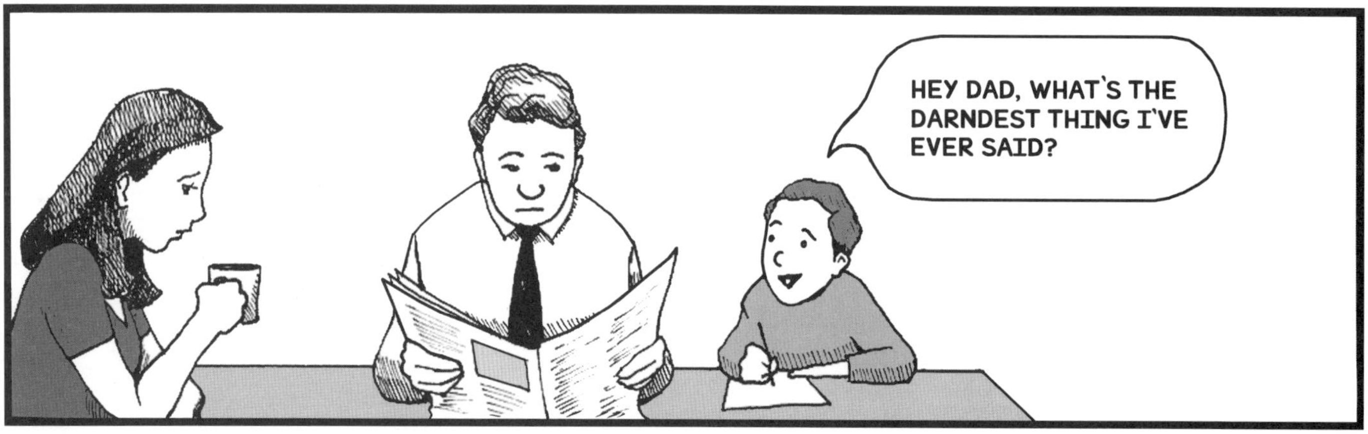
HEY DAD, WHAT'S THE DARNDEST THING I'VE EVER SAID?

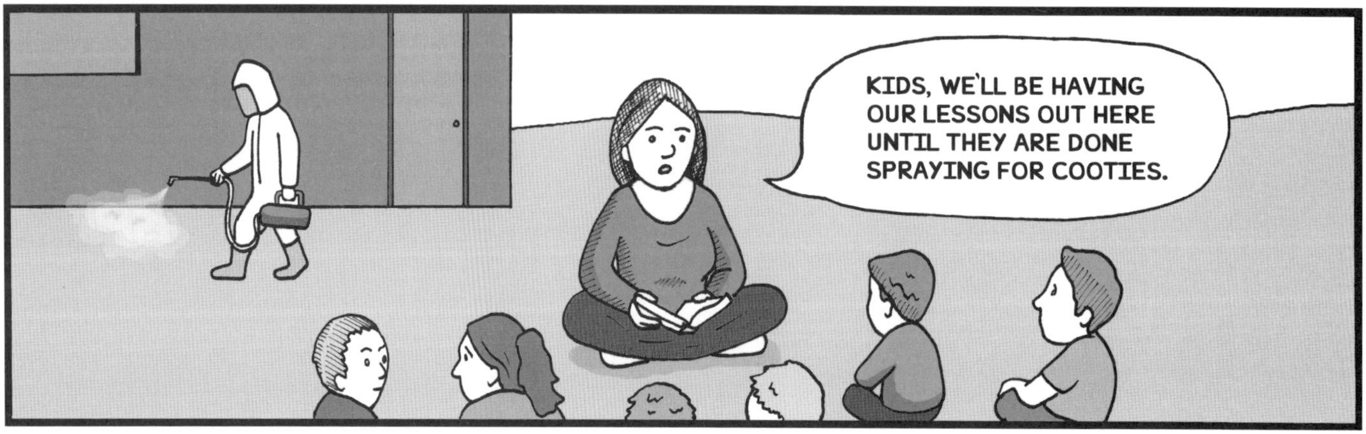
KIDS, WE'LL BE HAVING OUR LESSONS OUT HERE UNTIL THEY ARE DONE SPRAYING FOR COOTIES.

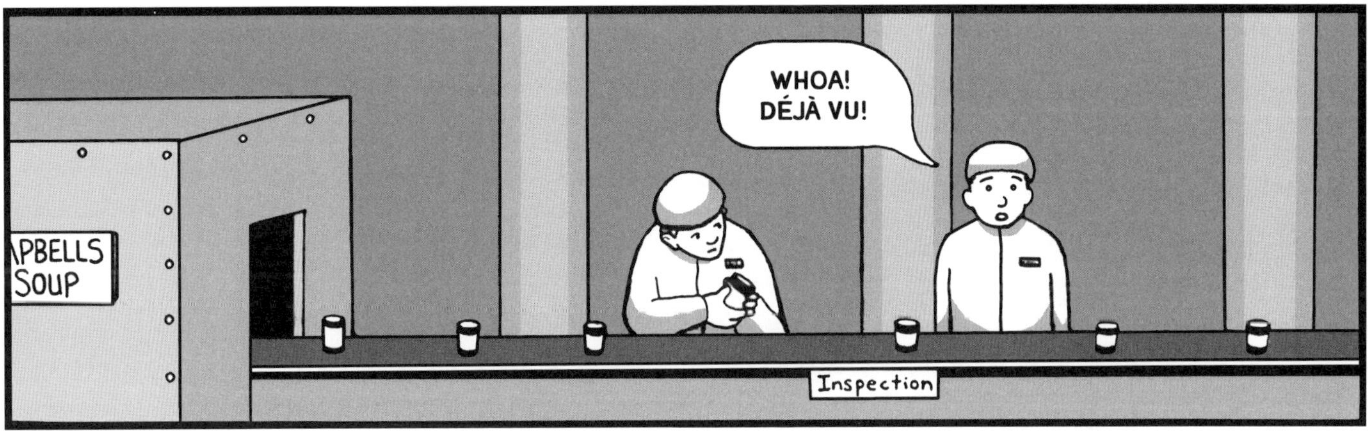
WHOA! DÉJÀ VU!
PBELLS SOUP
Inspection

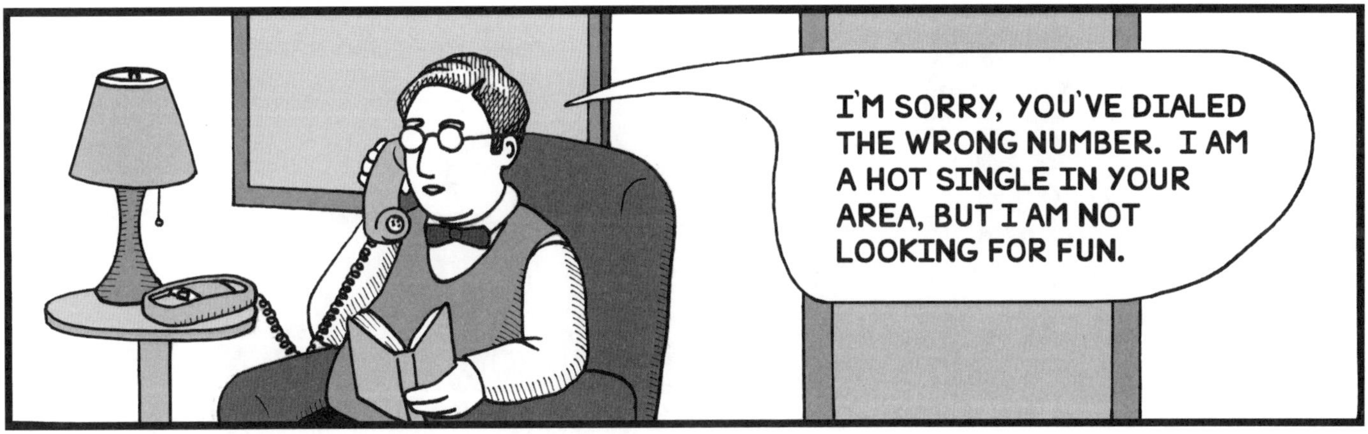
I'M SORRY, YOU'VE DIALED THE WRONG NUMBER. I AM A HOT SINGLE IN YOUR AREA, BUT I AM NOT LOOKING FOR FUN.

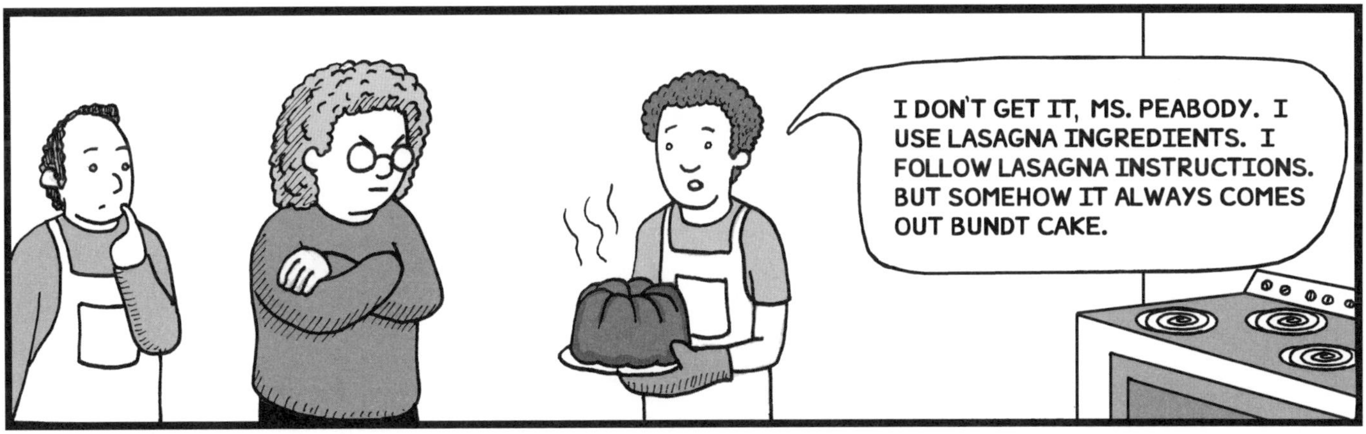
I DON'T GET IT, MS. PEABODY. I USE LASAGNA INGREDIENTS. I FOLLOW LASAGNA INSTRUCTIONS. BUT SOMEHOW IT ALWAYS COMES OUT BUNDT CAKE.

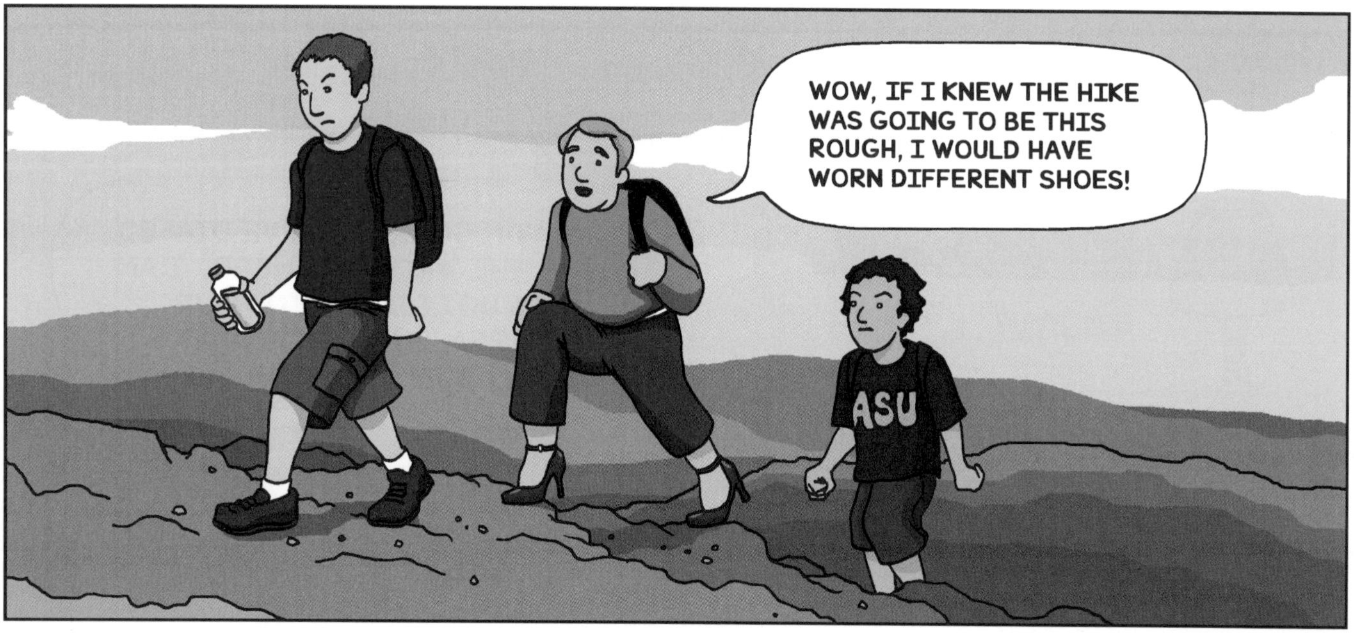
WOW, IF I KNEW THE HIKE WAS GOING TO BE THIS ROUGH, I WOULD HAVE WORN DIFFERENT SHOES!
ASU

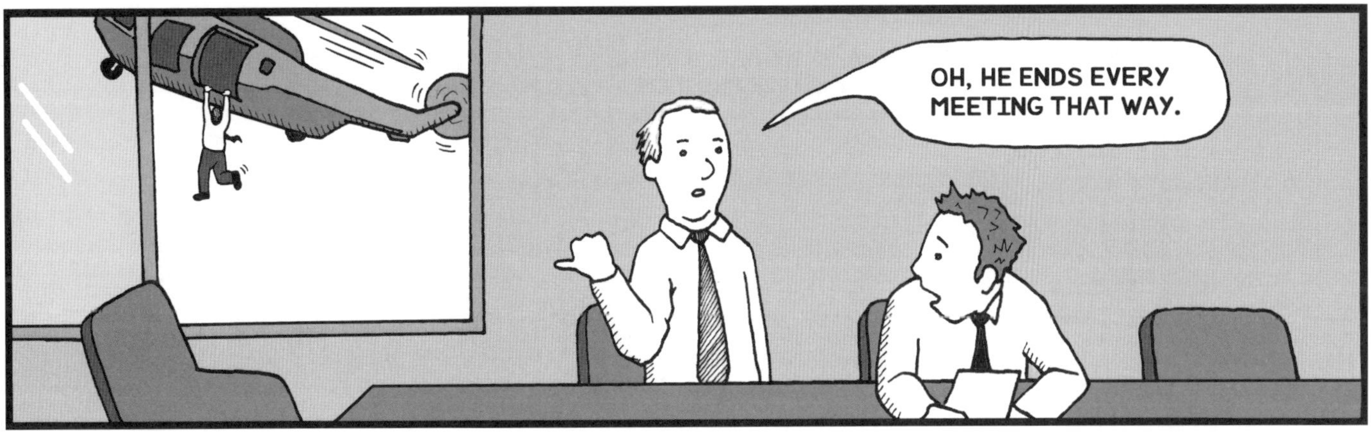
OH, HE ENDS EVERY MEETING THAT WAY.

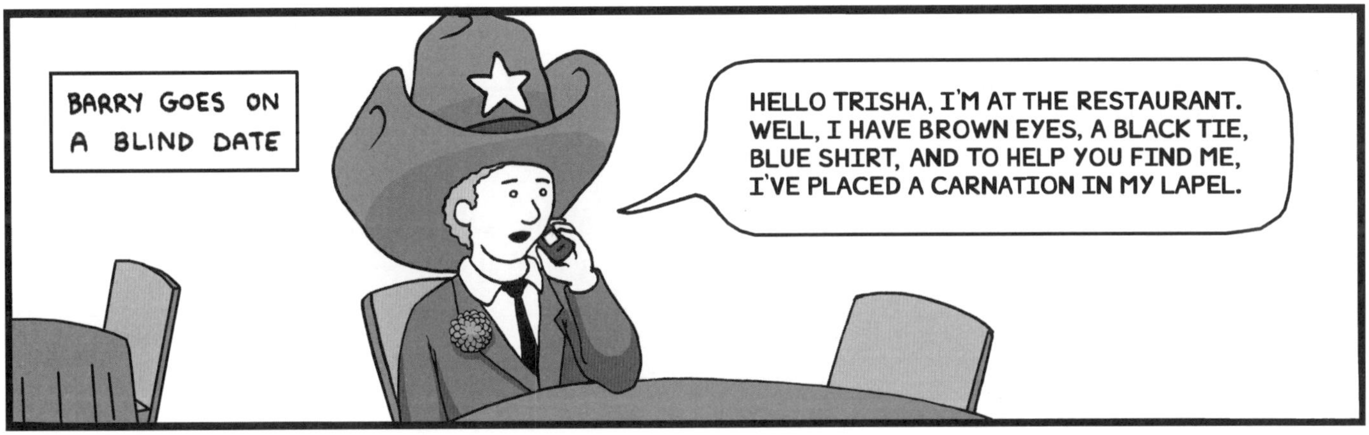
BARRY GOES ON A BLIND DATE
HELLO TRISHA, I'M AT THE RESTAURANT. WELL, I HAVE BROWN EYES, A BLACK TIE, BLUE SHIRT, AND TO HELP YOU FIND ME, I'VE PLACED A CARNATION IN MY LAPEL.

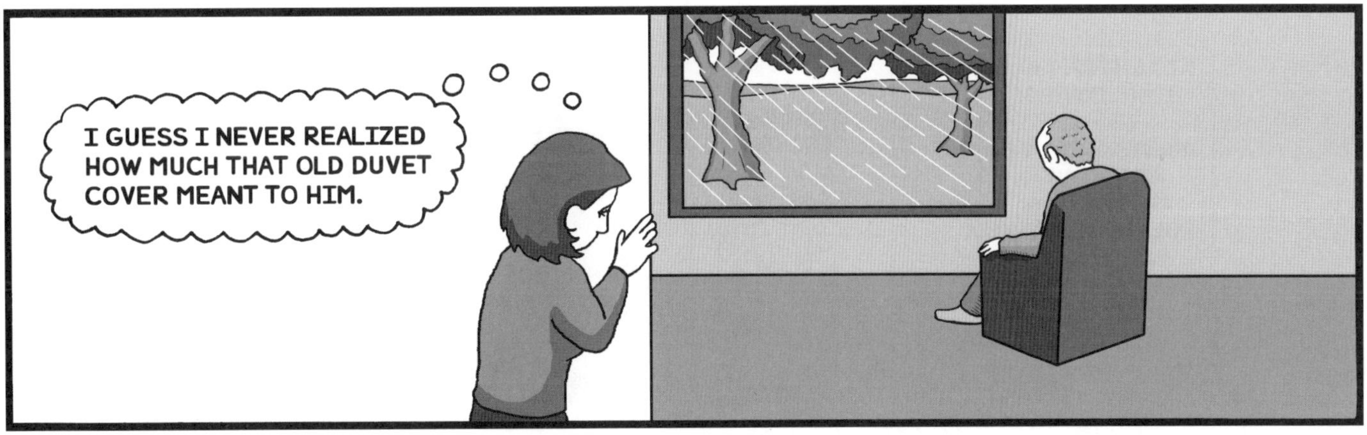
I GUESS I NEVER REALIZED HOW MUCH THAT OLD DUVET COVER MEANT TO HIM.

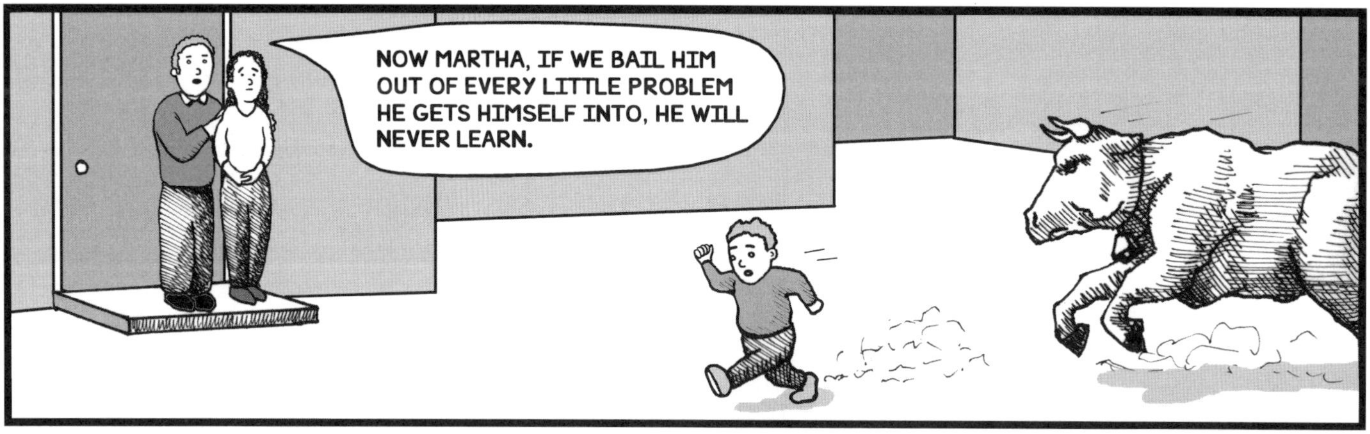
NOW MARTHA, IF WE BAIL HIM OUT OF EVERY LITTLE PROBLEM HE GETS HIMSELF INTO, HE WILL NEVER LEARN.

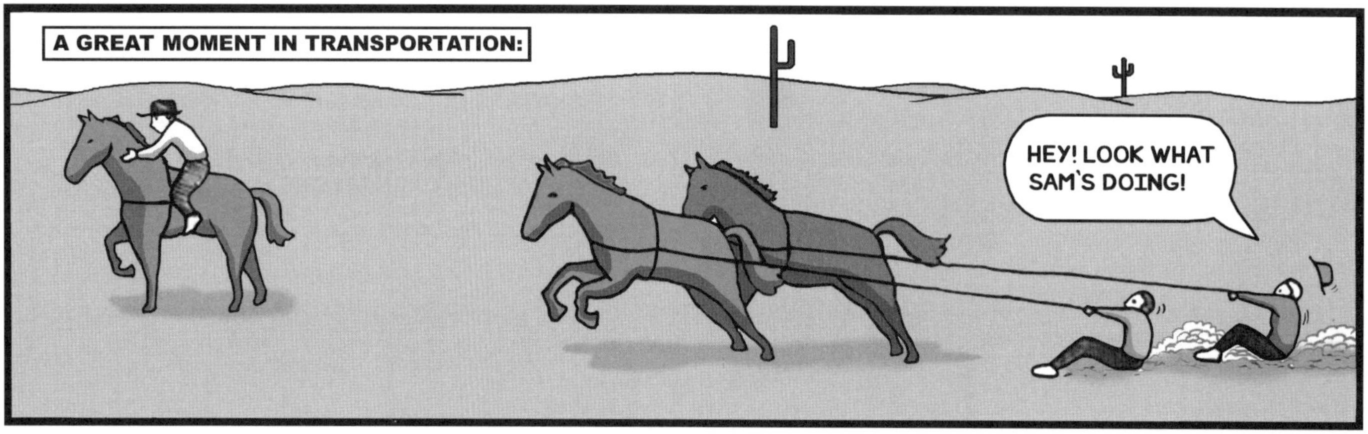
A GREAT MOMENT IN TRANSPORTATION:
HEY! LOOK WHAT SAM'S DOING!

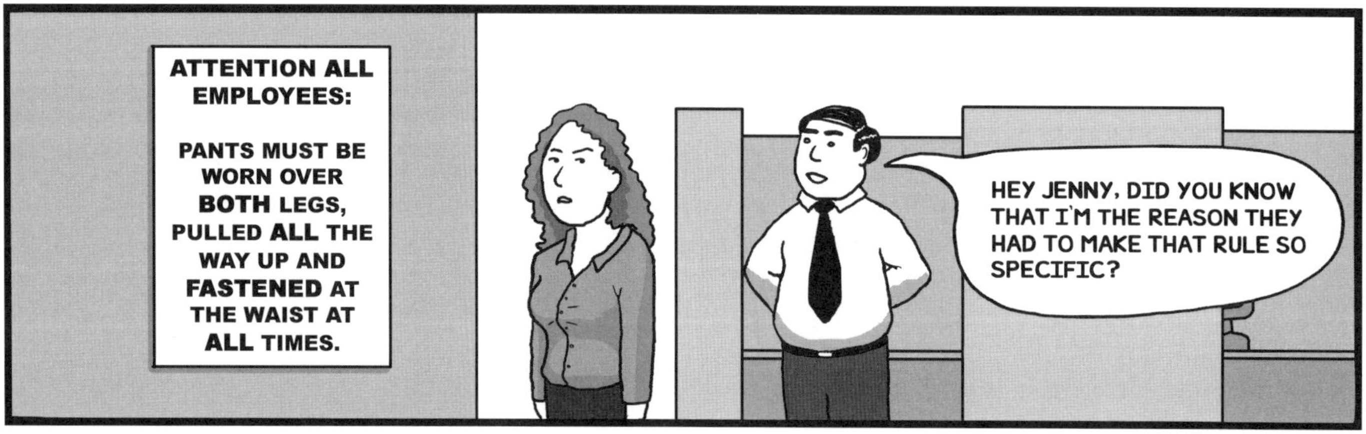
ATTENTION ALL EMPLOYEES:
PANTS MUST BE WORN OVER BOTH LEGS, PULLED ALL THE WAY UP AND FASTENED AT THE WAIST AT ALL TIMES.
HEY JENNY, DID YOU KNOW THAT I'M THE REASON THEY HAD TO MAKE THAT RULE SO SPECIFIC?

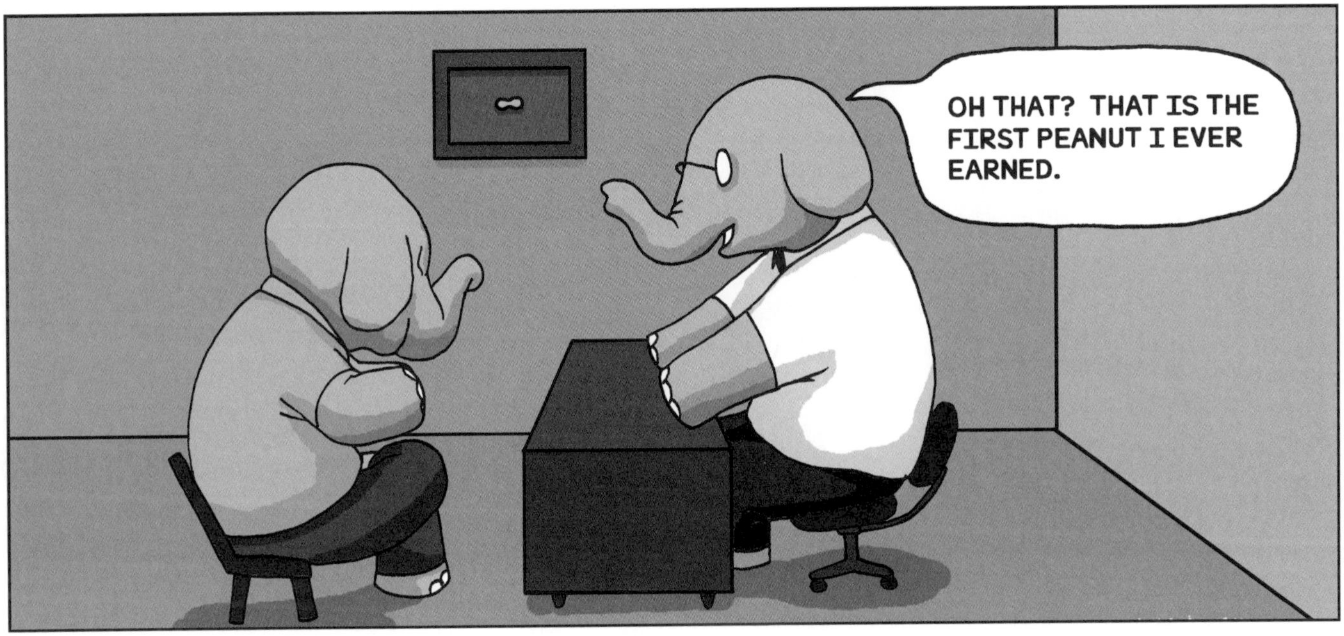
OH THAT? THAT IS THE FIRST PEANUT I EVER EARNED.

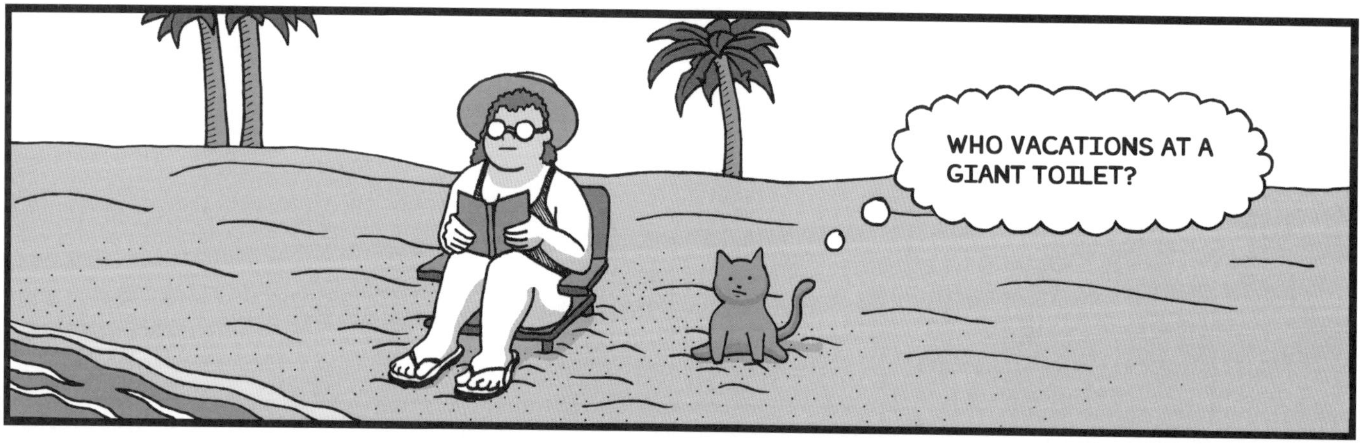
WHO VACATIONS AT A GIANT TOILET?

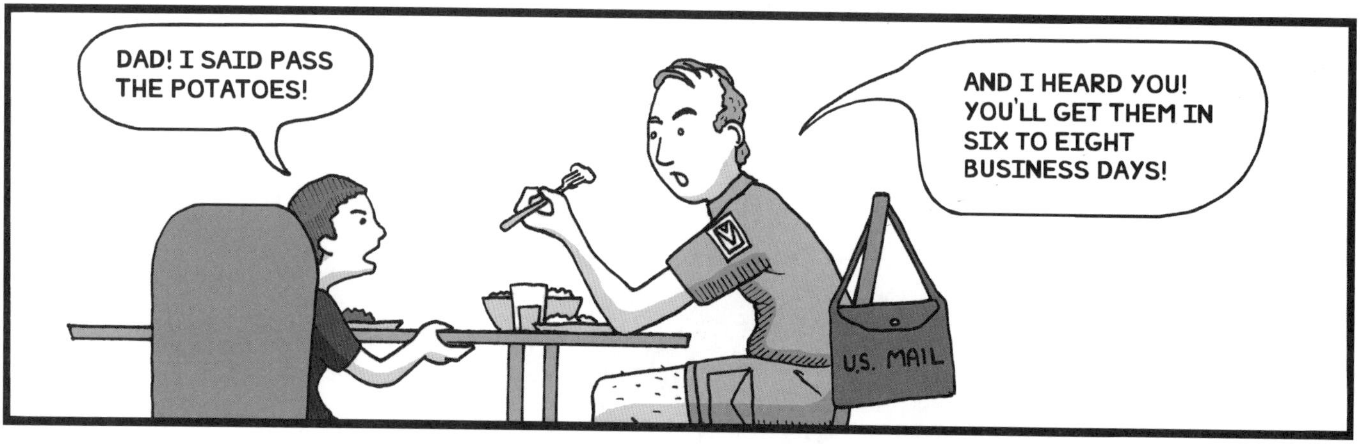
DAD! I SAID PASS THE POTATOES!
AND I HEARD YOU! YOU'LL GET THEM IN SIX TO EIGHT BUSINESS DAYS!
U.S. MAIL

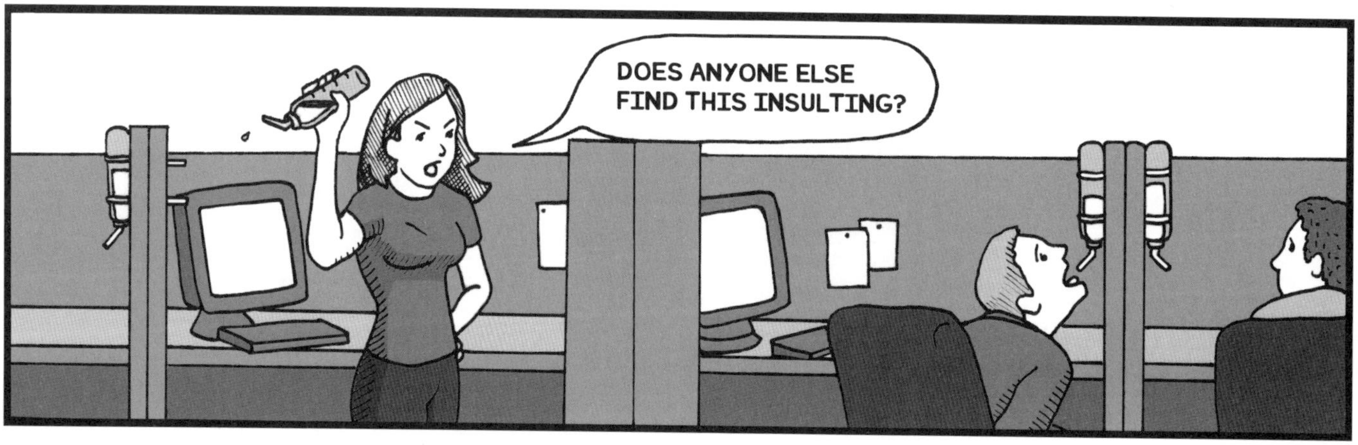
DOES ANYONE ELSE FIND THIS INSULTING?

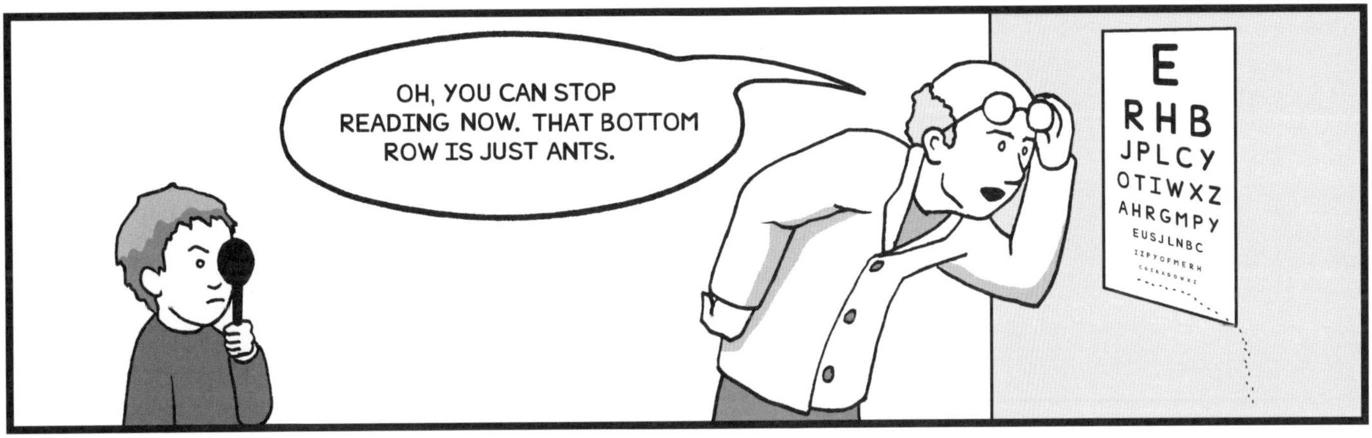
OH, YOU CAN STOP READING NOW. THAT BOTTOM ROW IS JUST ANTS.
E
RHB
JPLCY
OTIWXZ
AHRGMPY
EUSJLNBC

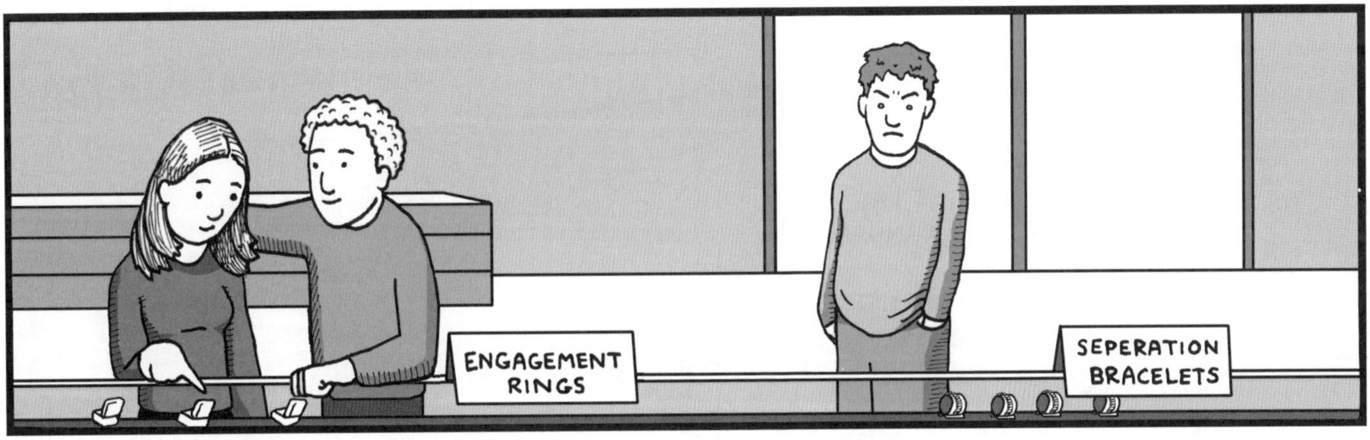
ENGAGEMENT RINGS
SEPERATION BRACELETS

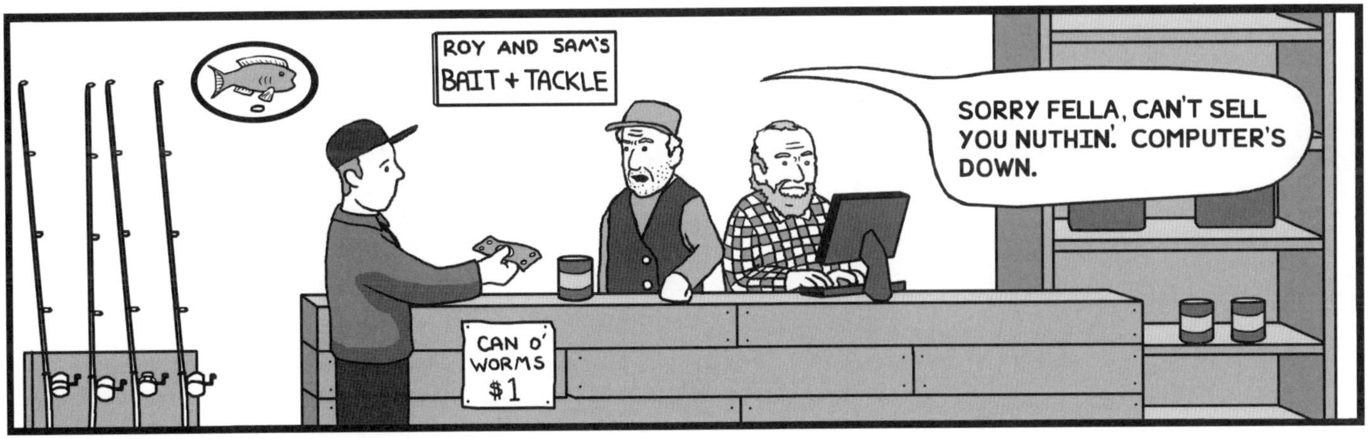
ROY AND SAM'S
BAIT + TACKLE
SORRY FELLA, CAN'T SELL YOU NUTHIN'. COMPUTER'S DOWN.
CAN O' WORMS $1

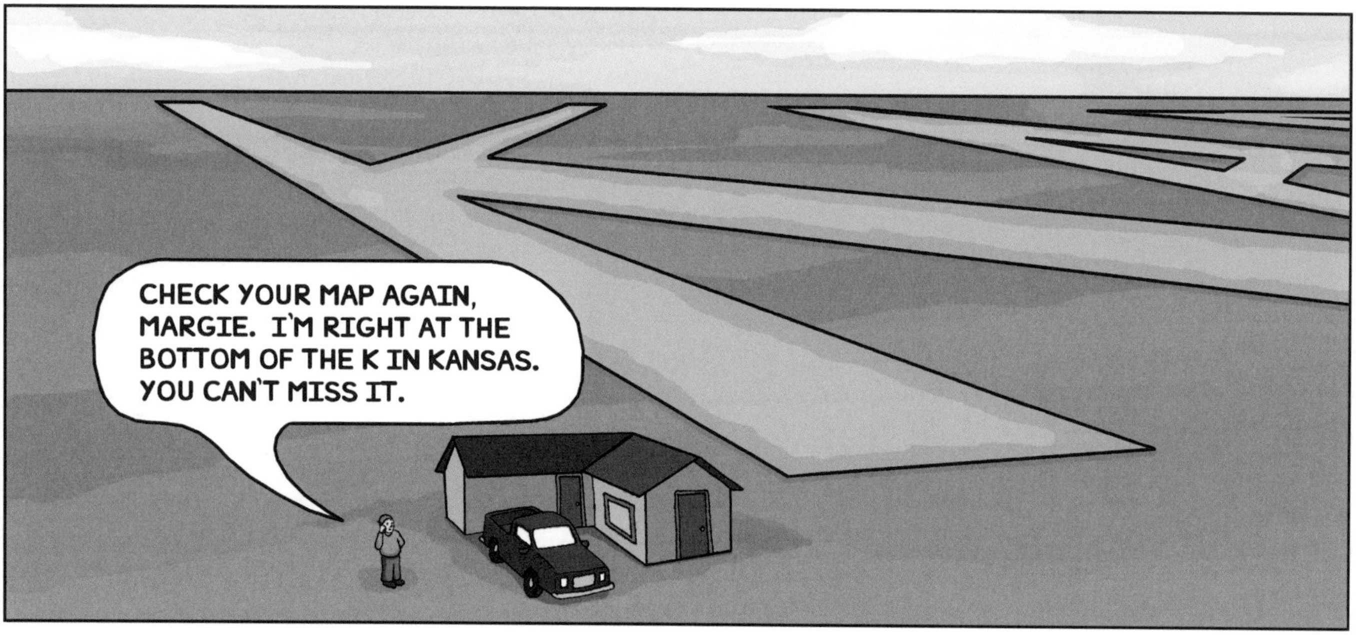
CHECK YOUR MAP AGAIN, MARGIE. I'M RIGHT AT THE BOTTOM OF THE K IN KANSAS. YOU CAN'T MISS IT.

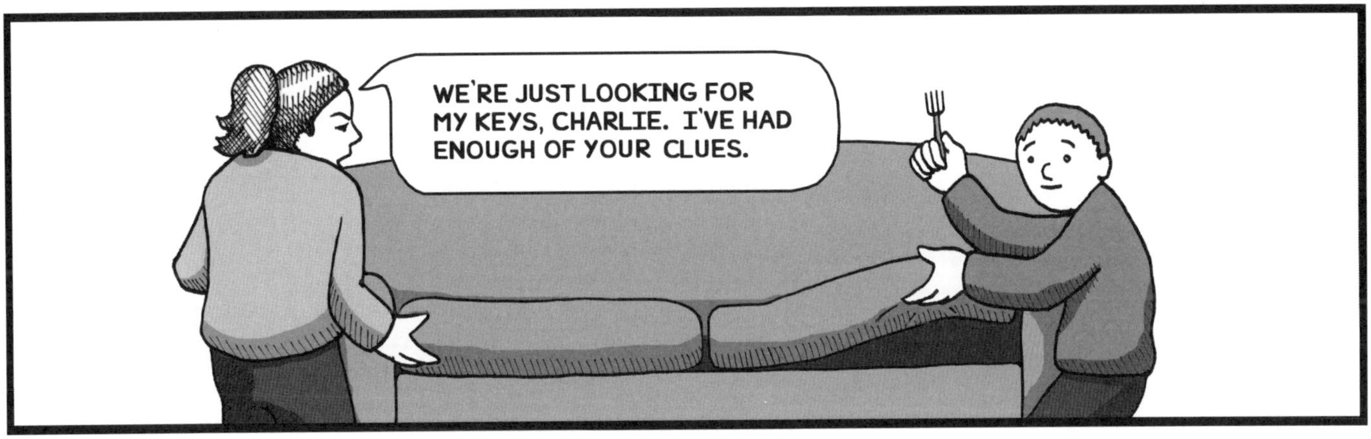
WE'RE JUST LOOKING FOR MY KEYS, CHARLIE. I'VE HAD ENOUGH OF YOUR CLUES.

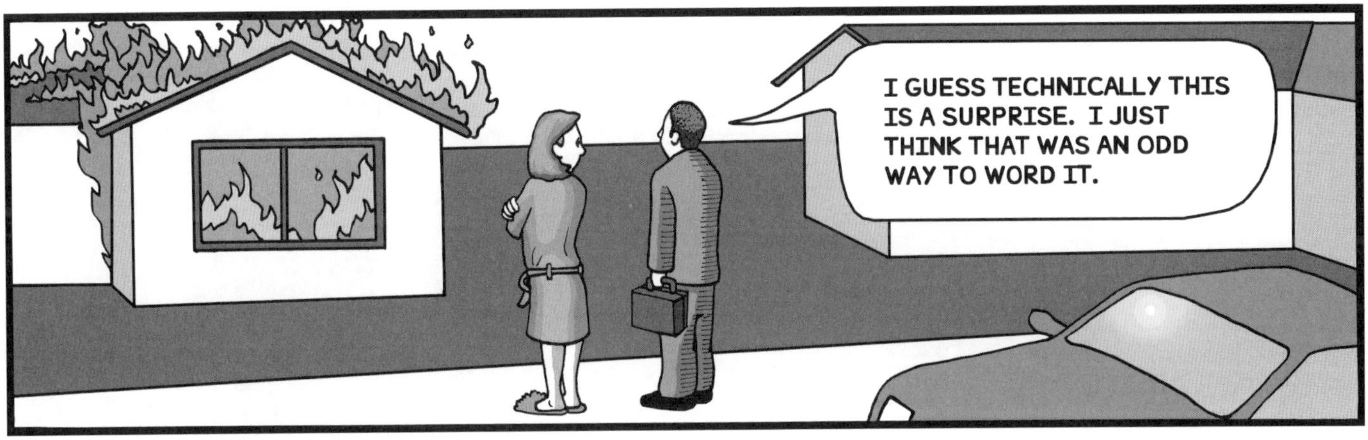
I GUESS TECHNICALLY THIS IS A SURPRISE. I JUST THINK THAT WAS AN ODD WAY TO WORD IT.

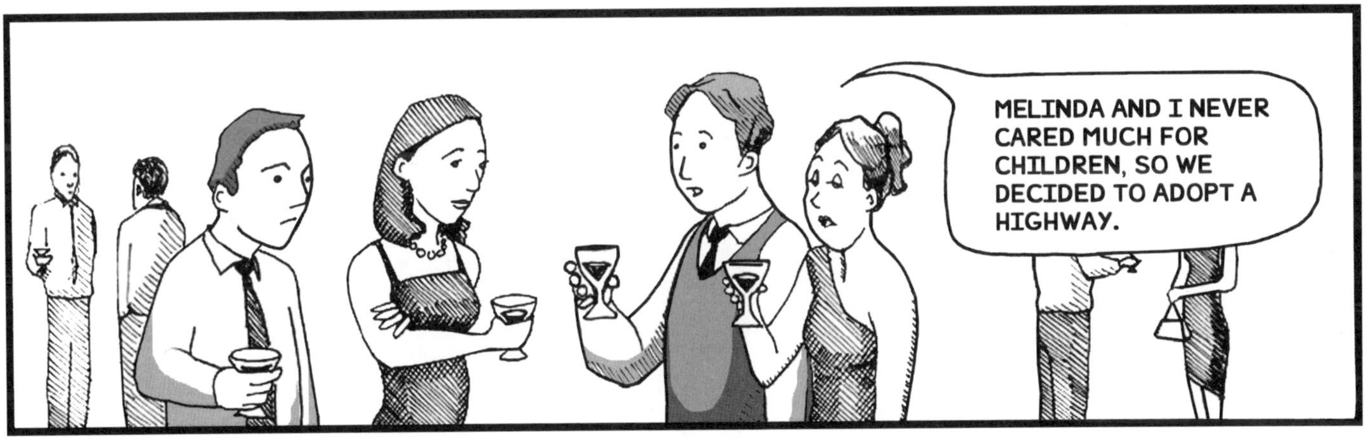
MELINDA AND I NEVER CARED MUCH FOR CHILDREN, SO WE DECIDED TO ADOPT A HIGHWAY.

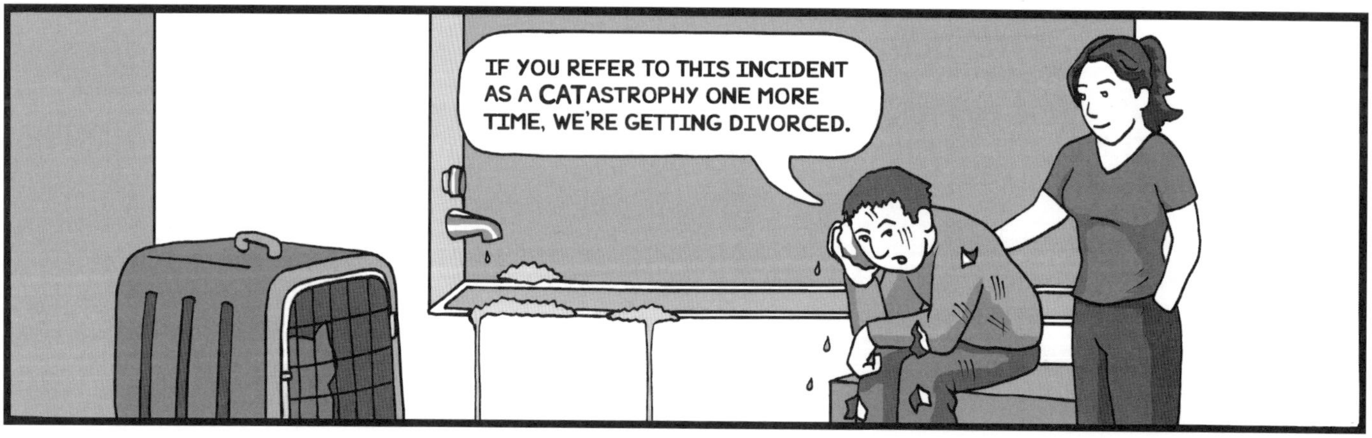
IF YOU REFER TO THIS INCIDENT AS A CATASTROPHY ONE MORE TIME, WE'RE GETTING DIVORCED.

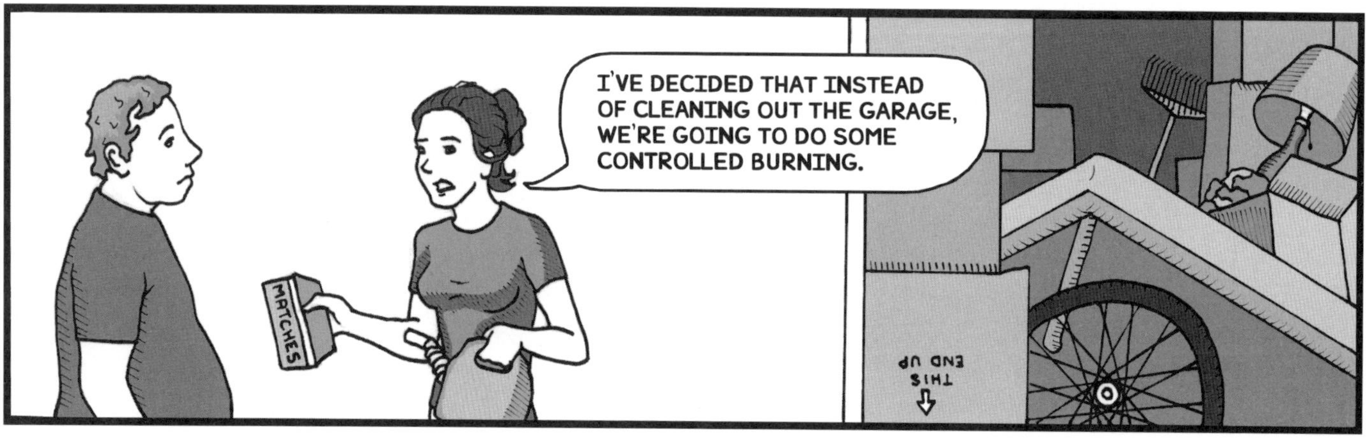
I'VE DECIDED THAT INSTEAD OF CLEANING OUT THE GARAGE, WE'RE GOING TO DO SOME CONTROLLED BURNING.
MATCHES
THIS END UP

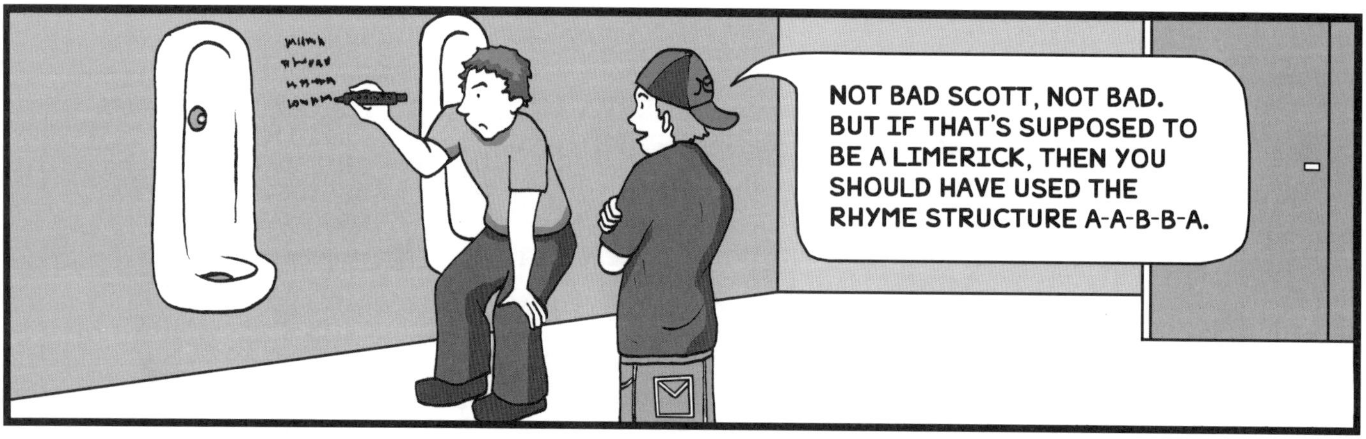
NOT BAD SCOTT, NOT BAD. BUT IF THAT'S SUPPOSED TO BE A LIMERICK, THEN YOU SHOULD HAVE USED THE RHYME STRUCTURE A-A-B-B-A.

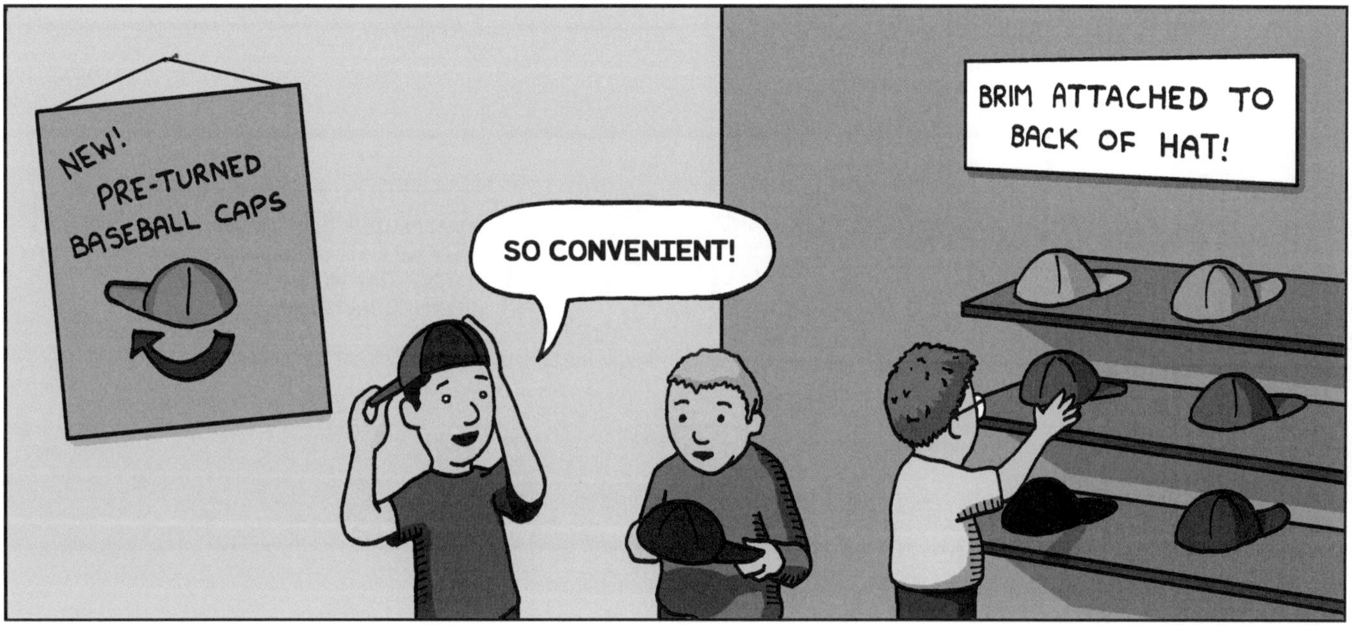
NEW! PRE-TURNED BASEBALL CAPS
SO CONVENIENT!
BRIM ATTACHED TO BACK OF HAT!

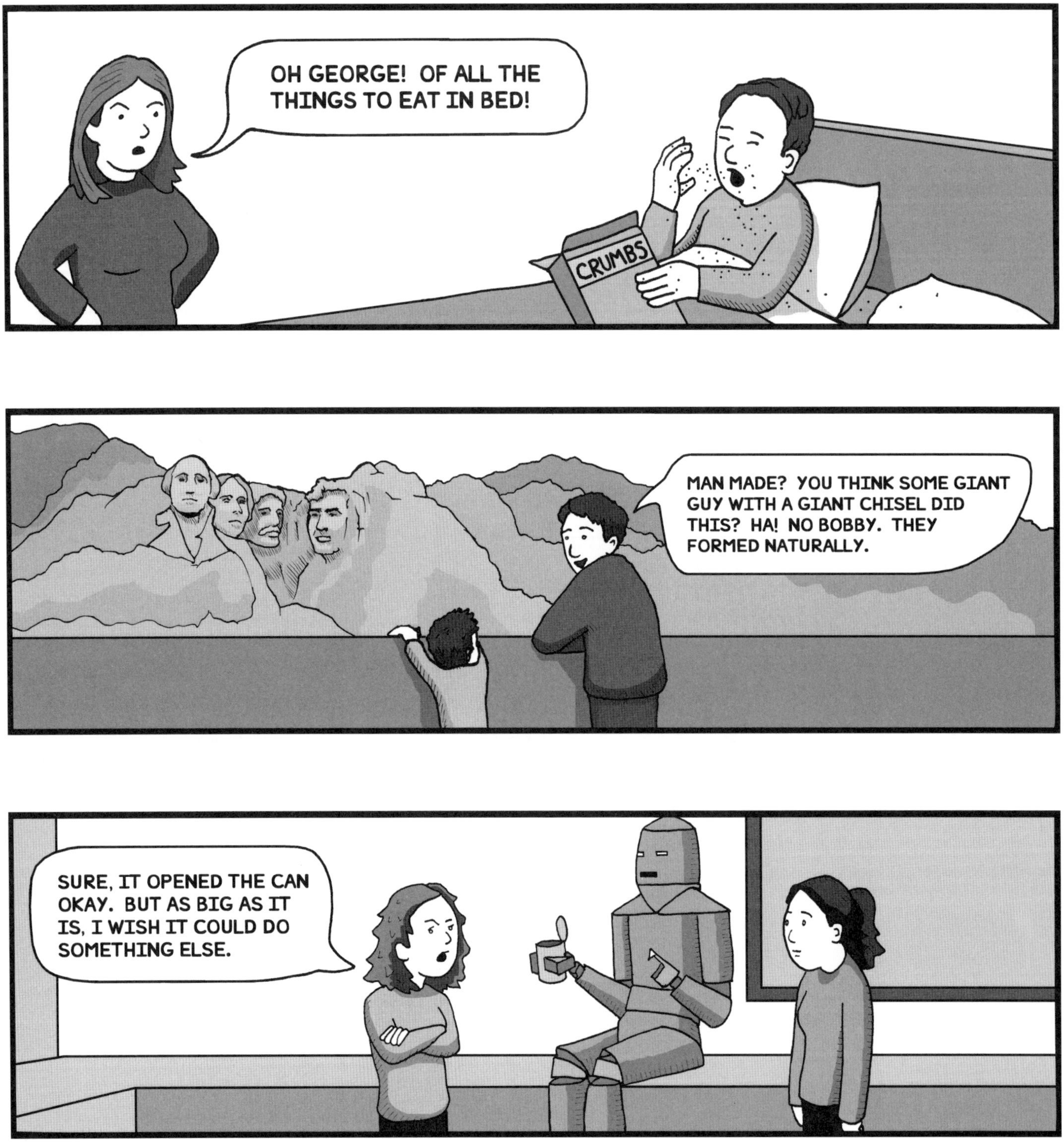
OH GEORGE! OF ALL THE THINGS TO EAT IN BED!
CRUMBS
MAN MADE? YOU THINK SOME GIANT GUY WITH A GIANT CHISEL DID THIS? HA! NO BOBBY. THEY FORMED NATURALLY.
SURE, IT OPENED THE CAN OKAY. BUT AS BIG AS IT IS, I WISH IT COULD DO SOMETHING ELSE.

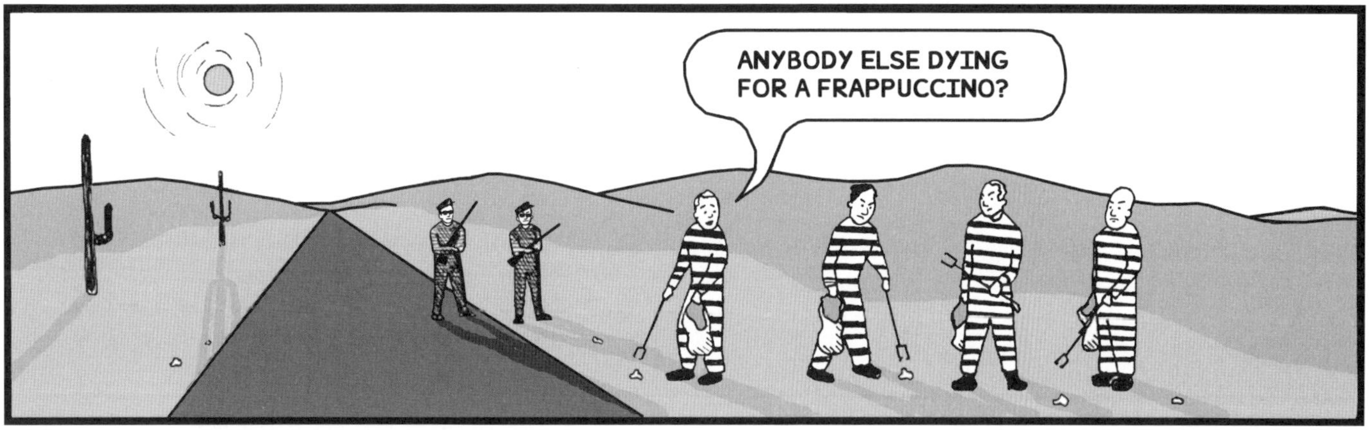
ANYBODY ELSE DYING FOR A FRAPPUCCINO?

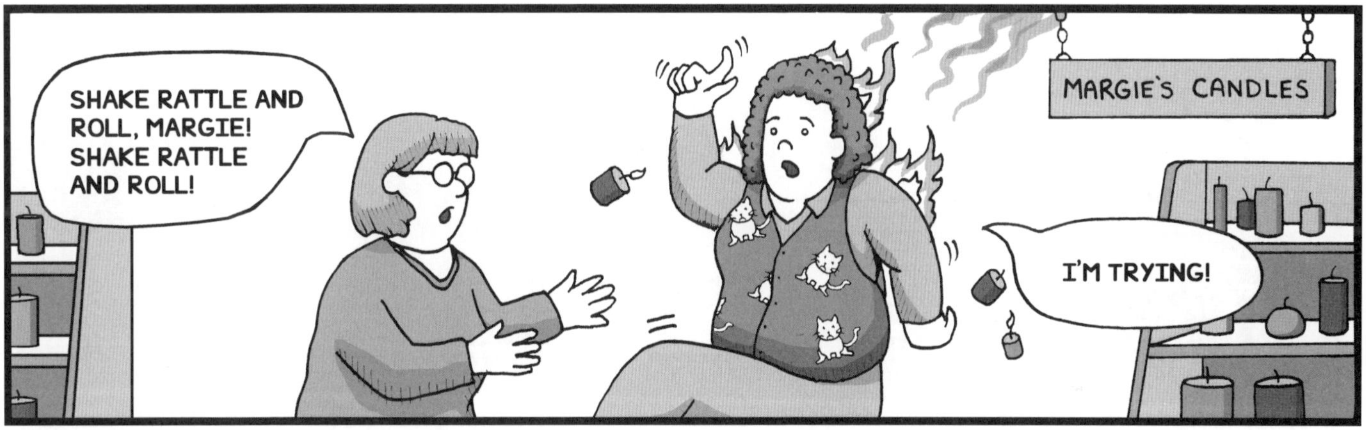
SHAKE RATTLE AND ROLL, MARGIE! SHAKE RATTLE AND ROLL!
MARGIE'S CANDLES
I'M TRYING!

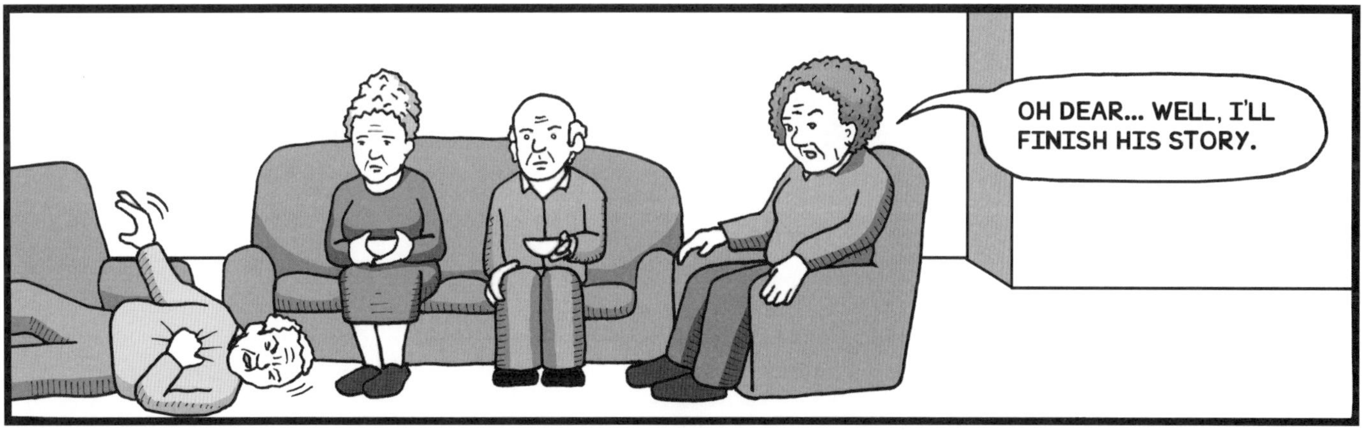
OH DEAR... WELL, I'LL FINISH HIS STORY.

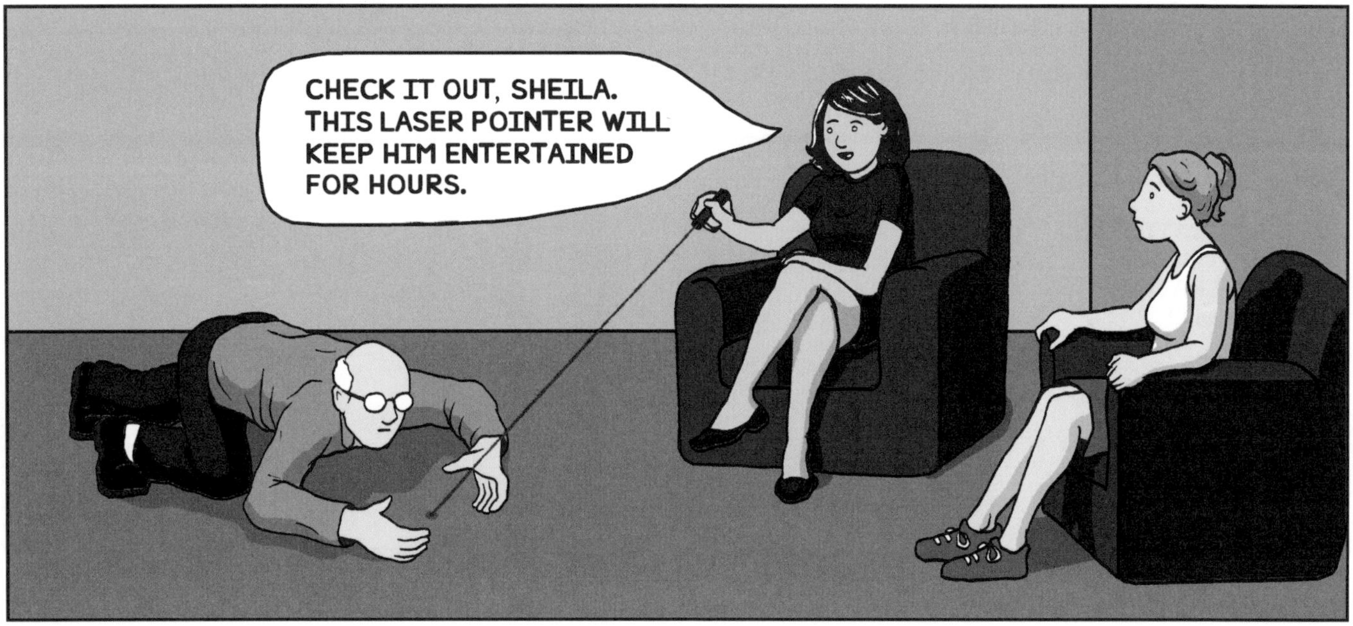
CHECK IT OUT, SHEILA. THIS LASER POINTER WILL KEEP HIM ENTERTAINED FOR HOURS.

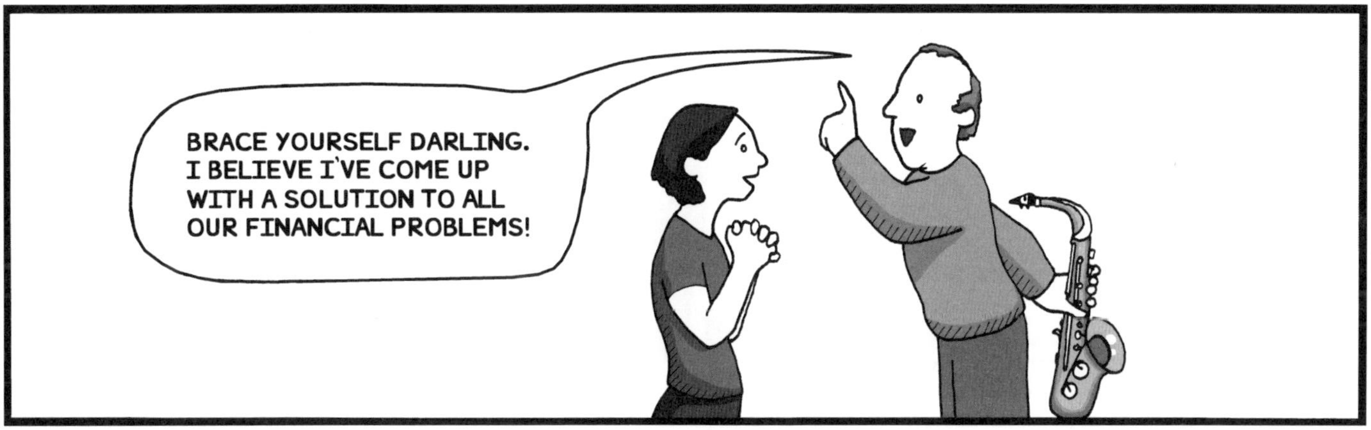
BRACE YOURSELF DARLING. I BELIEVE I'VE COME UP WITH A SOLUTION TO ALL OUR FINANCIAL PROBLEMS!

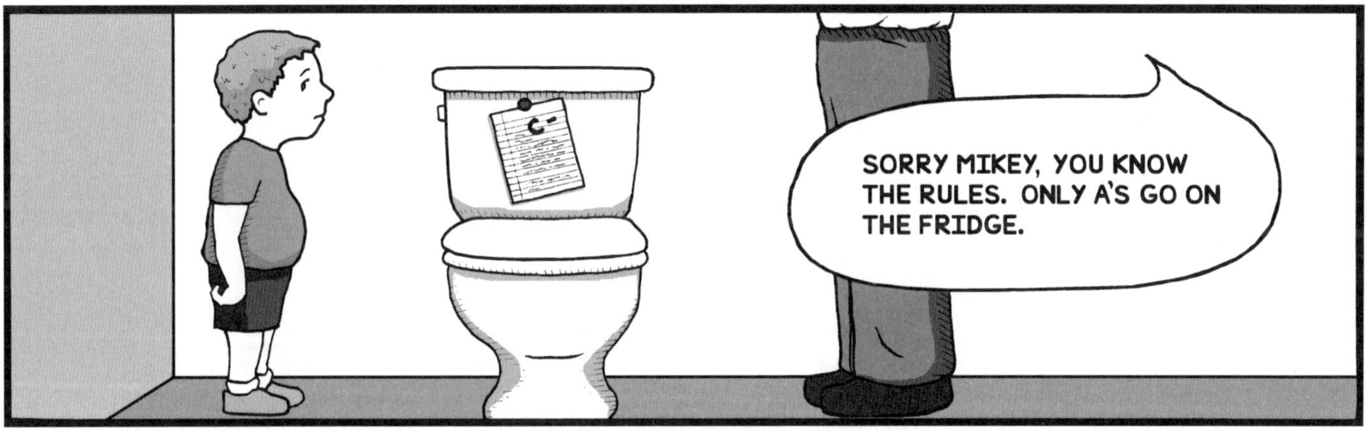
C-
SORRY MIKEY, YOU KNOW THE RULES. ONLY A'S GO ON THE FRIDGE.

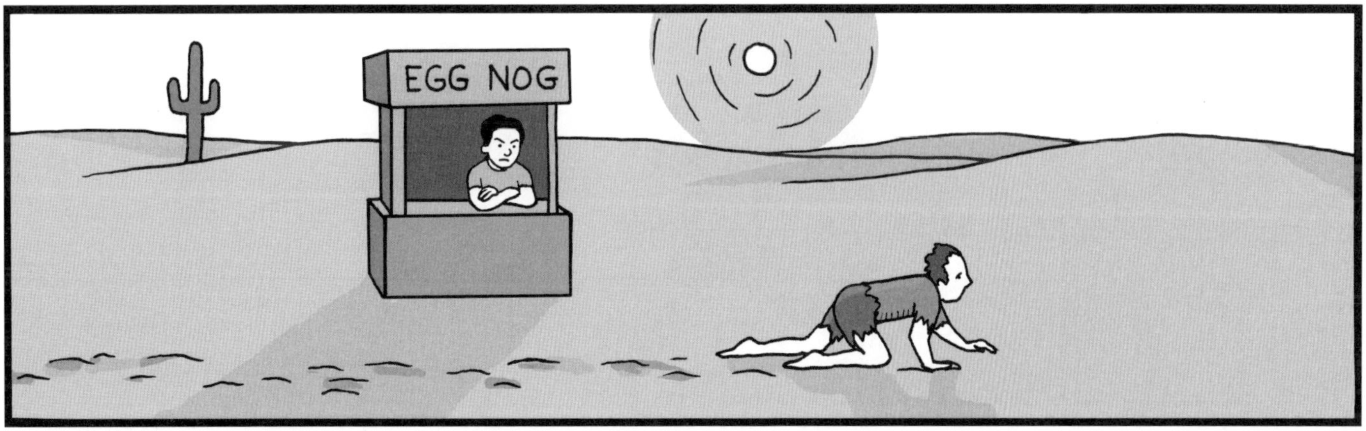
EGG NOG

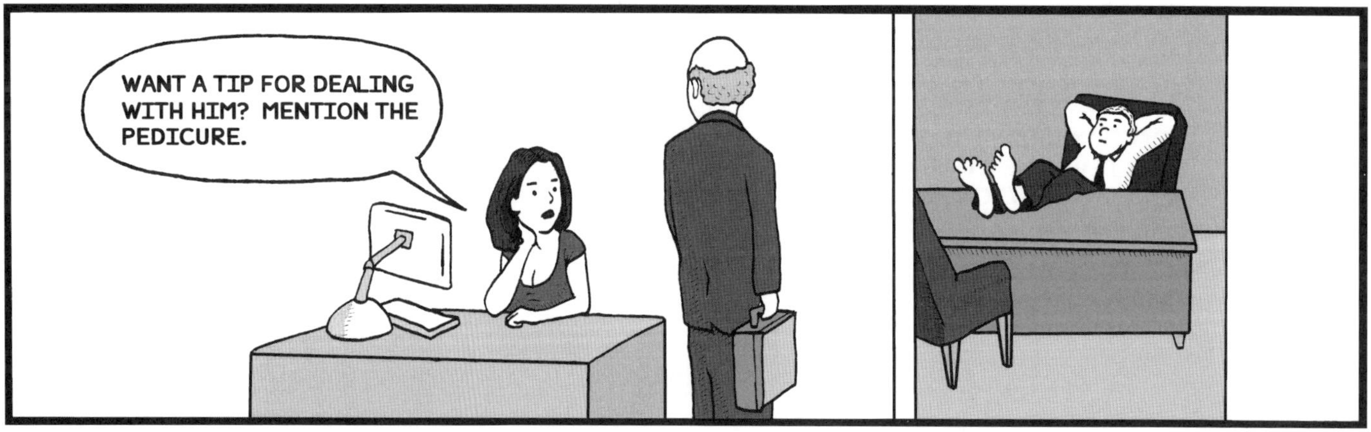
WANT A TIP FOR DEALING WITH HIM? MENTION THE PEDICURE.

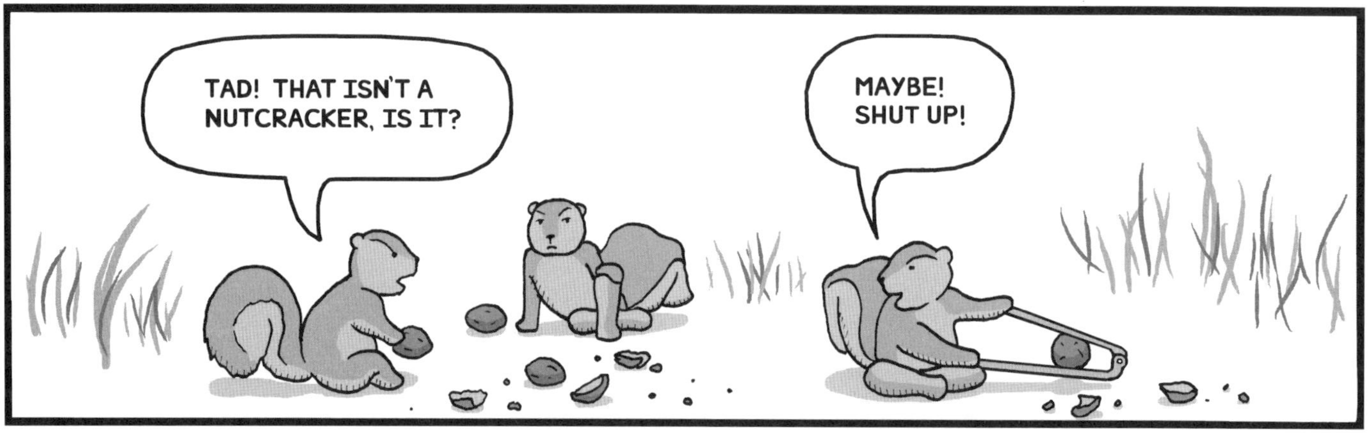
TAD! THAT ISN'T A NUTCRACKER, IS IT?
MAYBE! SHUT UP!

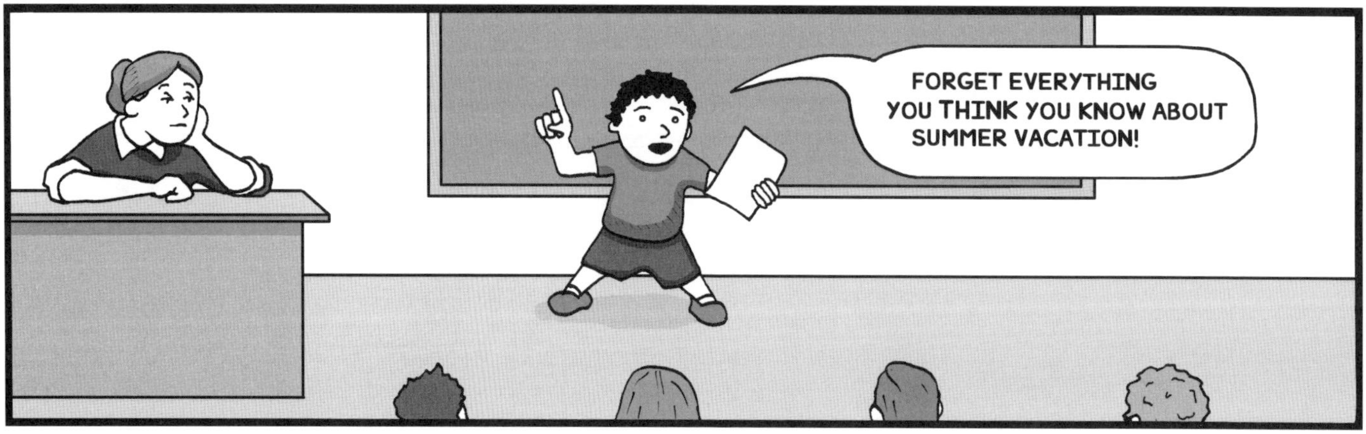
FORGET EVERYTHING YOU THINK YOU KNOW ABOUT SUMMER VACATION!

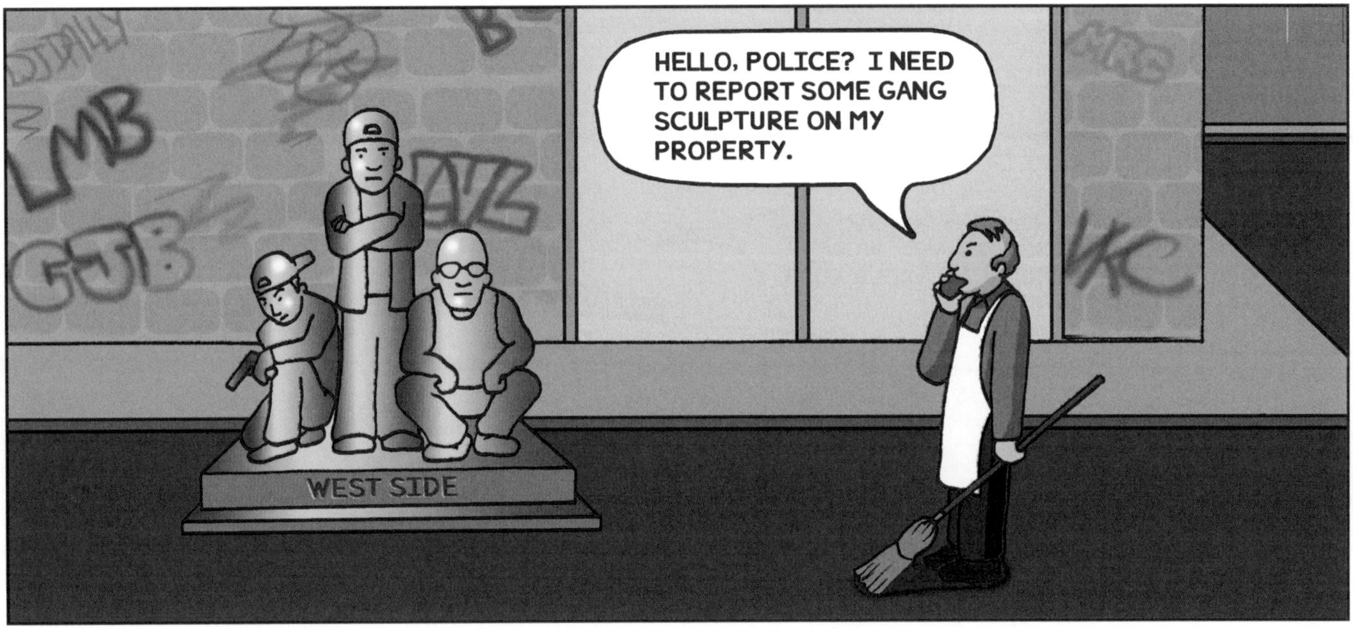
HELLO, POLICE? I NEED TO REPORT SOME GANG SCULPTURE ON MY PROPERTY.
WEST SIDE

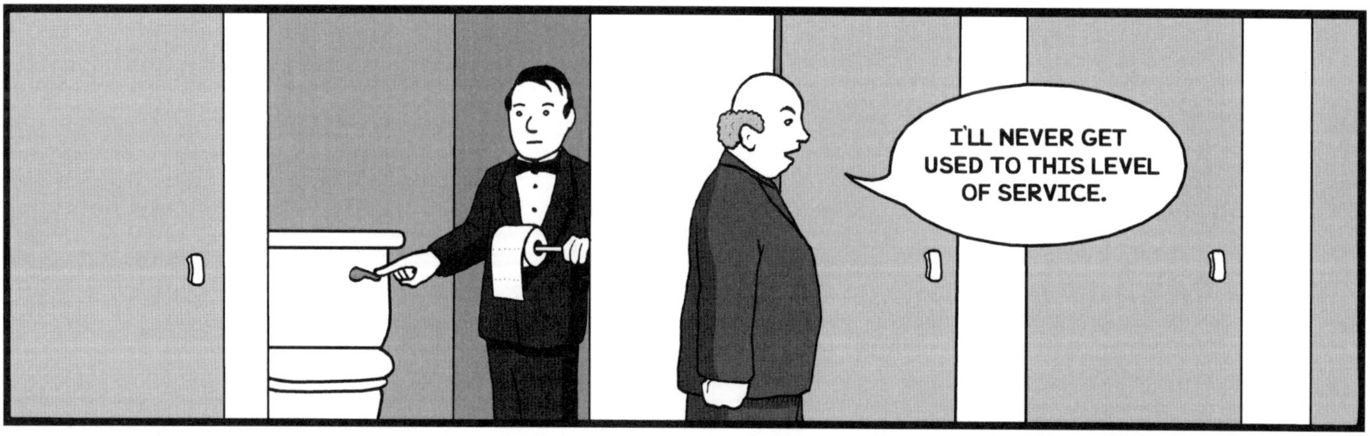
I'LL NEVER GET USED TO THIS LEVEL OF SERVICE.

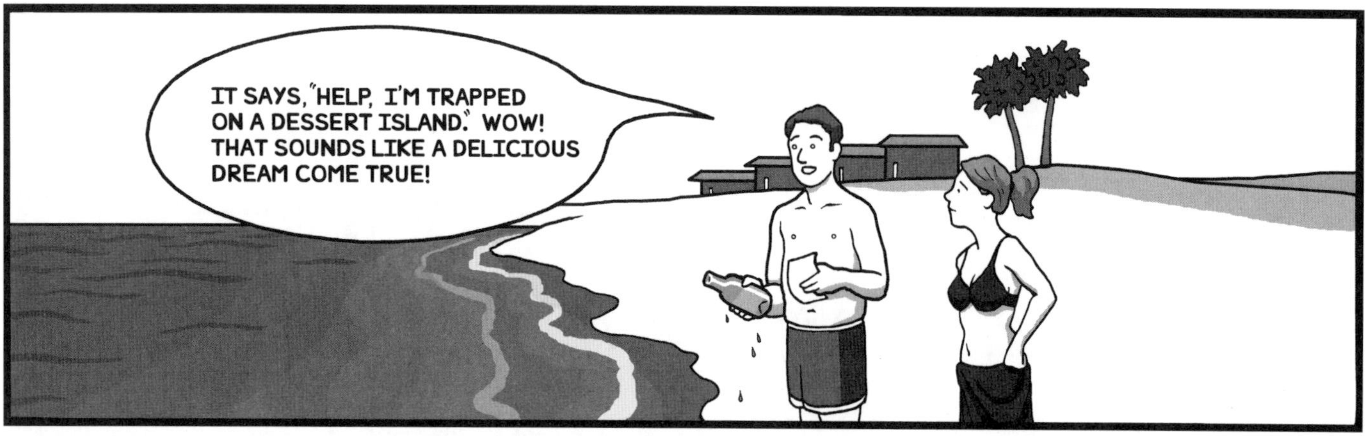
IT SAYS, "HELP, I'M TRAPPED ON A DESSERT ISLAND." WOW! THAT SOUNDS LIKE A DELICIOUS DREAM COME TRUE!

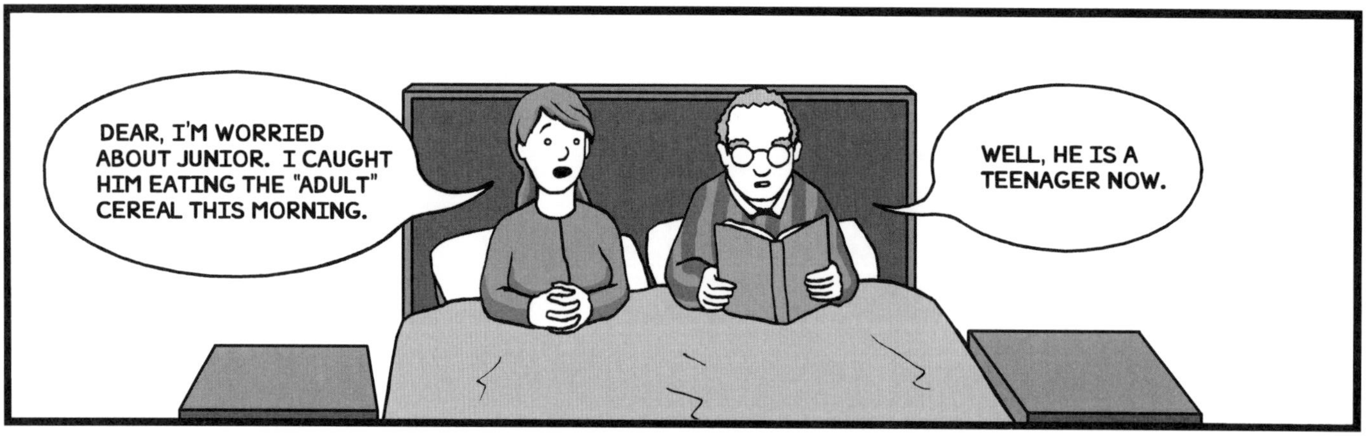
DEAR, I'M WORRIED ABOUT JUNIOR. I CAUGHT HIM EATING THE "ADULT" CEREAL THIS MORNING.
WELL, HE IS A TEENAGER NOW.

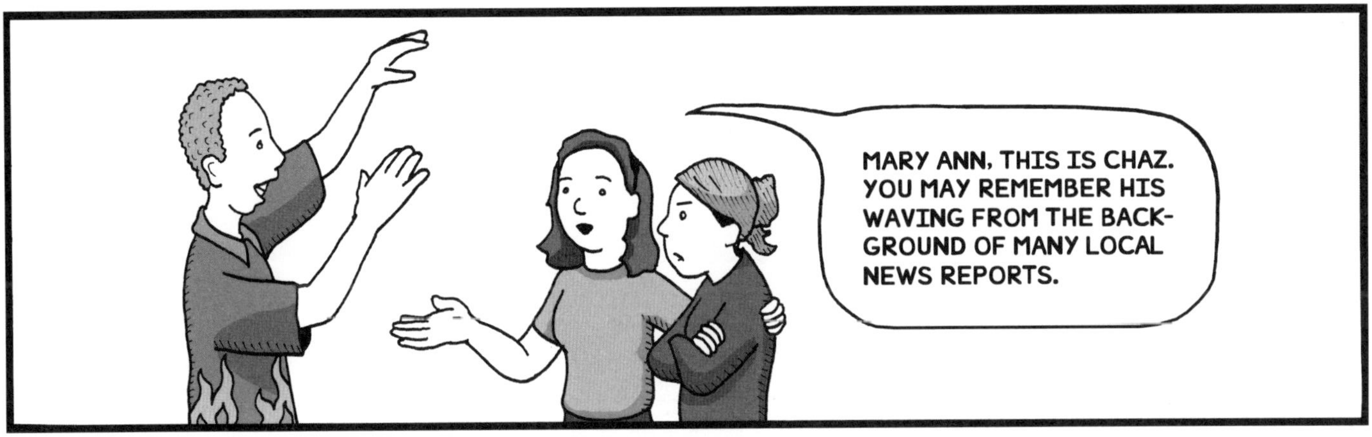
MARY ANN, THIS IS CHAZ. YOU MAY REMEMBER HIS WAVING FROM THE BACK-GROUND OF MANY LOCAL NEWS REPORTS.

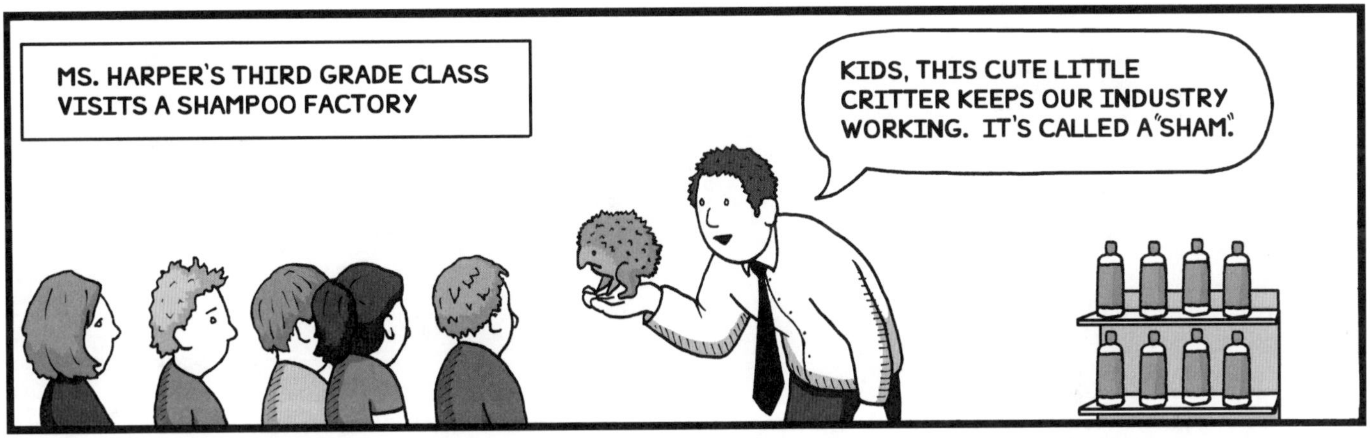
MS. HARPER'S THIRD GRADE CLASS VISITS A SHAMPOO FACTORY
KIDS, THIS CUTE LITTLE CRITTER KEEPS OUR INDUSTRY WORKING. IT'S CALLED A "SHAM."

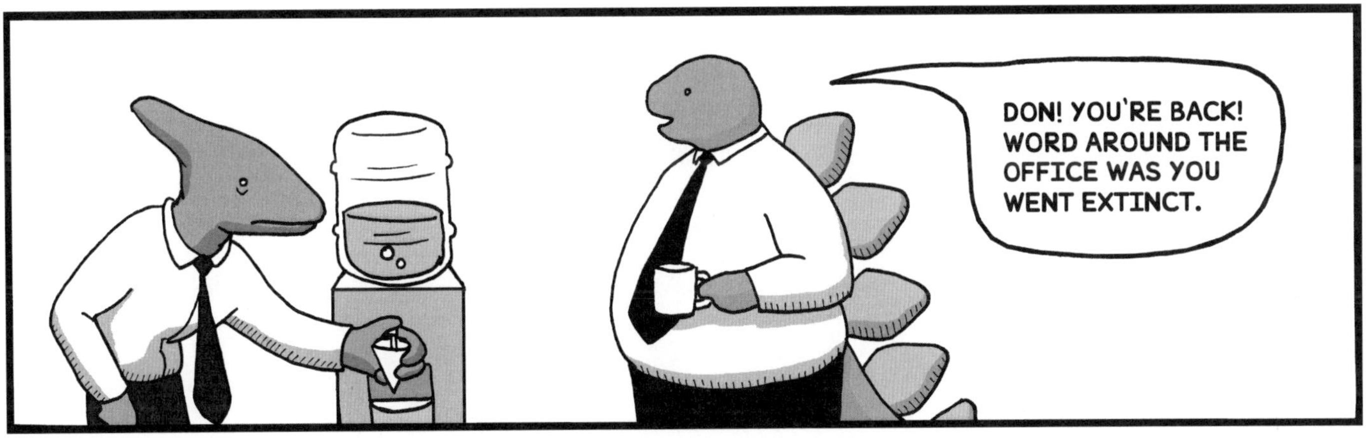
DON! YOU'RE BACK! WORD AROUND THE OFFICE WAS YOU WENT EXTINCT.

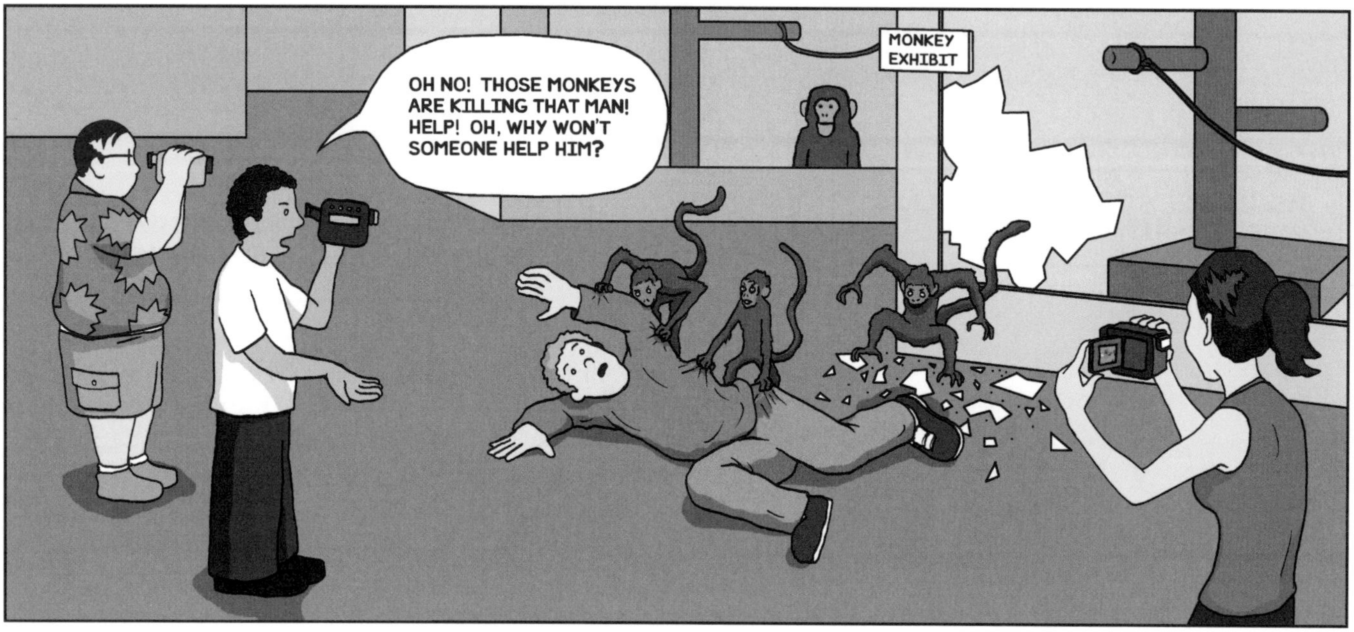
MONKEY EXHIBIT
OH NO! THOSE MONKEYS ARE KILLING THAT MAN! HELP! OH, WHY WON'T SOMEONE HELP HIM?

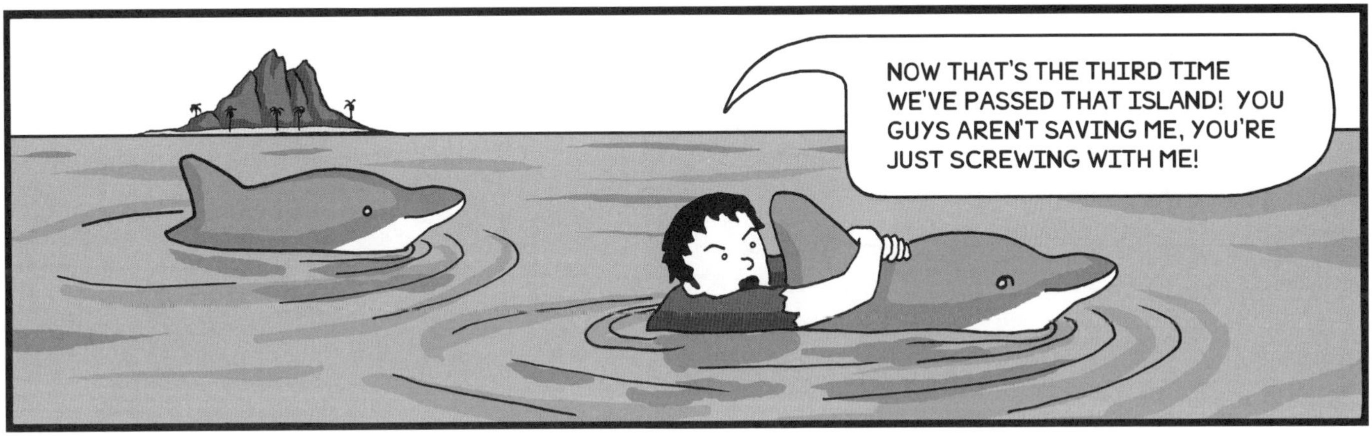
NOW THAT'S THE THIRD TIME WE'VE PASSED THAT ISLAND! YOU GUYS AREN'T SAVING ME, YOU'RE JUST SCREWING WITH ME!

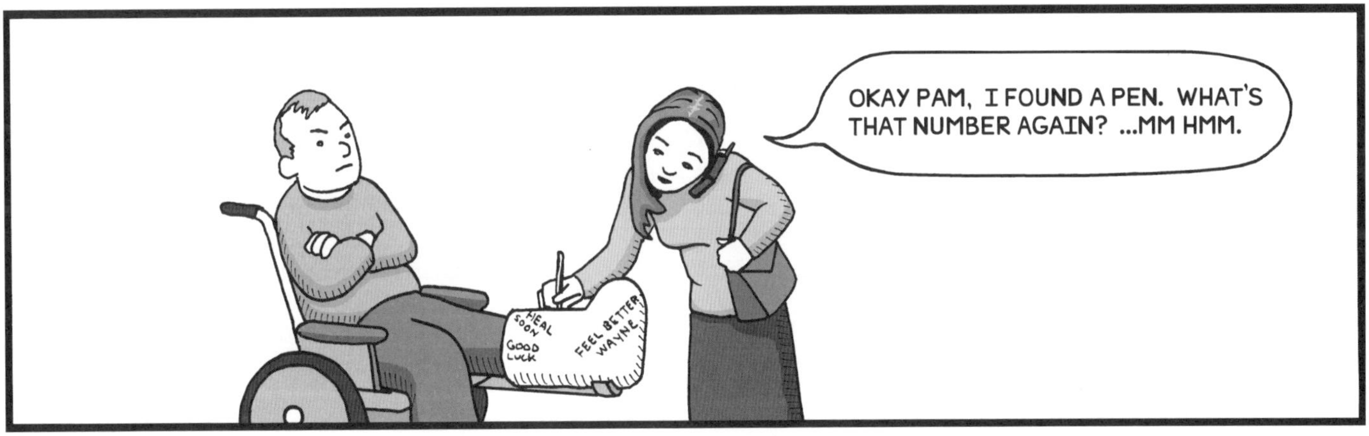
OKAY PAM, I FOUND A PEN. WHAT'S THAT NUMBER AGAIN? ...MM HMM.
HEAL SOON
GOOD LUCK
FEEL BETTER WAYNE

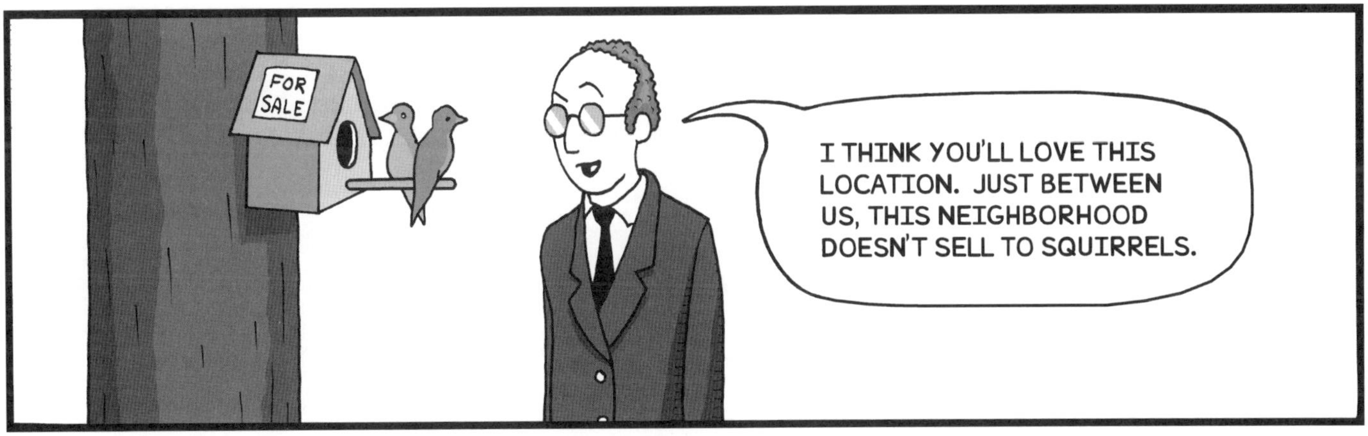
FOR SALE
I THINK YOU'LL LOVE THIS LOCATION. JUST BETWEEN US, THIS NEIGHBORHOOD DOESN'T SELL TO SQUIRRELS.

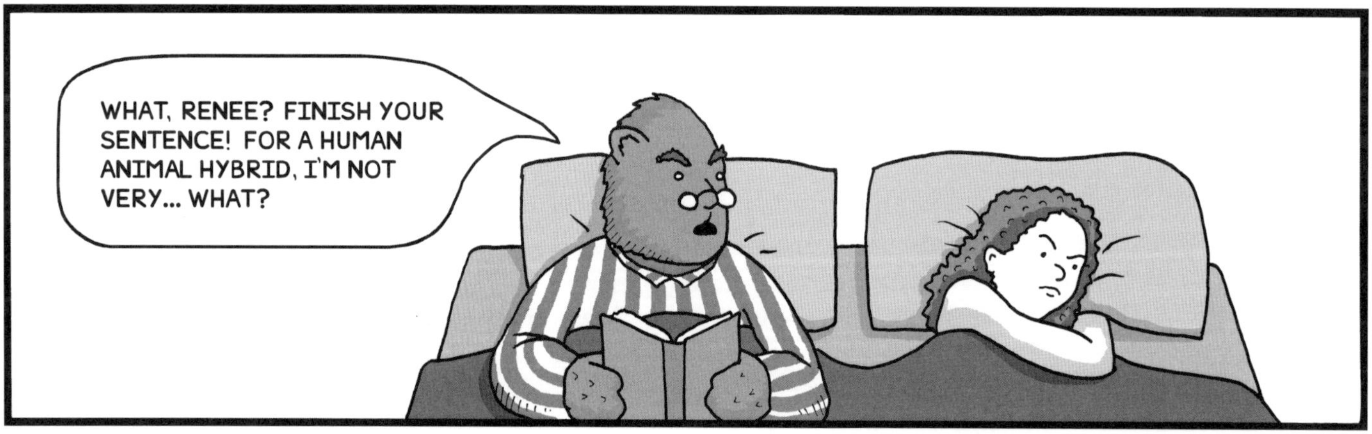
WHAT, RENEE? FINISH YOUR SENTENCE! FOR A HUMAN ANIMAL HYBRID, I'M NOT VERY... WHAT?

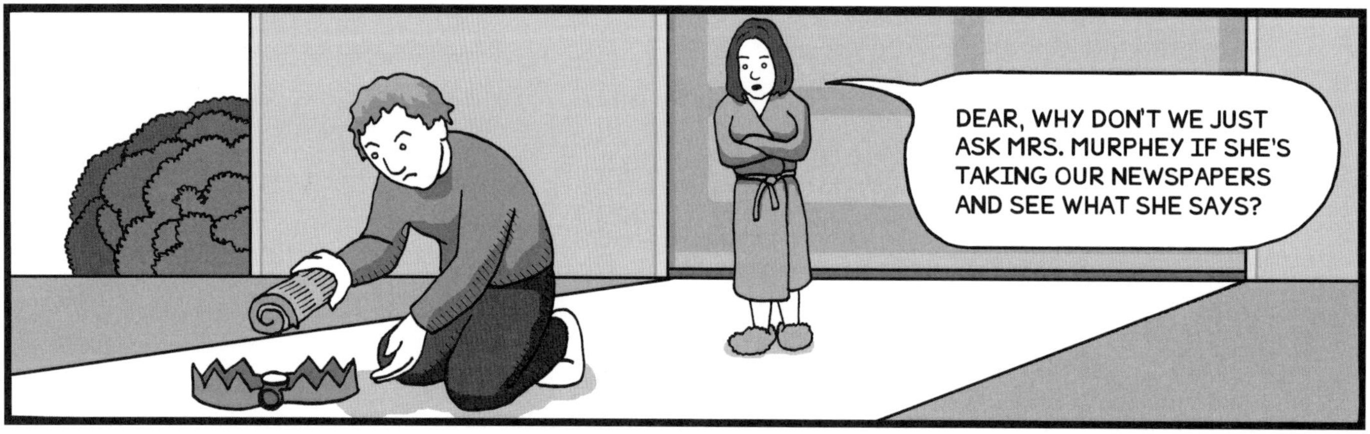
DEAR, WHY DON'T WE JUST ASK MRS. MURPHEY IF SHE'S TAKING OUR NEWSPAPERS AND SEE WHAT SHE SAYS?

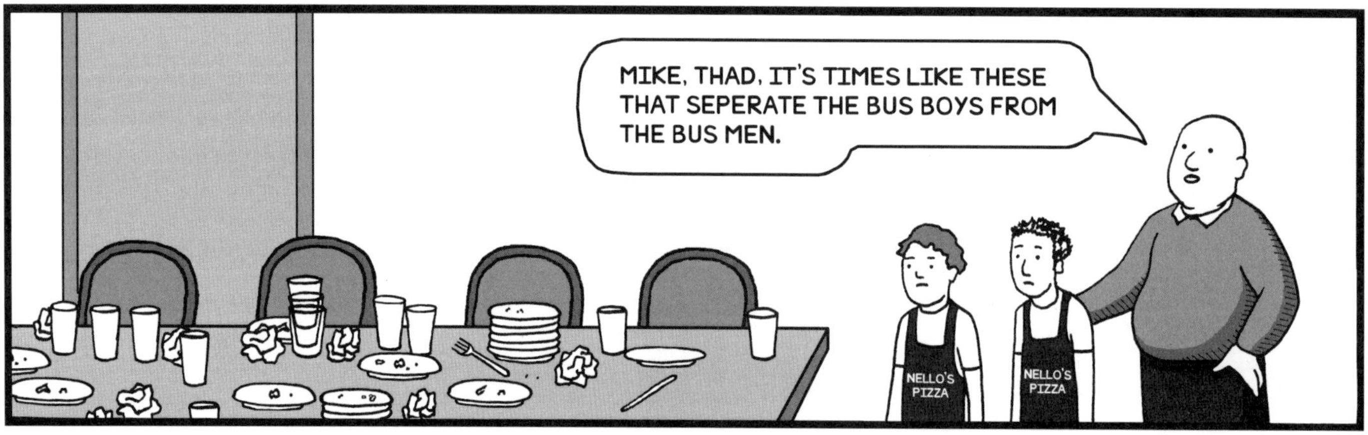
MIKE, THAD, IT'S TIMES LIKE THESE THAT SEPERATE THE BUS BOYS FROM THE BUS MEN.
NELLO'S PIZZA
NELLO'S PIZZA

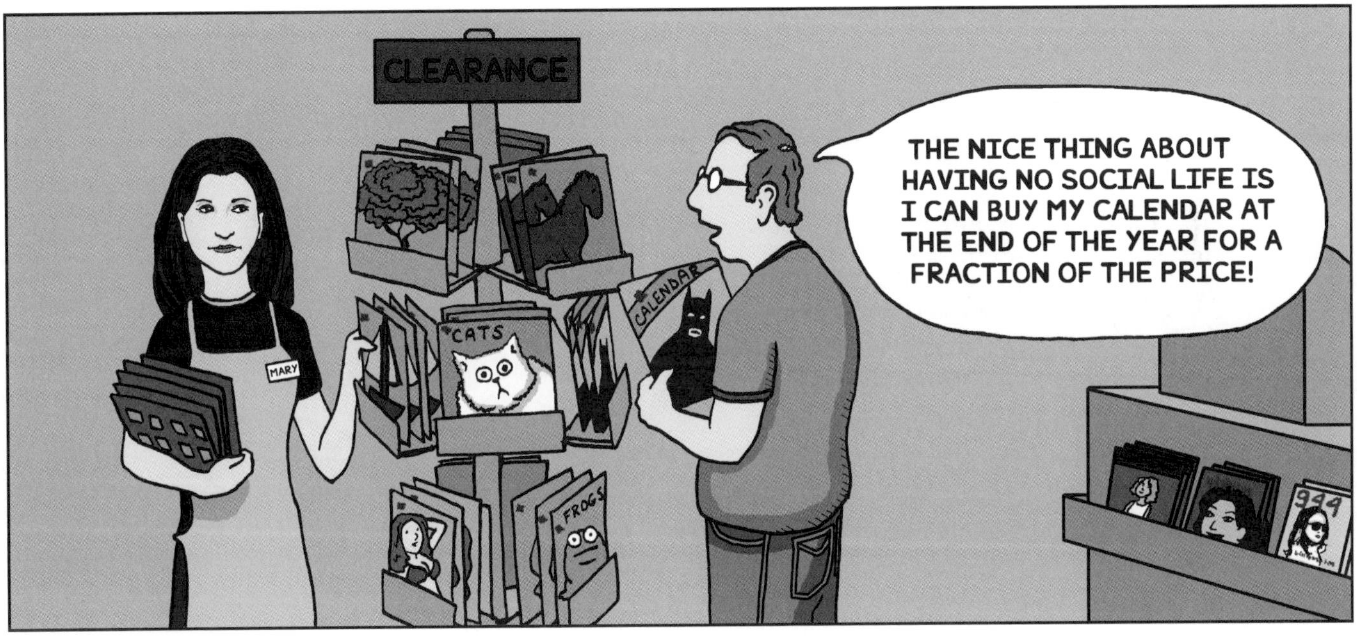
CLEARANCE
MARY
CATS
CALENDAR
FROGS
THE NICE THING ABOUT HAVING NO SOCIAL LIFE IS I CAN BUY MY CALENDAR AT THE END OF THE YEAR FOR A FRACTION OF THE PRICE!

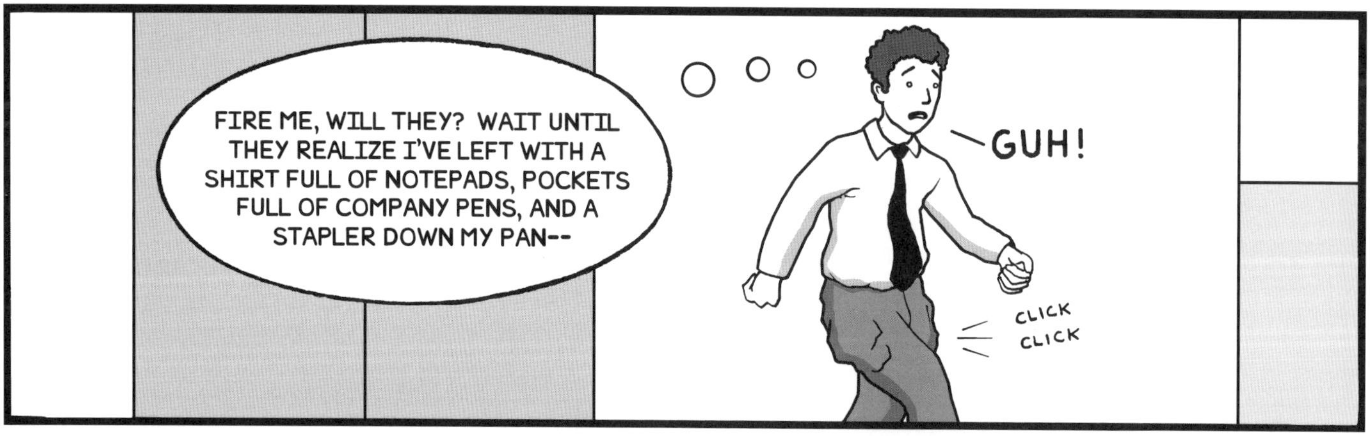
FIRE ME, WILL THEY? WAIT UNTIL THEY REALIZE I'VE LEFT WITH A SHIRT FULL OF NOTEPADS, POCKETS FULL OF COMPANY PENS, AND A STAPLER DOWN MY PAN--
GUH!
CLICK
CLICK

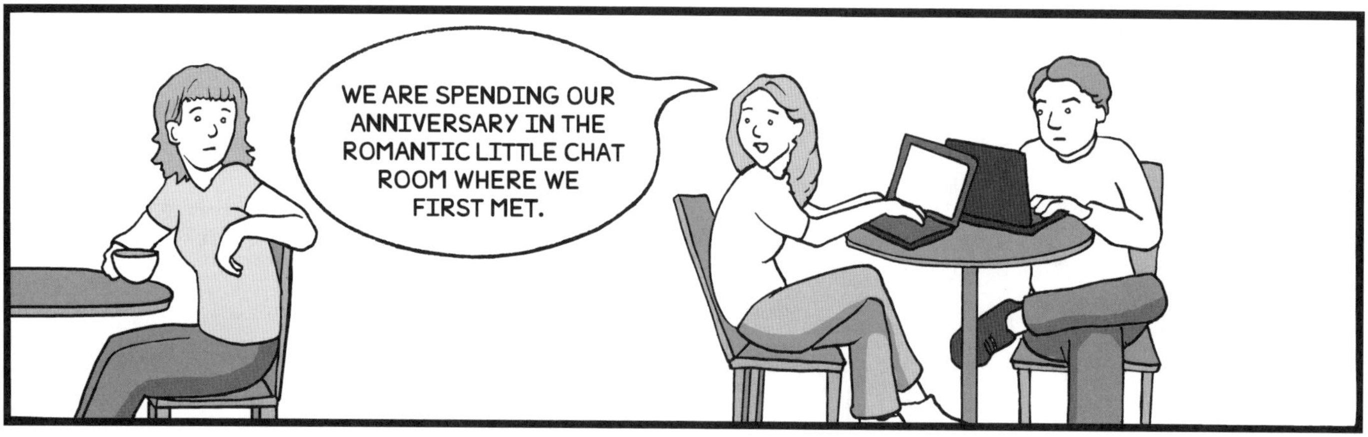
WE ARE SPENDING OUR ANNIVERSARY IN THE ROMANTIC LITTLE CHAT ROOM WHERE WE FIRST MET.

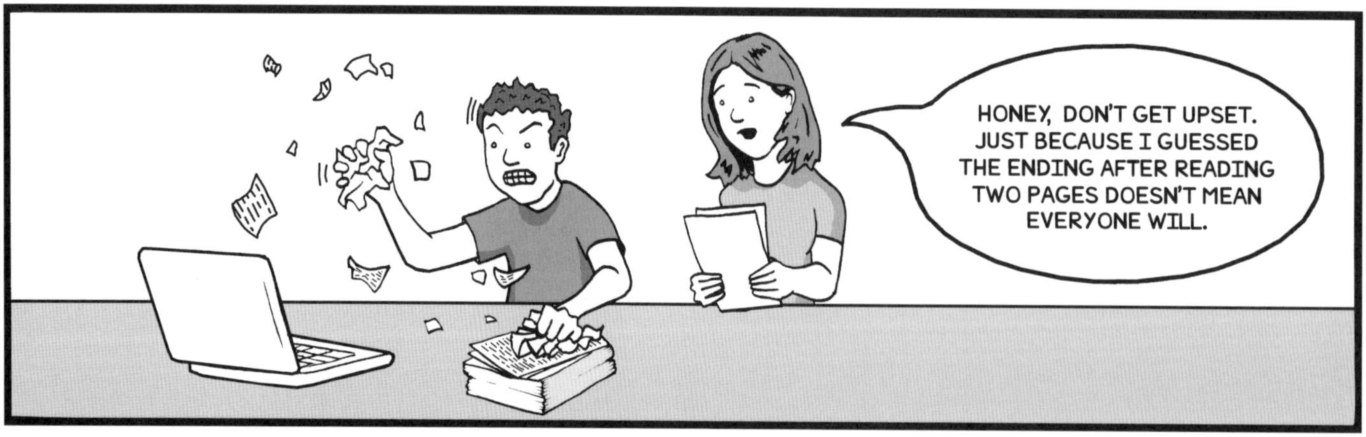
HONEY, DON'T GET UPSET. JUST BECAUSE I GUESSED THE ENDING AFTER READING TWO PAGES DOESN'T MEAN EVERYONE WILL.

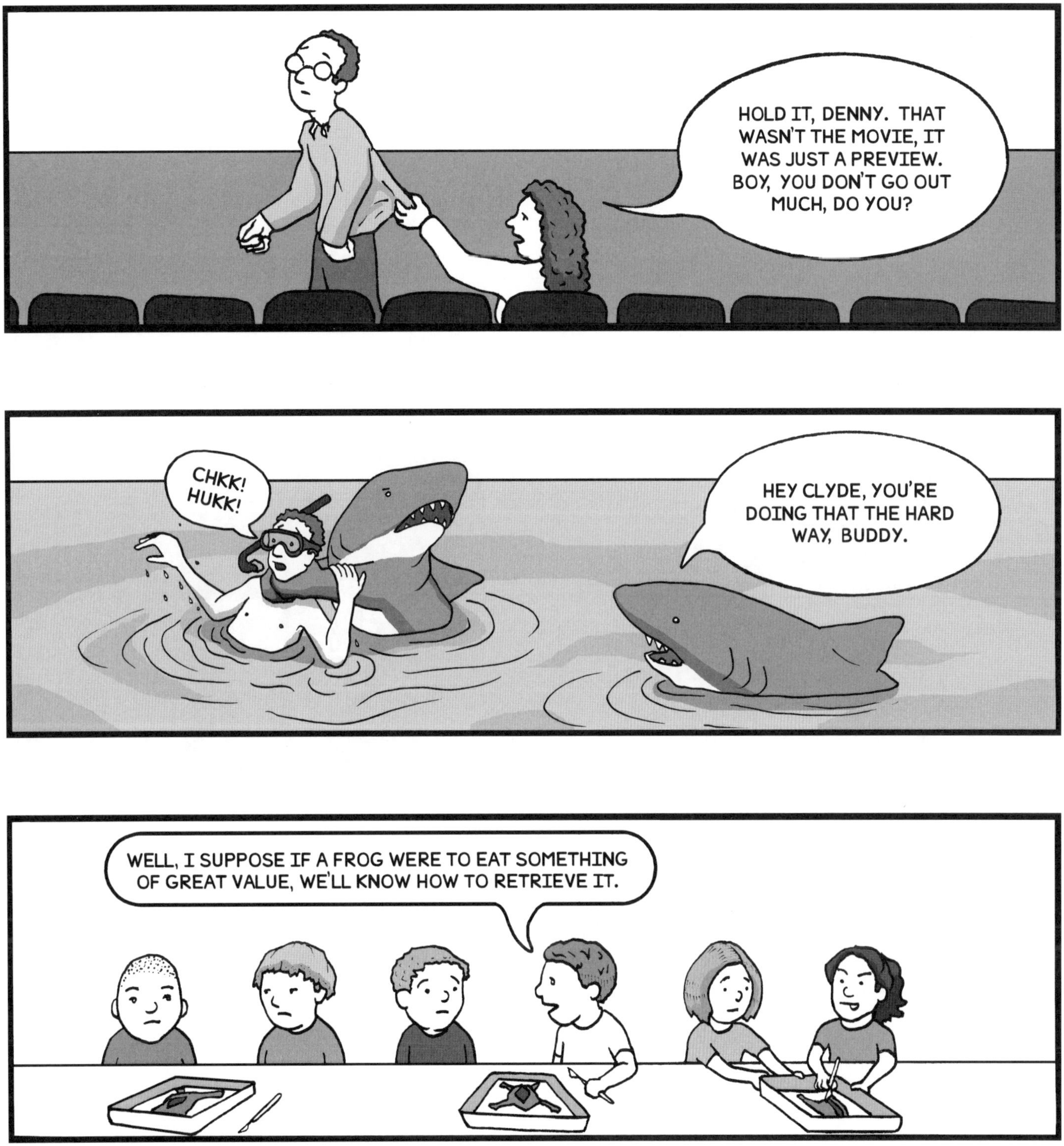
HOLD IT, DENNY. THAT WASN'T THE MOVIE, IT WAS JUST A PREVIEW. BOY, YOU DON'T GO OUT MUCH, DO YOU?
CHKK! HUKK!
HEY CLYDE, YOU'RE DOING THAT THE HARD WAY, BUDDY.
WELL, I SUPPOSE IF A FROG WERE TO EAT SOMETHING OF GREAT VALUE, WE'LL KNOW HOW TO RETRIEVE IT.

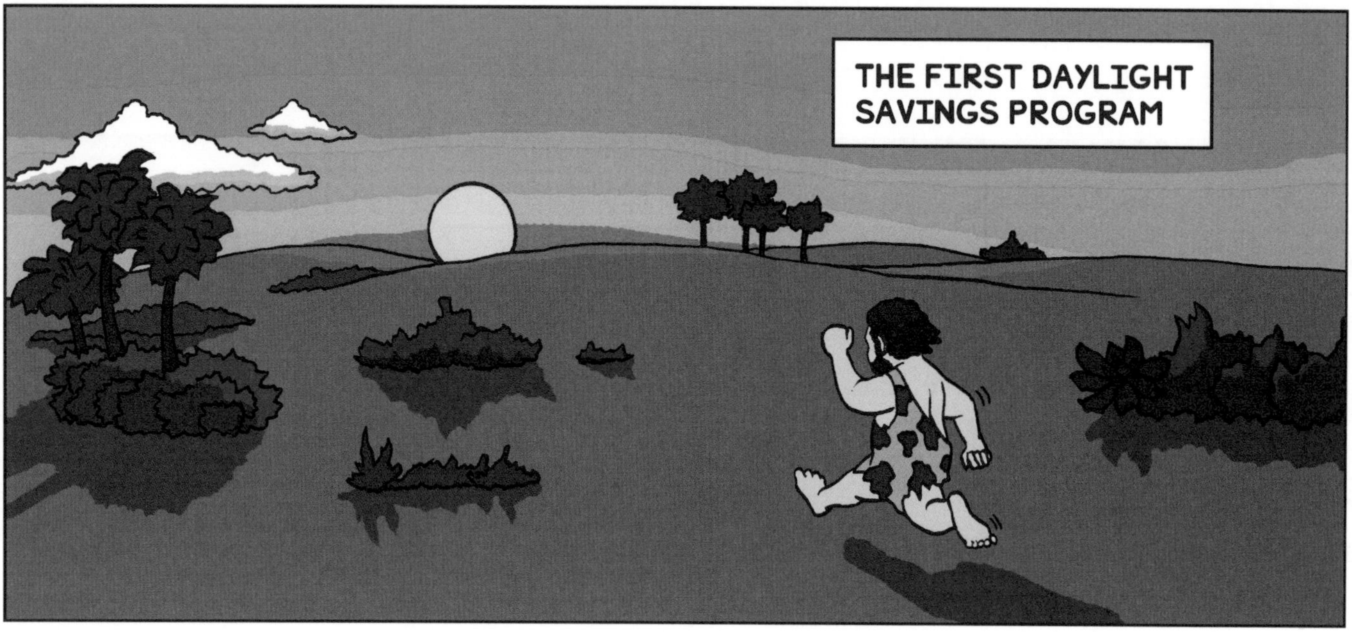
THE FIRST DAYLIGHT SAVINGS PROGRAM

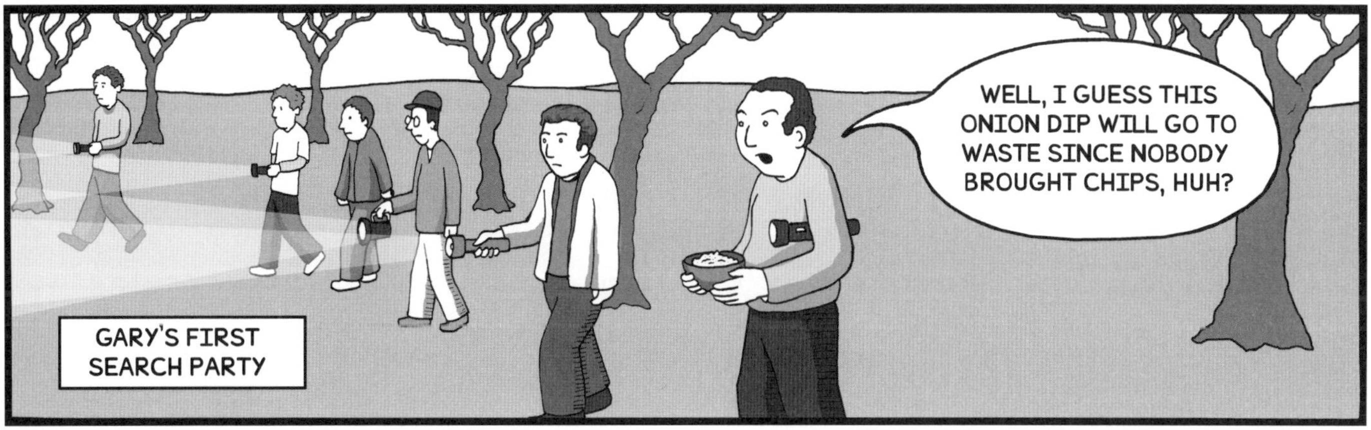
GARY'S FIRST SEARCH PARTY
WELL, I GUESS THIS ONION DIP WILL GO TO WASTE SINCE NOBODY BROUGHT CHIPS, HUH?

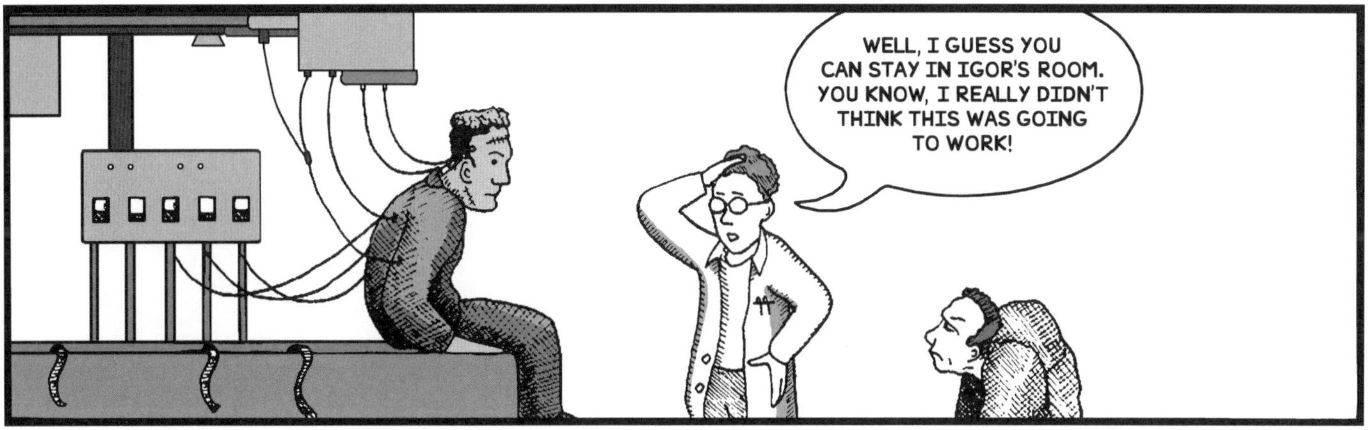
WELL, I GUESS YOU CAN STAY IN IGOR'S ROOM. YOU KNOW, I REALLY DIDN'T THINK THIS WAS GOING TO WORK!

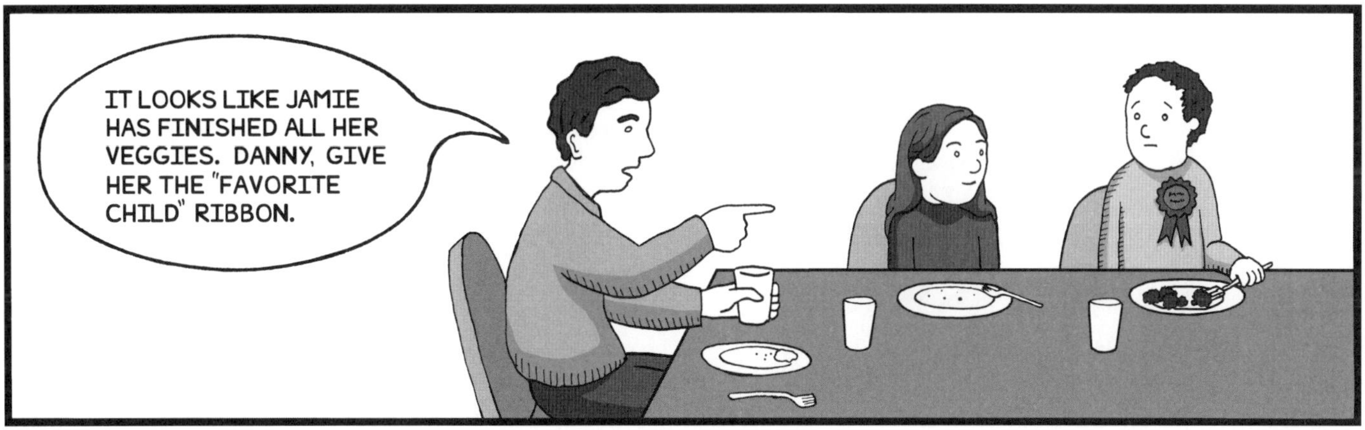
IT LOOKS LIKE JAMIE HAS FINISHED ALL HER VEGGIES. DANNY, GIVE HER THE "FAVORITE CHILD" RIBBON.

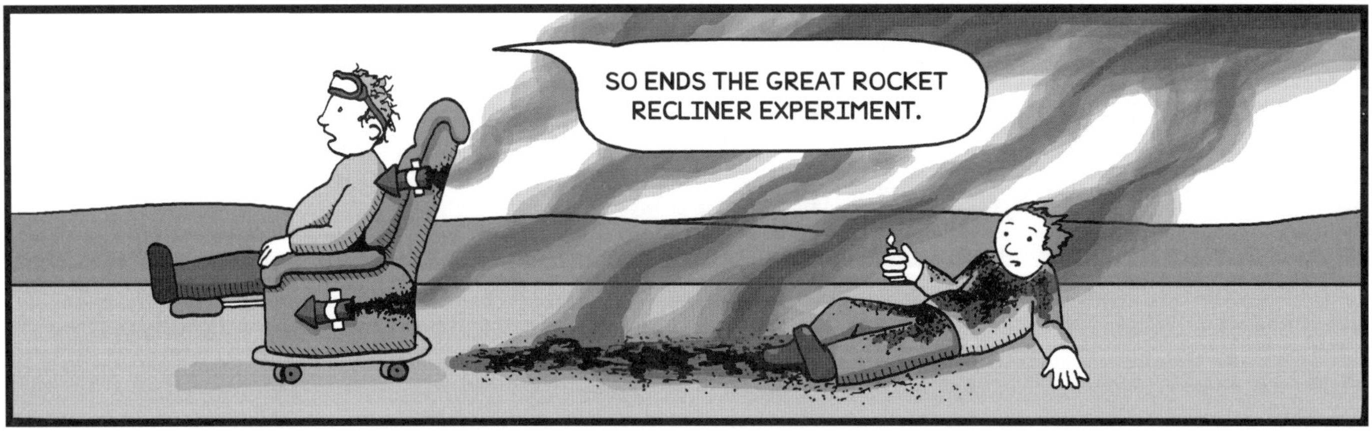
SO ENDS THE GREAT ROCKET RECLINER EXPERIMENT.

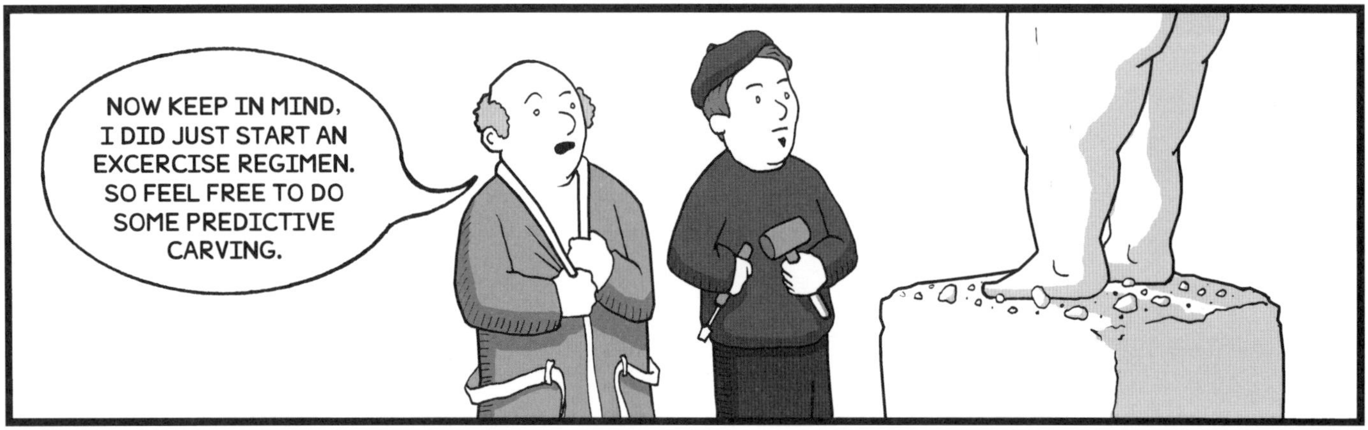
NOW KEEP IN MIND, I DID JUST START AN EXCERCISE REGIMEN. SO FEEL FREE TO DO SOME PREDICTIVE CARVING.

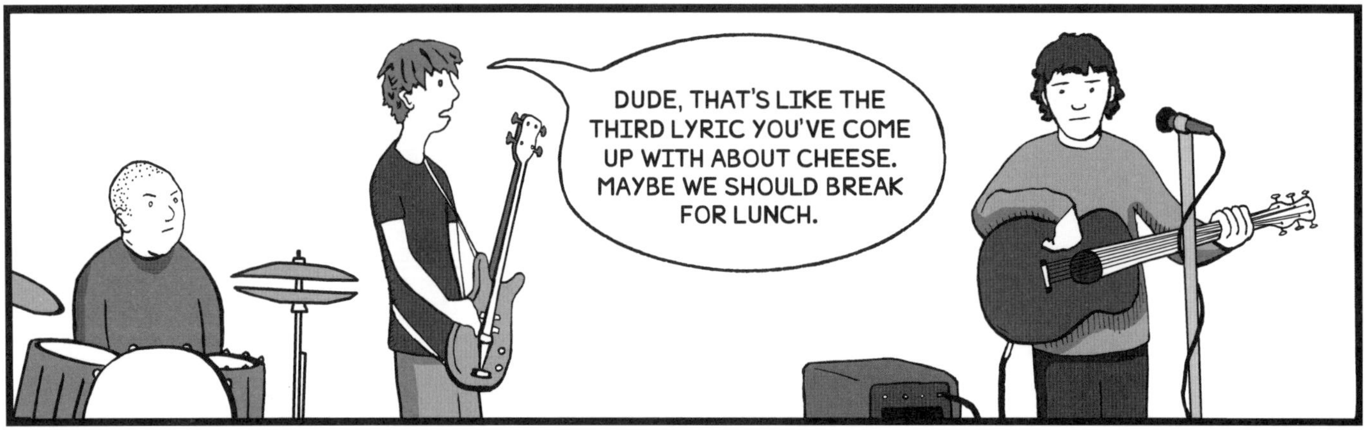
DUDE, THAT'S LIKE THE THIRD LYRIC YOU'VE COME UP WITH ABOUT CHEESE. MAYBE WE SHOULD BREAK FOR LUNCH.

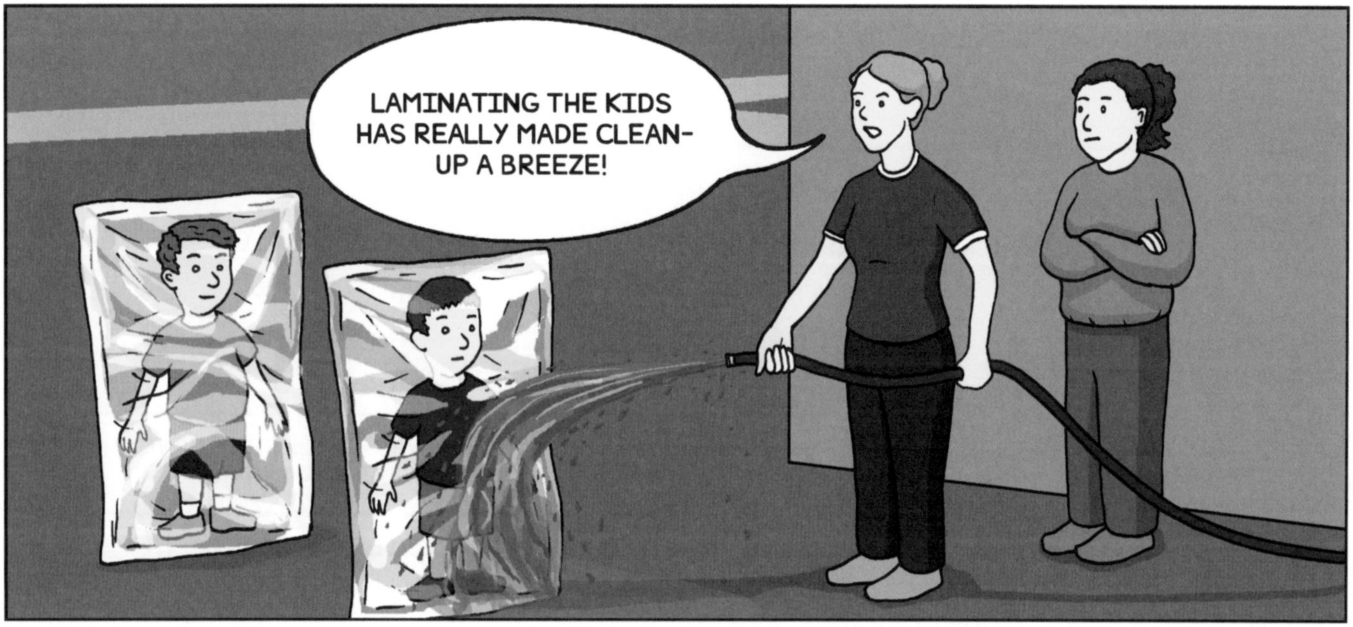
LAMINATING THE KIDS HAS REALLY MADE CLEAN-UP A BREEZE!

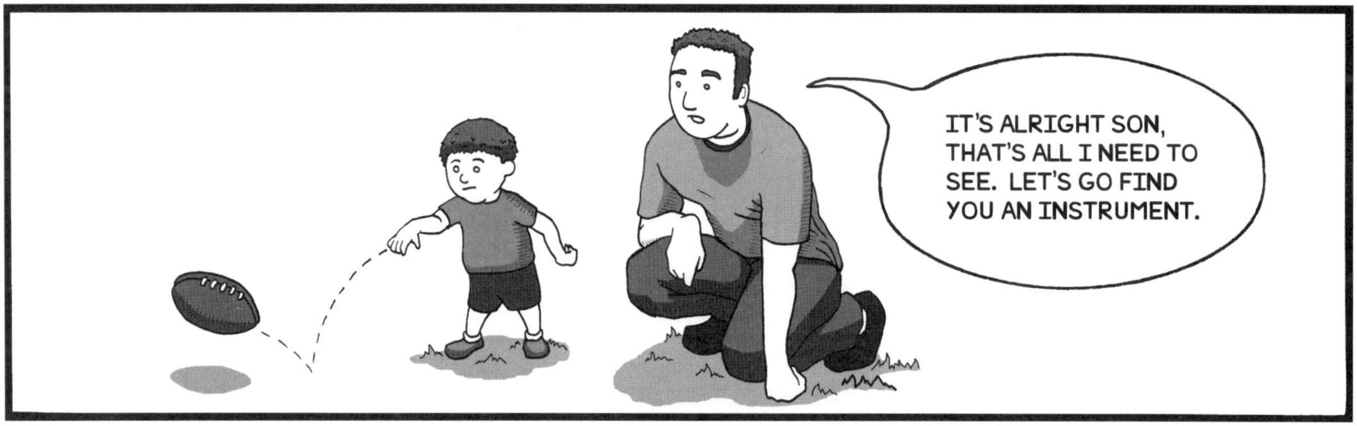
IT'S ALRIGHT SON, THAT'S ALL I NEED TO SEE. LET'S GO FIND YOU AN INSTRUMENT.

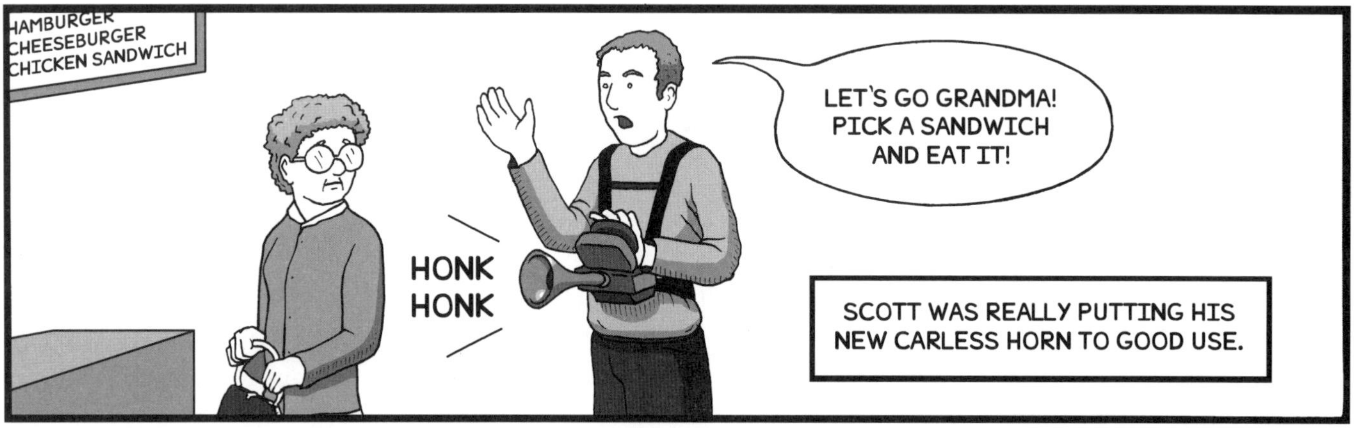
HAMBURGER
CHEESEBURGER
CHICKEN SANDWICH
LET'S GO GRANDMA! PICK A SANDWICH AND EAT IT!
HONK HONK
SCOTT WAS REALLY PUTTING HIS NEW CARLESS HORN TO GOOD USE.

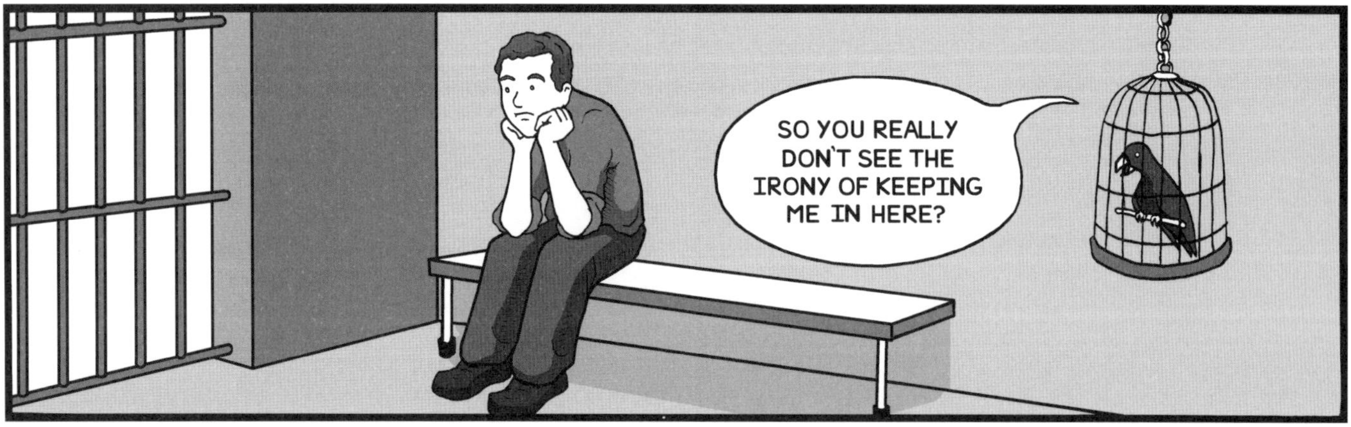
SO YOU REALLY DON'T SEE THE IRONY OF KEEPING ME IN HERE?

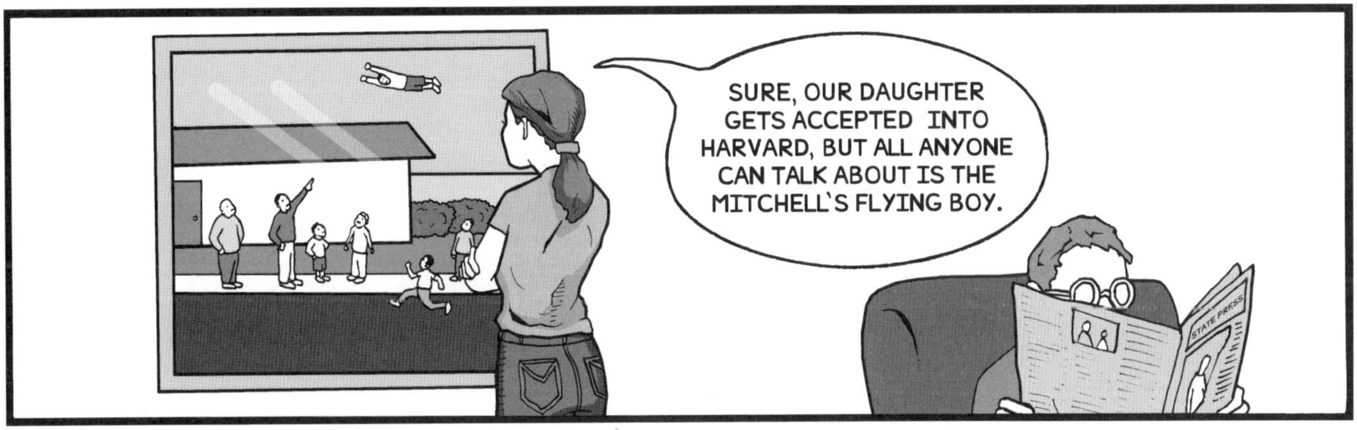
SURE, OUR DAUGHTER GETS ACCEPTED INTO HARVARD, BUT ALL ANYONE CAN TALK ABOUT IS THE MITCHELL'S FLYING BOY.
STATE PRESS

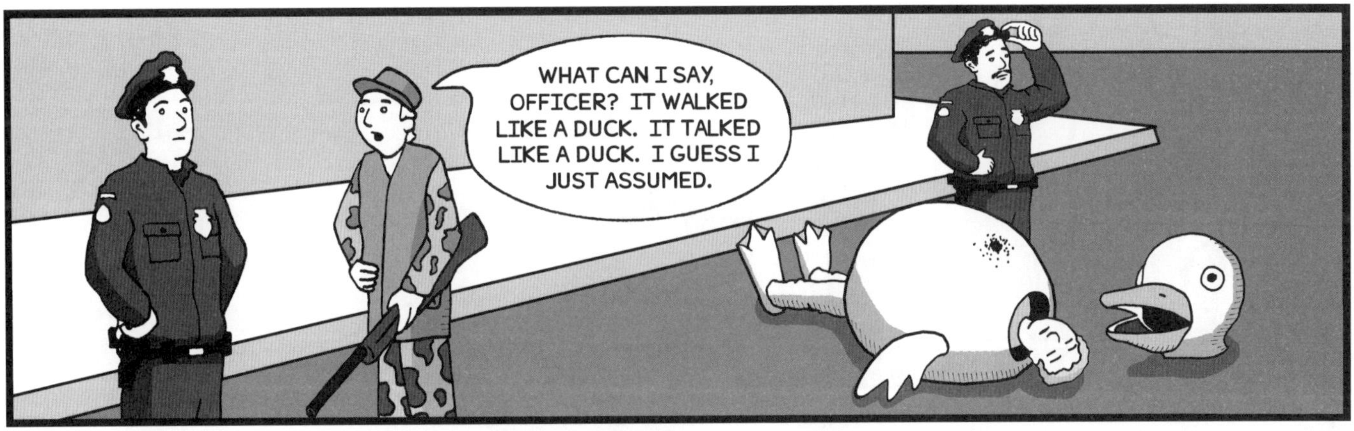
WHAT CAN I SAY, OFFICER? IT WALKED LIKE A DUCK. IT TALKED LIKE A DUCK. I GUESS I JUST ASSUMED.

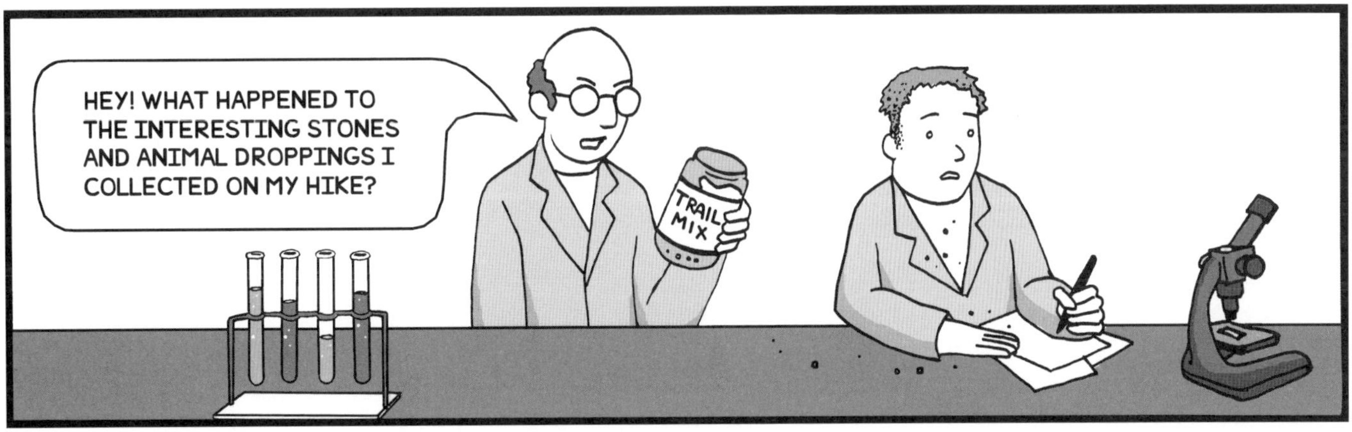
HEY! WHAT HAPPENED TO THE INTERESTING STONES AND ANIMAL DROPPINGS I COLLECTED ON MY HIKE?
TRAIL MIX

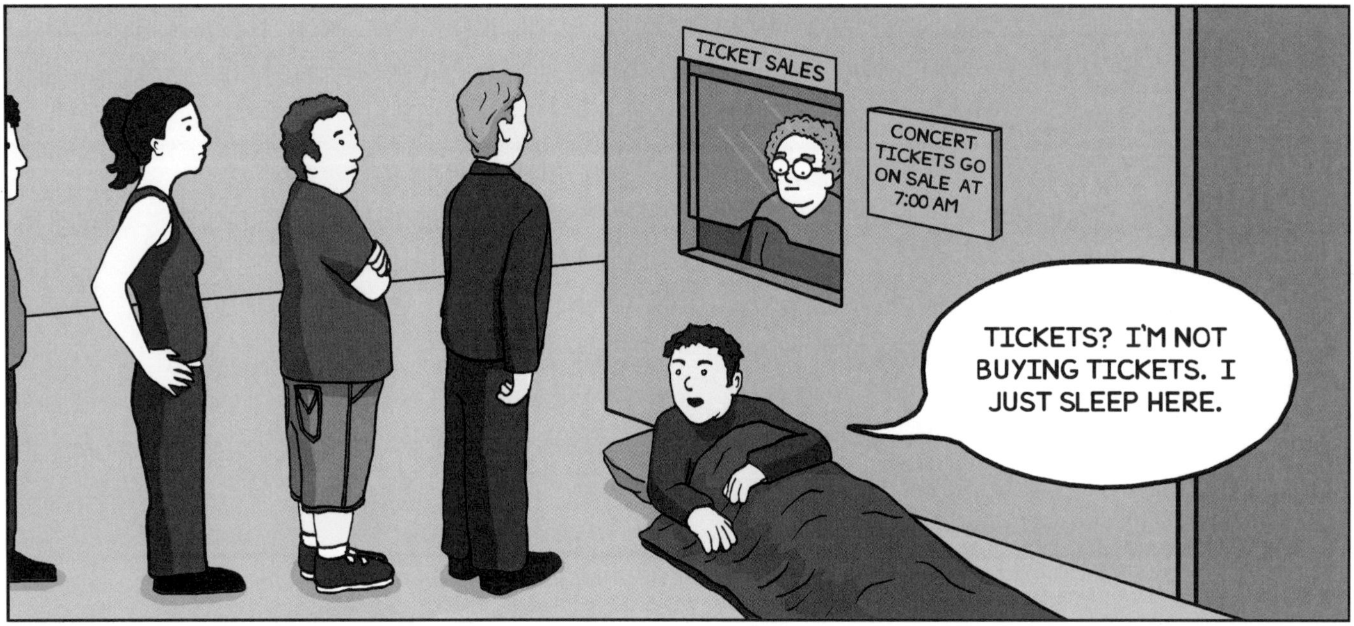
TICKET SALES
CONCERT TICKETS GO ON SALE AT 7:00 AM
TICKETS? I'M NOT BUYING TICKETS. I JUST SLEEP HERE.

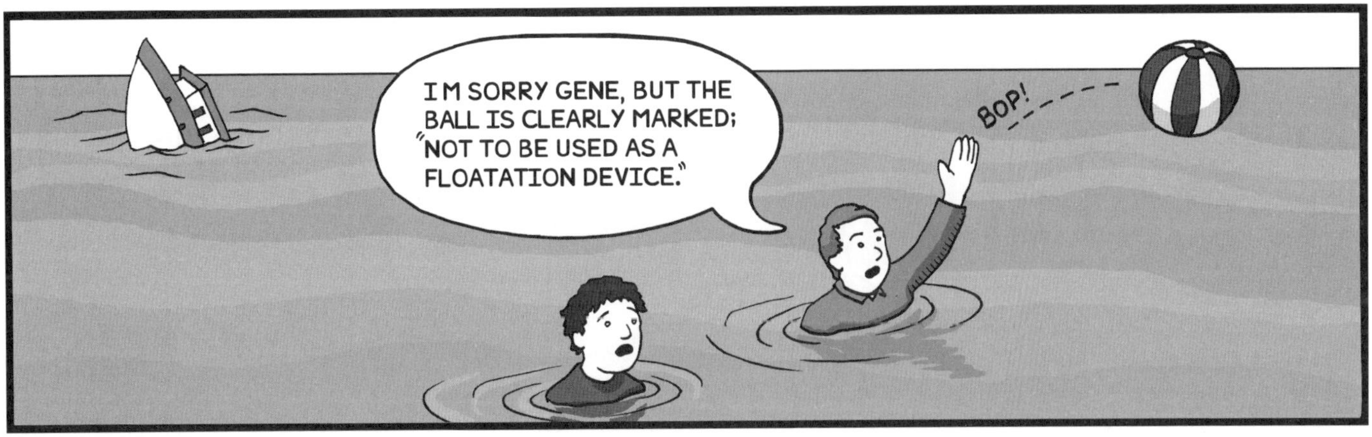
I M SORRY GENE, BUT THE BALL IS CLEARLY MARKED; "NOT TO BE USED AS A FLOATATION DEVICE."
BOP!

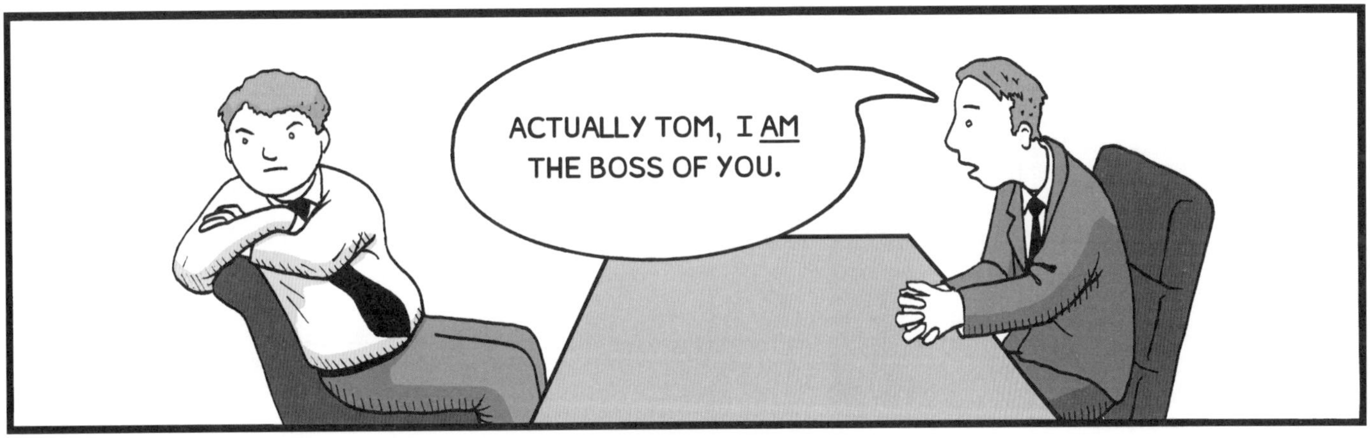
ACTUALLY TOM, I AM THE BOSS OF YOU.

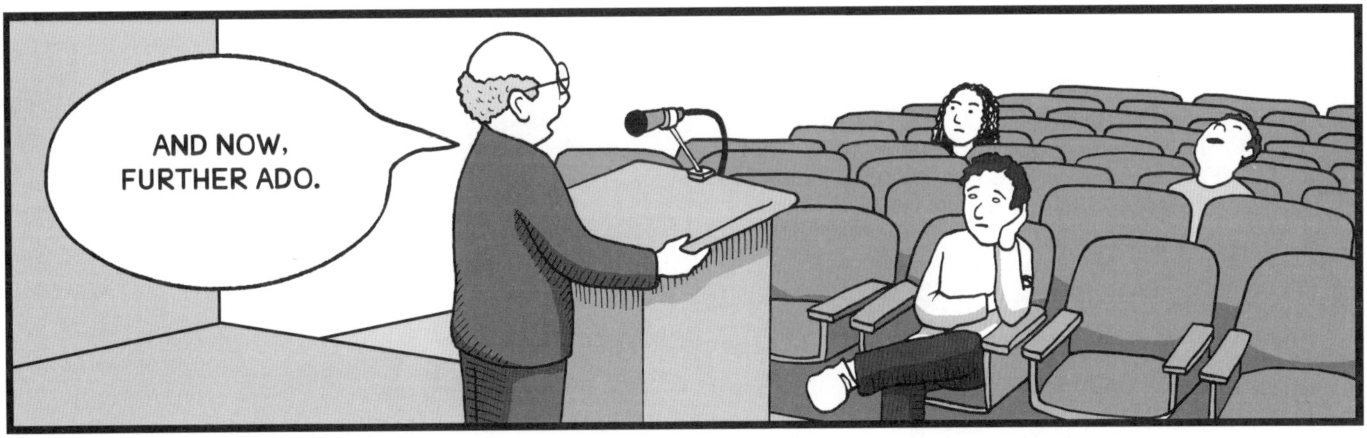
AND NOW, FURTHER ADO.

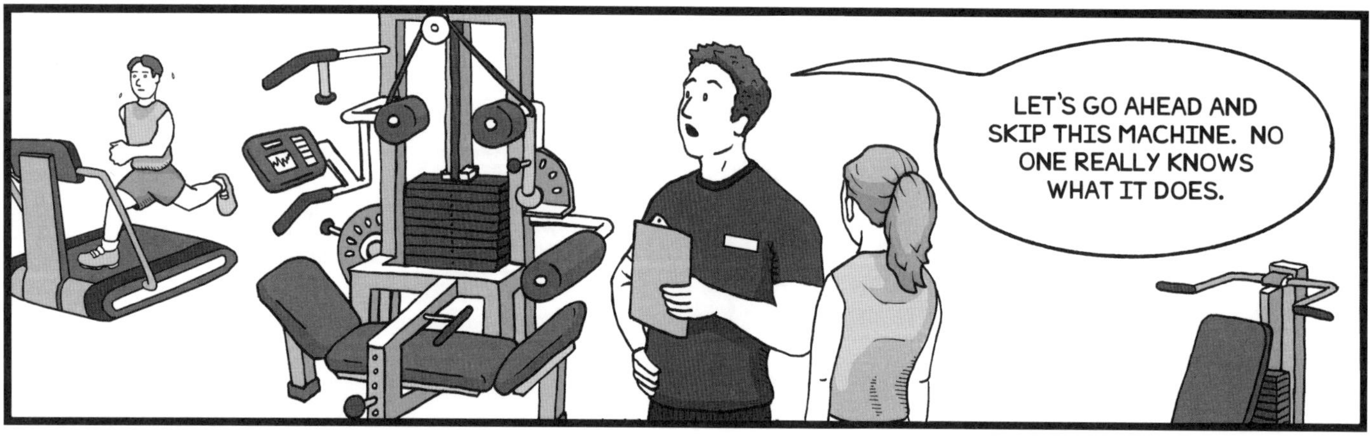
LET'S GO AHEAD AND SKIP THIS MACHINE. NO ONE REALLY KNOWS WHAT IT DOES.

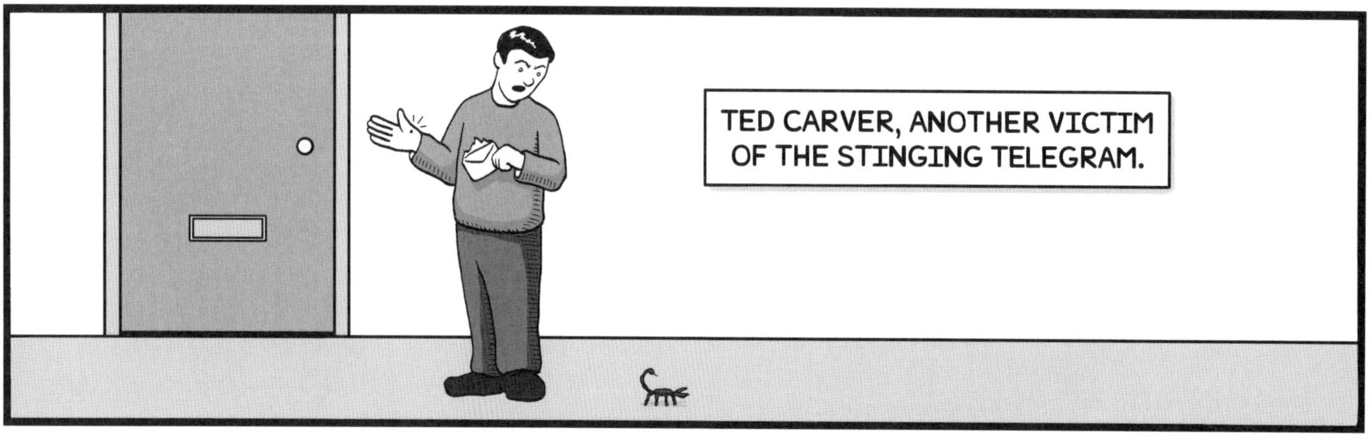
TED CARVER, ANOTHER VICTIM OF THE STINGING TELEGRAM.

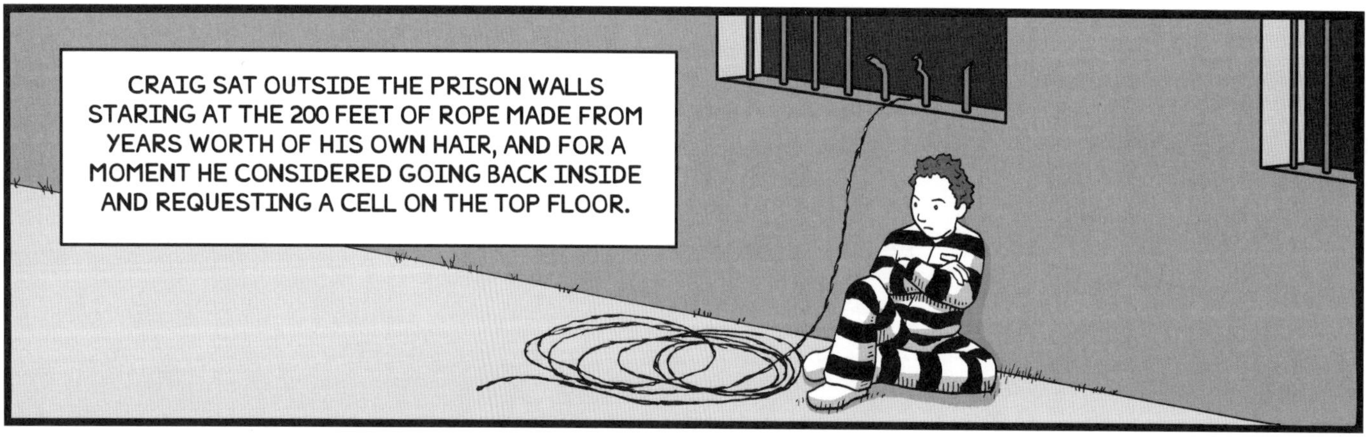
CRAIG SAT OUTSIDE THE PRISON WALLS STARING AT THE 200 FEET OF ROPE MADE FROM YEARS WORTH OF HIS OWN HAIR, AND FOR A MOMENT HE CONSIDERED GOING BACK INSIDE AND REQUESTING A CELL ON THE TOP FLOOR.

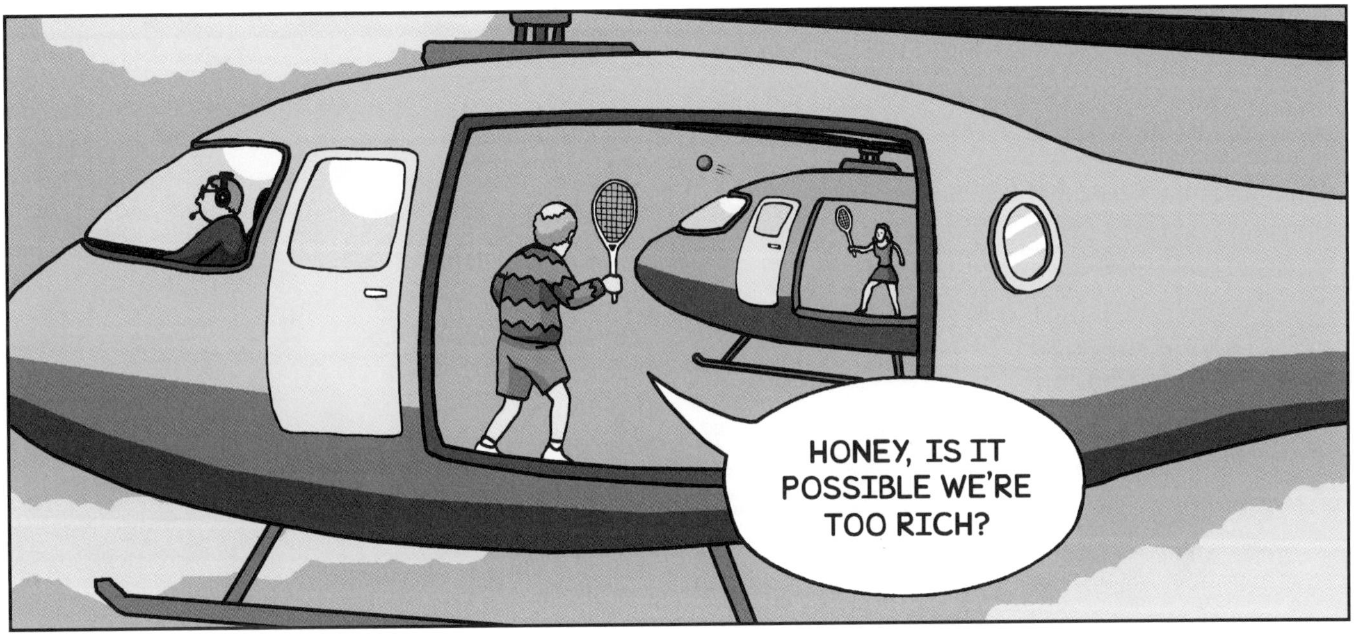
HONEY, IS IT POSSIBLE WE'RE TOO RICH?

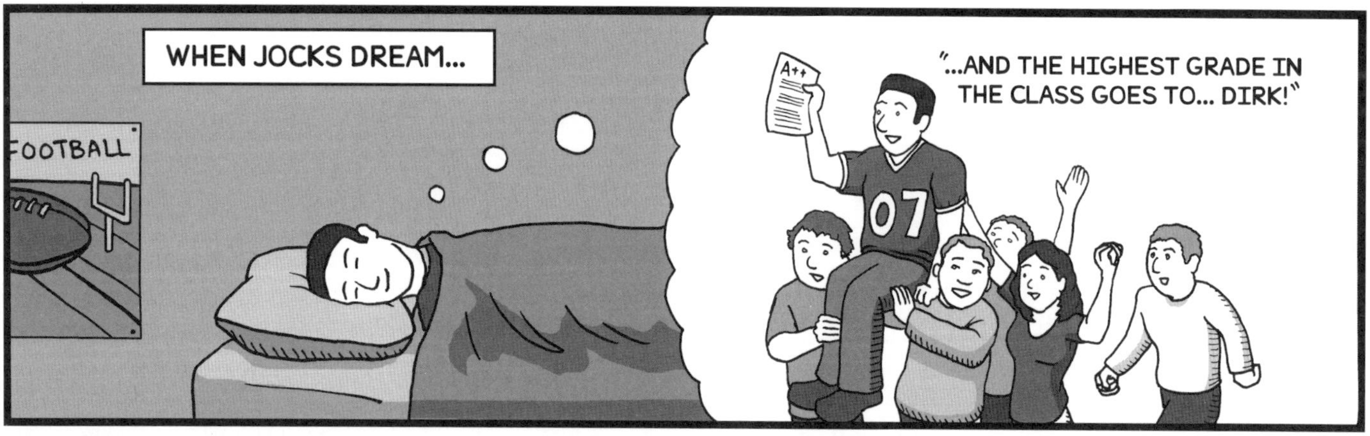
WHEN JOCKS DREAM...
FOOTBALL
A++
"...AND THE HIGHEST GRADE IN THE CLASS GOES TO... DIRK!"
07

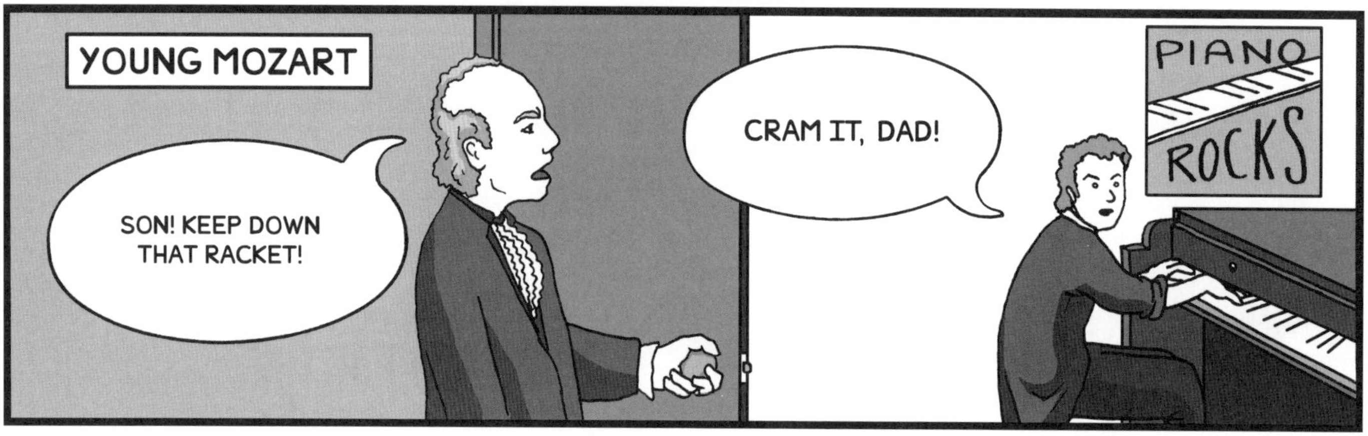
YOUNG MOZART
SON! KEEP DOWN THAT RACKET!
CRAM IT, DAD!
PIANO ROCKS

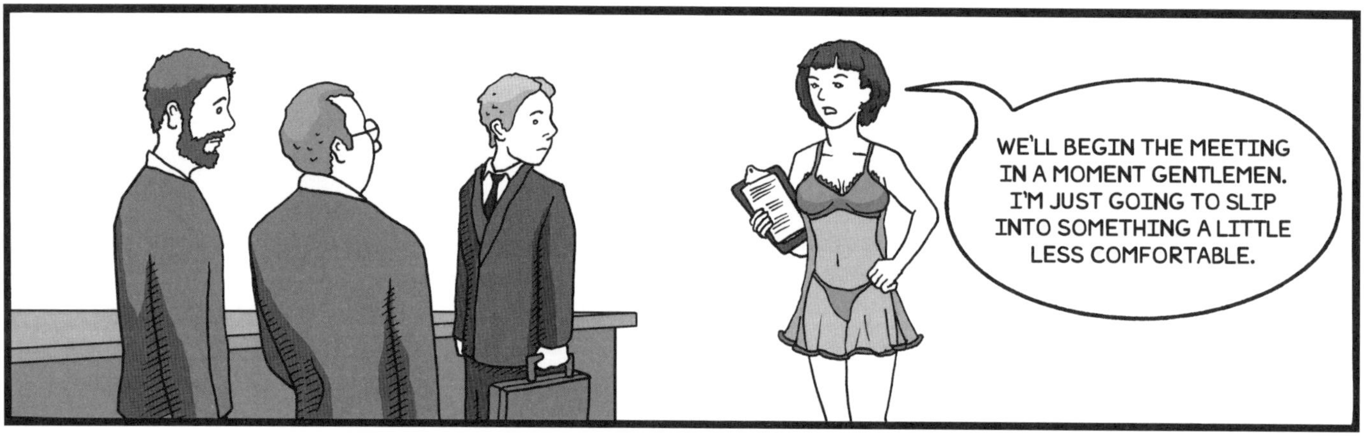
WE'LL BEGIN THE MEETING IN A MOMENT GENTLEMEN. I'M JUST GOING TO SLIP INTO SOMETHING A LITTLE LESS COMFORTABLE.

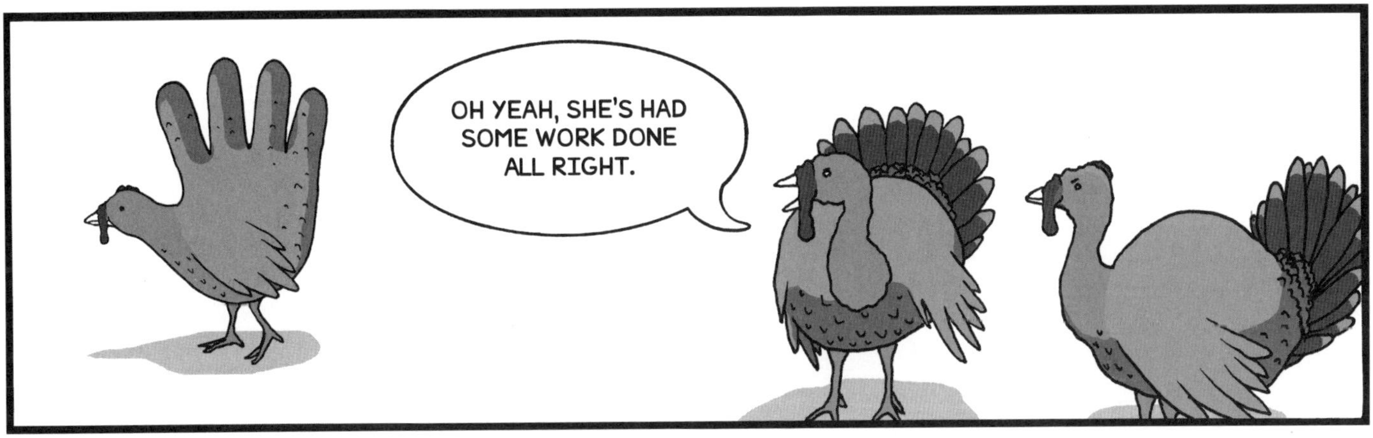
OH YEAH, SHE'S HAD SOME WORK DONE ALL RIGHT.

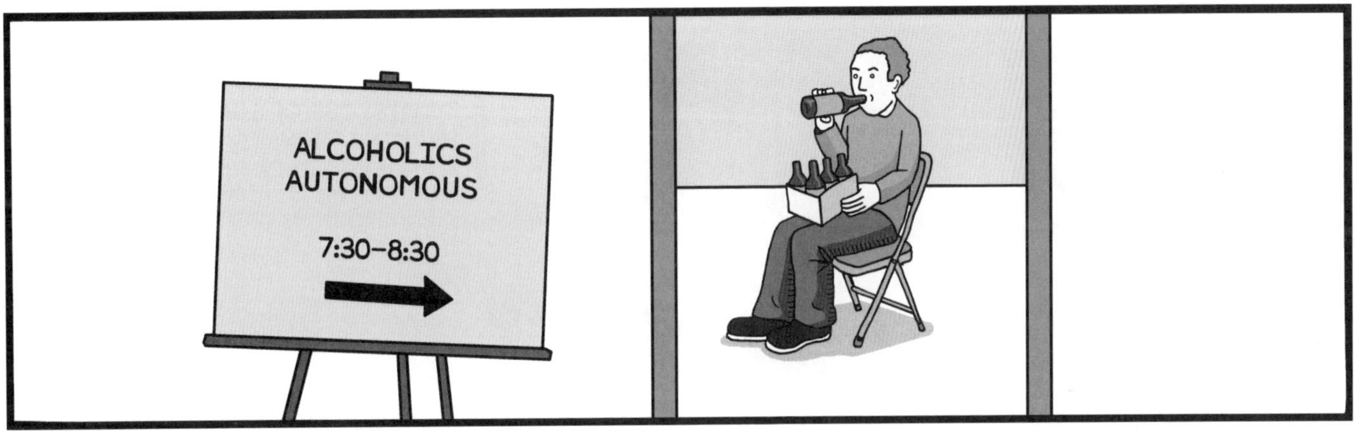
ALCOHOLICS AUTONOMOUS
7:30–8:30

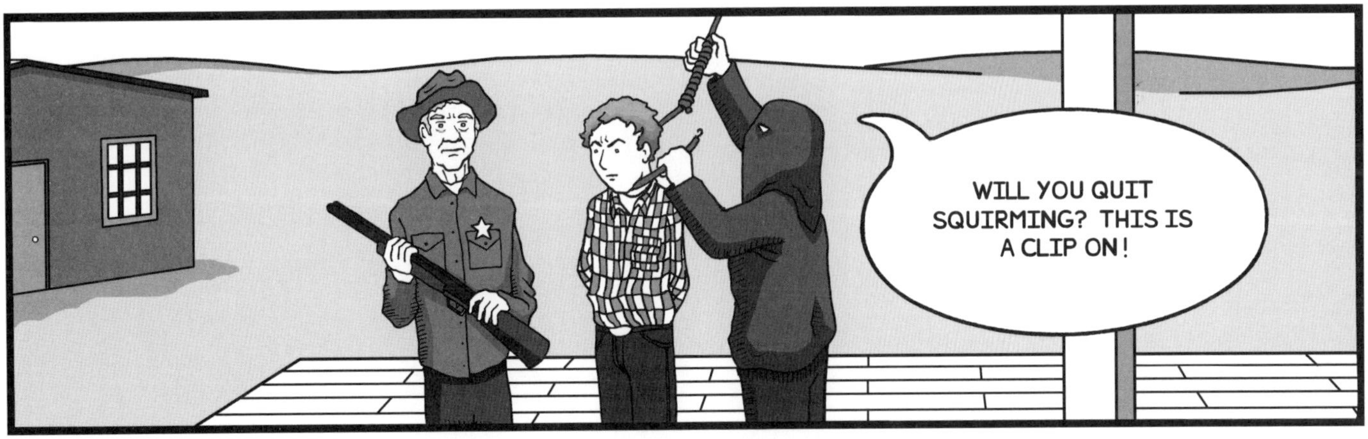
WILL YOU QUIT SQUIRMING? THIS IS A CLIP ON!

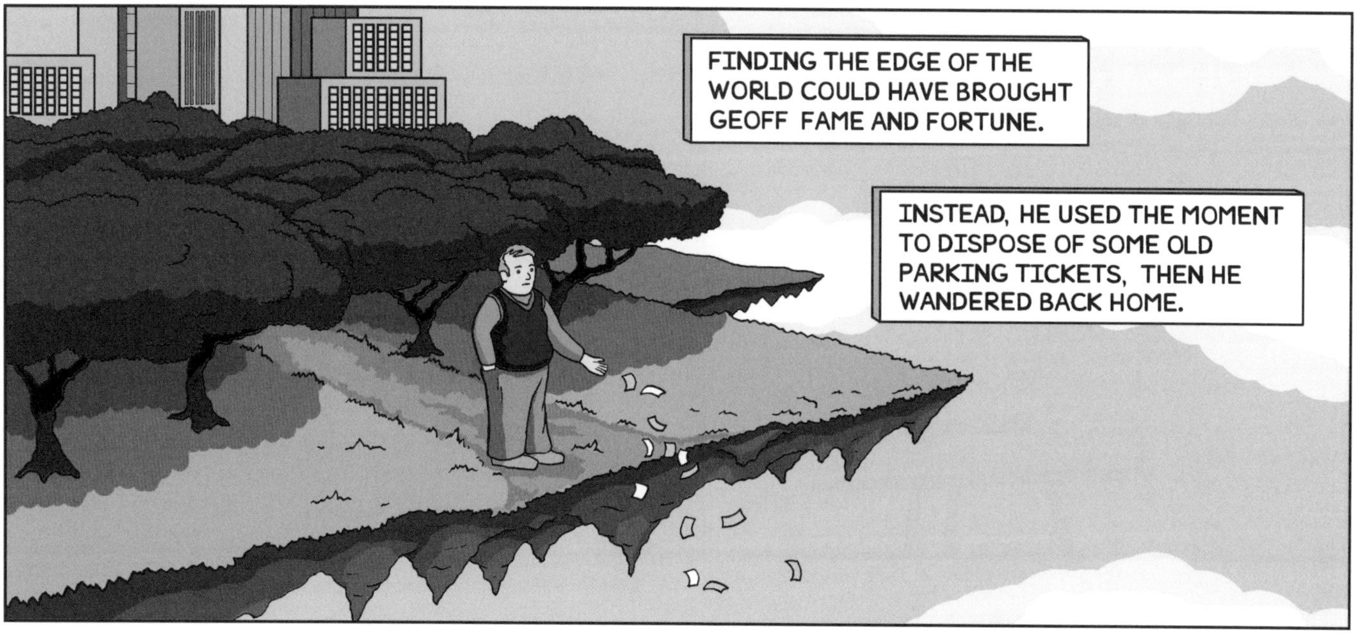
FINDING THE EDGE OF THE WORLD COULD HAVE BROUGHT GEOFF FAME AND FORTUNE.
INSTEAD, HE USED THE MOMENT TO DISPOSE OF SOME OLD PARKING TICKETS, THEN HE WANDERED BACK HOME.

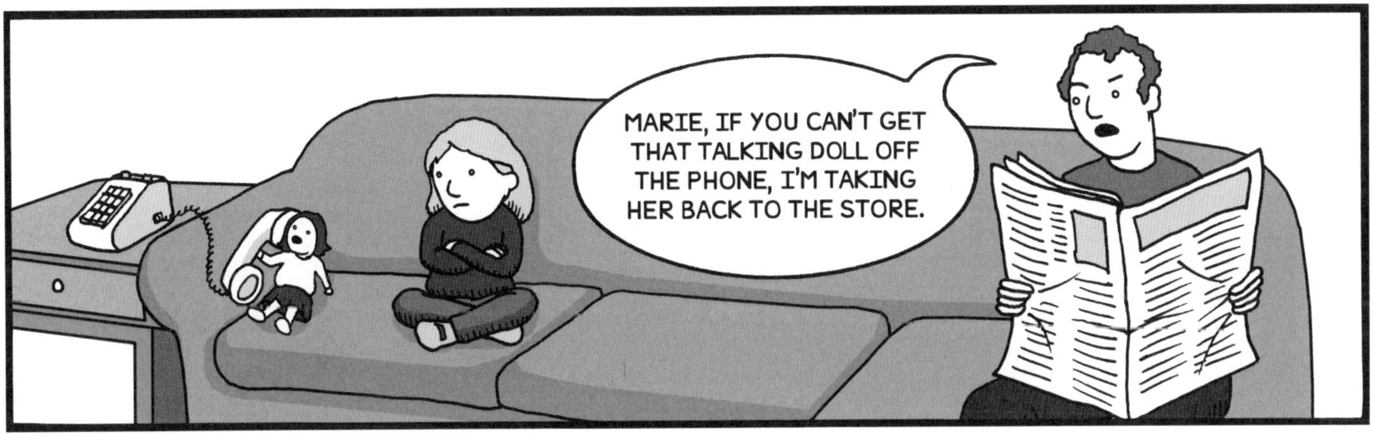
MARIE, IF YOU CAN'T GET THAT TALKING DOLL OFF THE PHONE, I'M TAKING HER BACK TO THE STORE.

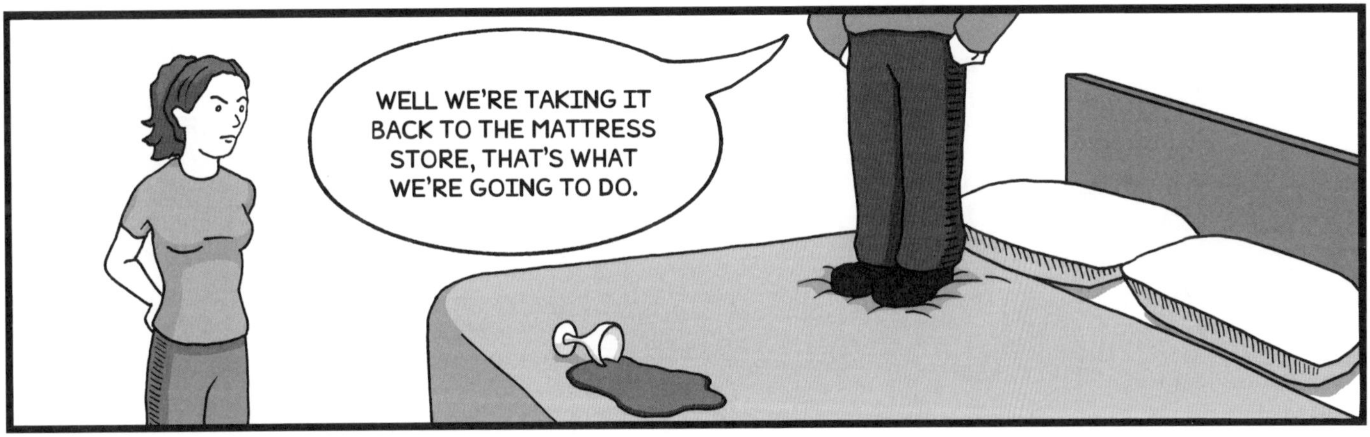
WELL WE'RE TAKING IT BACK TO THE MATTRESS STORE, THAT'S WHAT WE'RE GOING TO DO.

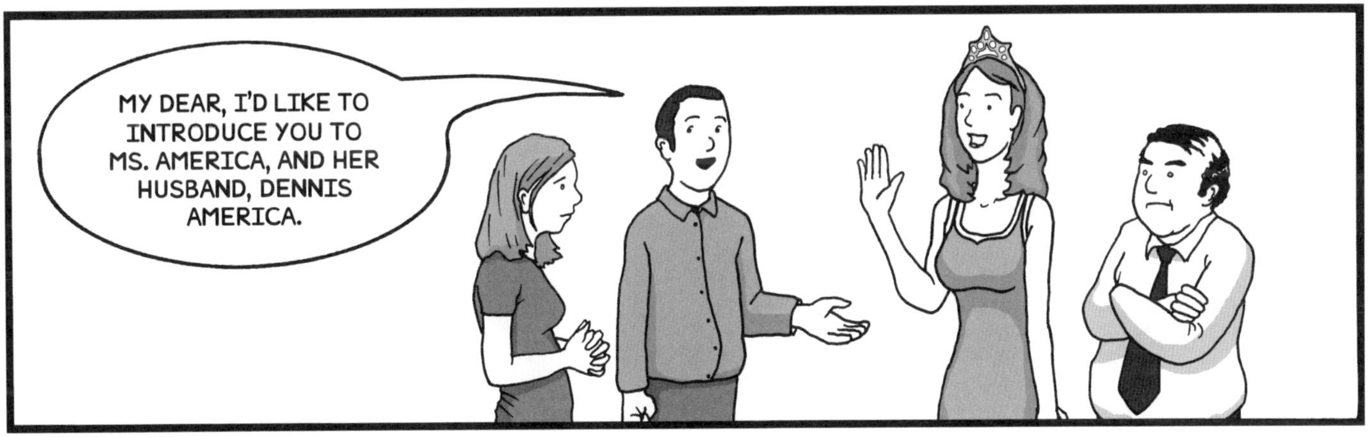
MY DEAR, I'D LIKE TO INTRODUCE YOU TO MS. AMERICA, AND HER HUSBAND, DENNIS AMERICA.

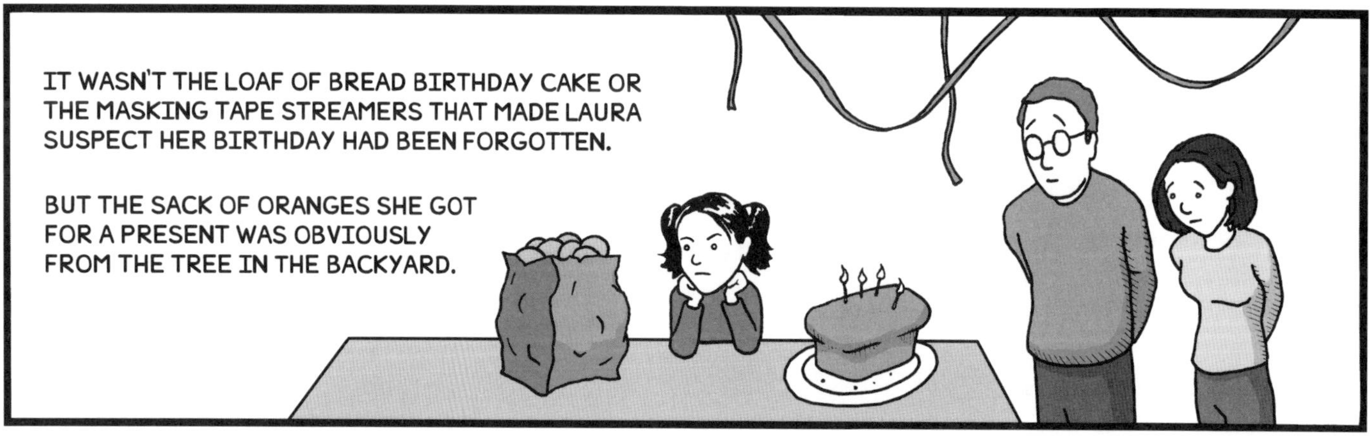
IT WASN'T THE LOAF OF BREAD BIRTHDAY CAKE OR THE MASKING TAPE STREAMERS THAT MADE LAURA SUSPECT HER BIRTHDAY HAD BEEN FORGOTTEN.
BUT THE SACK OF ORANGES SHE GOT FOR A PRESENT WAS OBVIOUSLY FROM THE TREE IN THE BACKYARD.

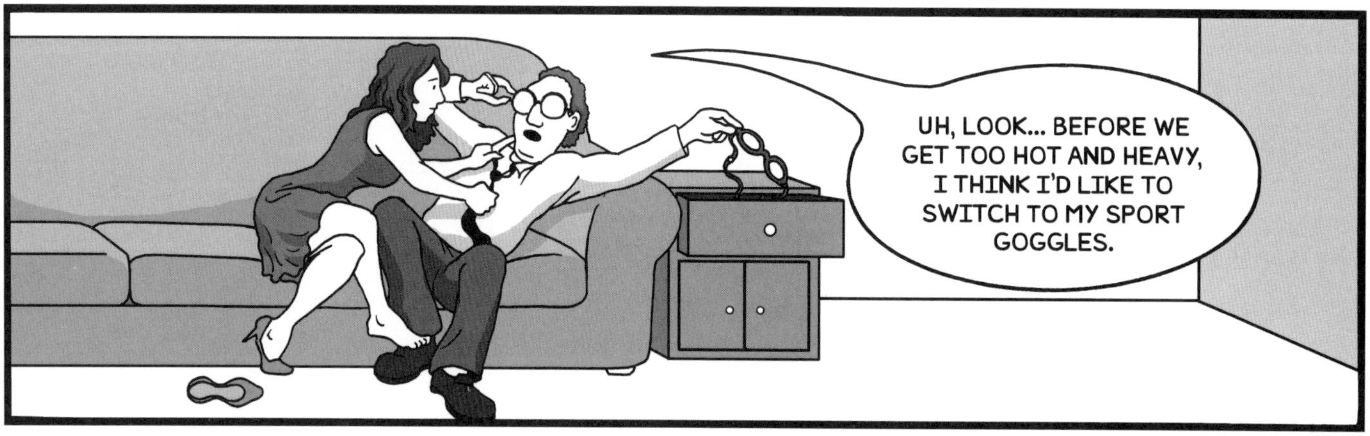
UH, LOOK... BEFORE WE GET TOO HOT AND HEAVY, I THINK I'D LIKE TO SWITCH TO MY SPORT GOGGLES.

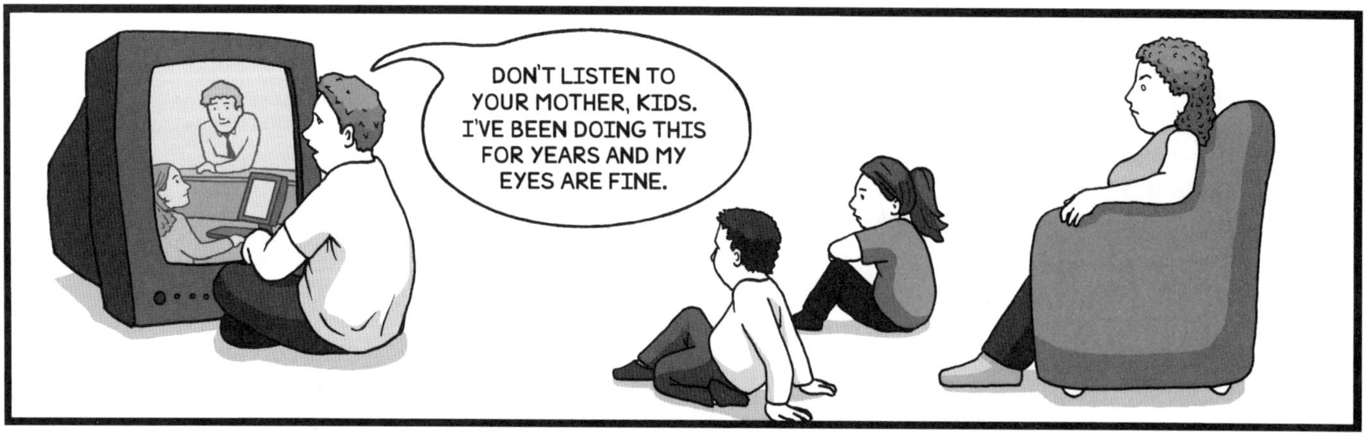
DON'T LISTEN TO YOUR MOTHER, KIDS. I'VE BEEN DOING THIS FOR YEARS AND MY EYES ARE FINE.

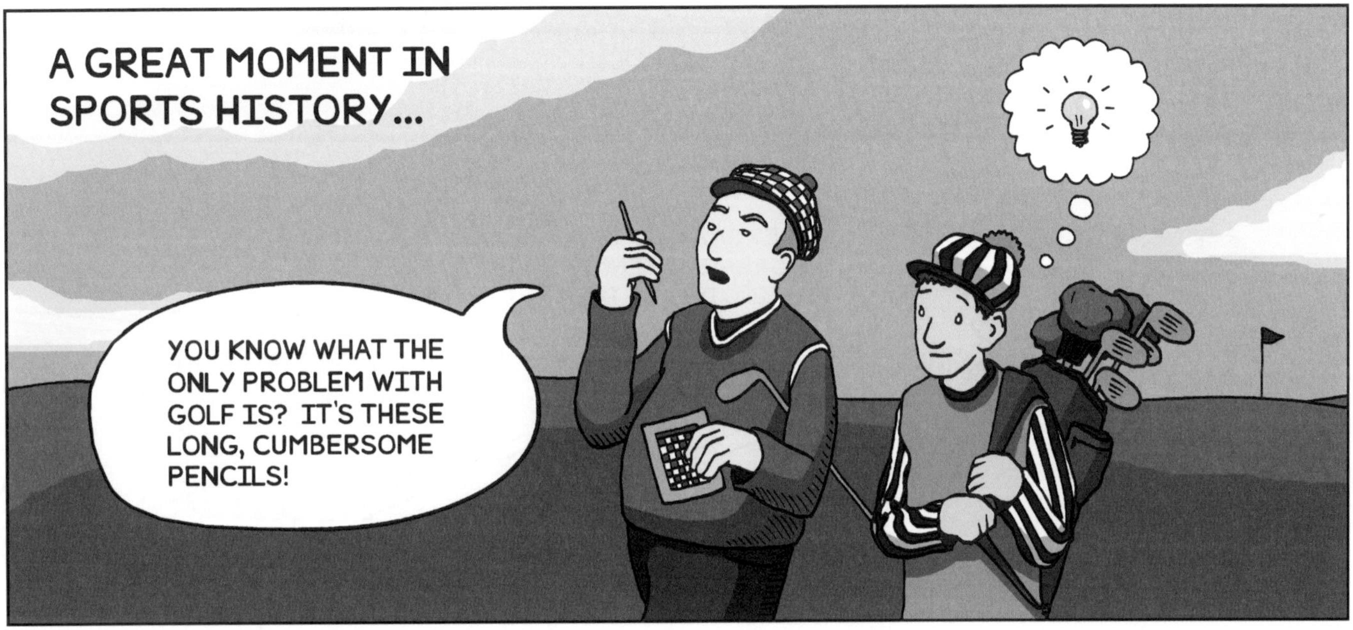
A GREAT MOMENT IN SPORTS HISTORY...
YOU KNOW WHAT THE ONLY PROBLEM WITH GOLF IS? IT'S THESE LONG, CUMBERSOME PENCILS!

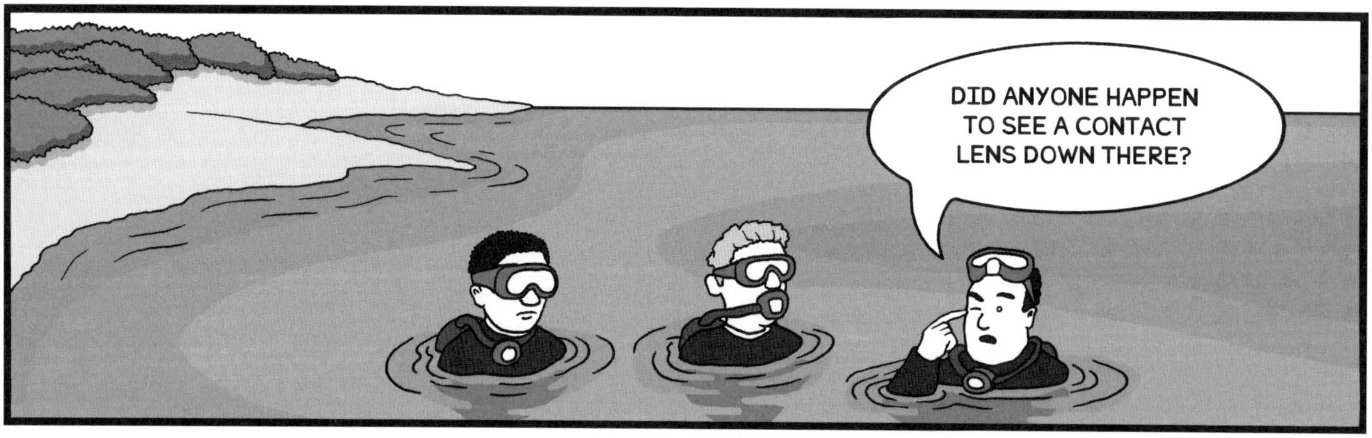
DID ANYONE HAPPEN TO SEE A CONTACT LENS DOWN THERE?

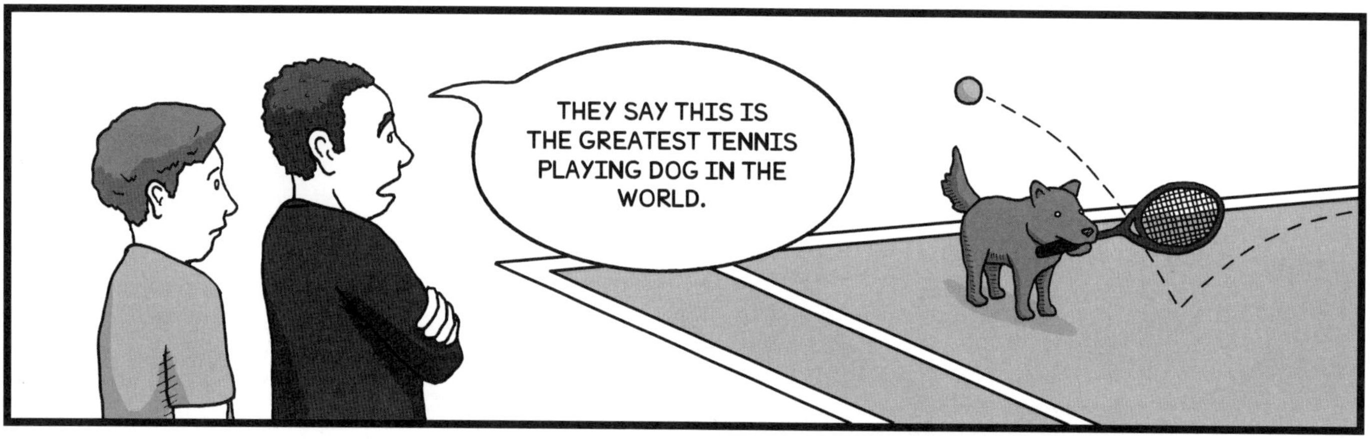
THEY SAY THIS IS THE GREATEST TENNIS PLAYING DOG IN THE WORLD.

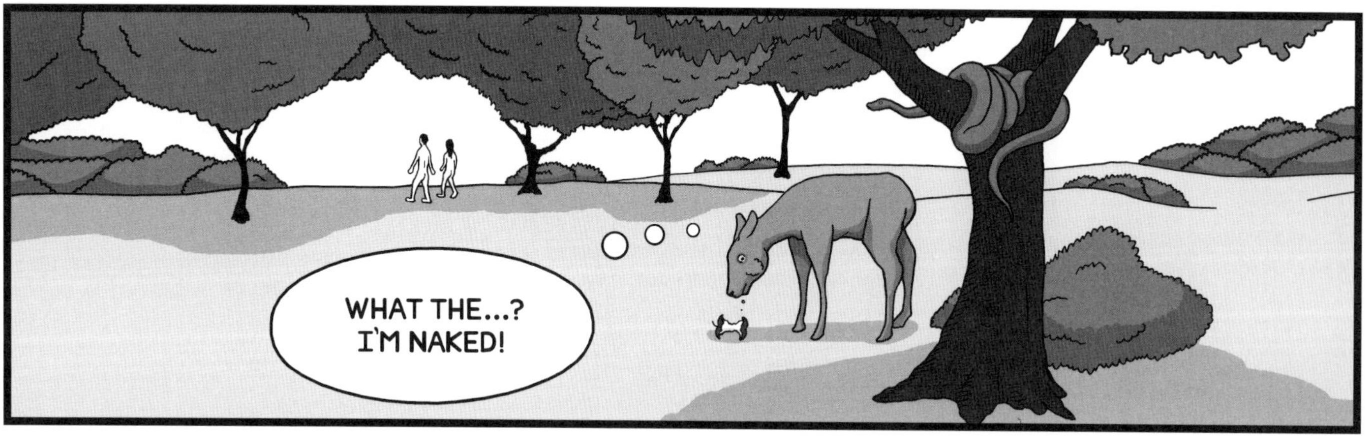
WHAT THE...? I'M NAKED!

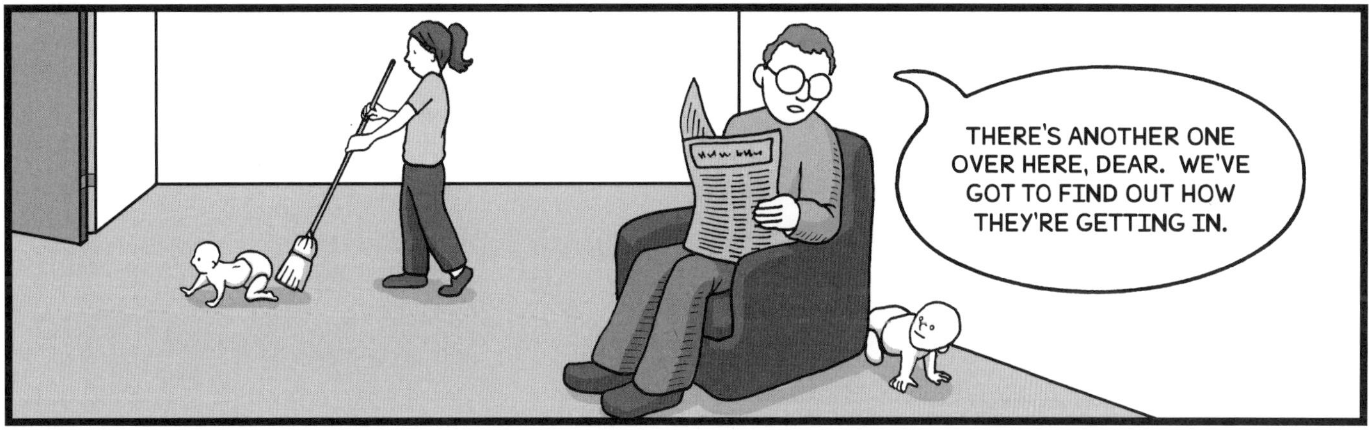
THERE'S ANOTHER ONE OVER HERE, DEAR. WE'VE GOT TO FIND OUT HOW THEY'RE GETTING IN.

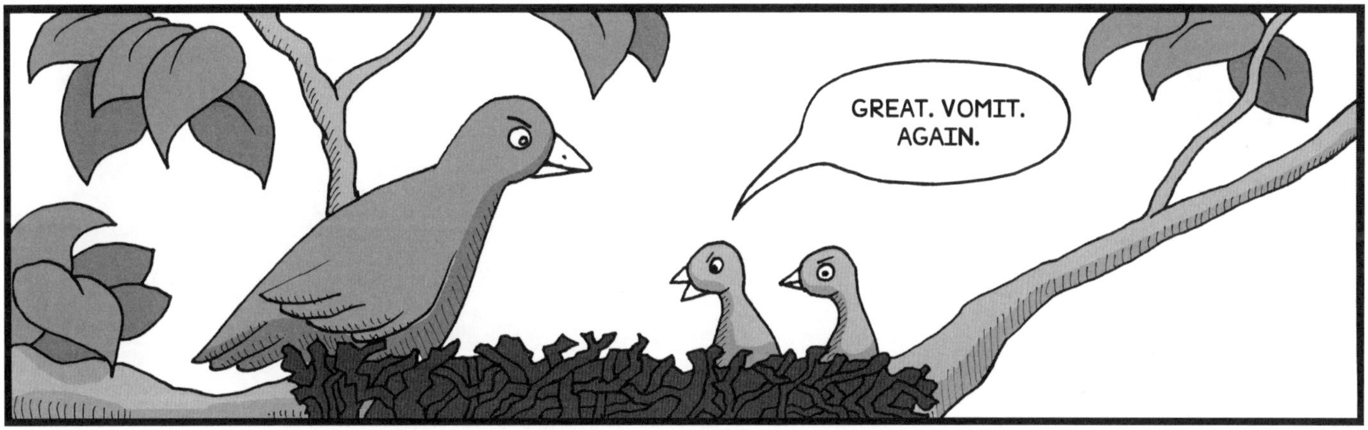
GREAT. VOMIT. AGAIN.

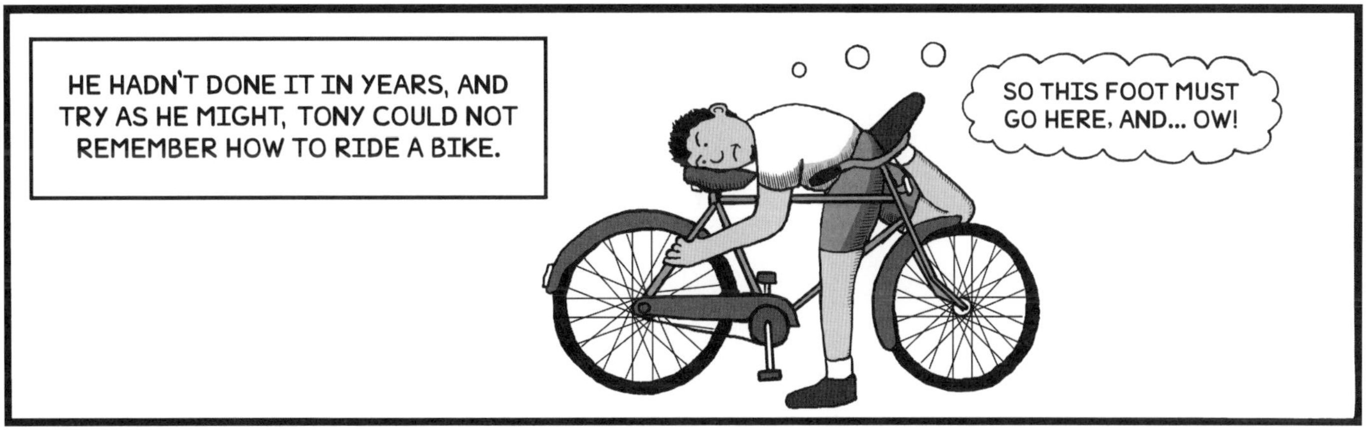
HE HADN'T DONE IT IN YEARS, AND TRY AS HE MIGHT, TONY COULD NOT REMEMBER HOW TO RIDE A BIKE.
SO THIS FOOT MUST GO HERE, AND... OW!

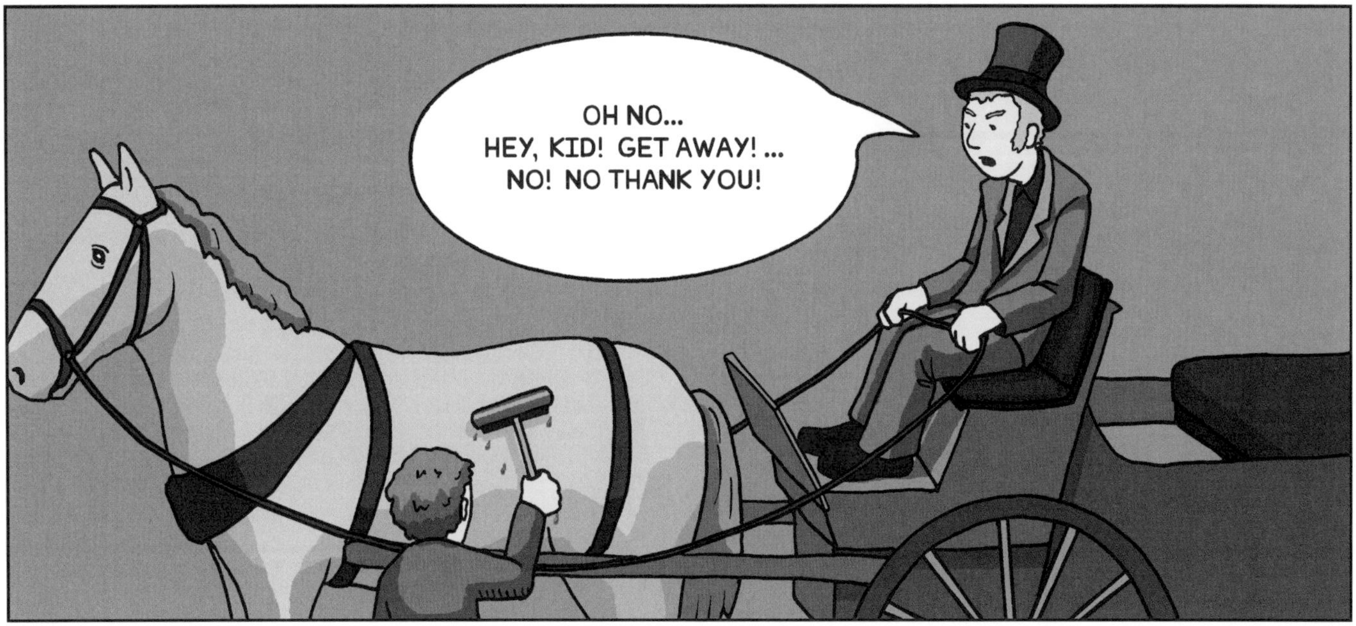
OH NO...
HEY, KID! GET AWAY! ...
NO! NO THANK YOU!

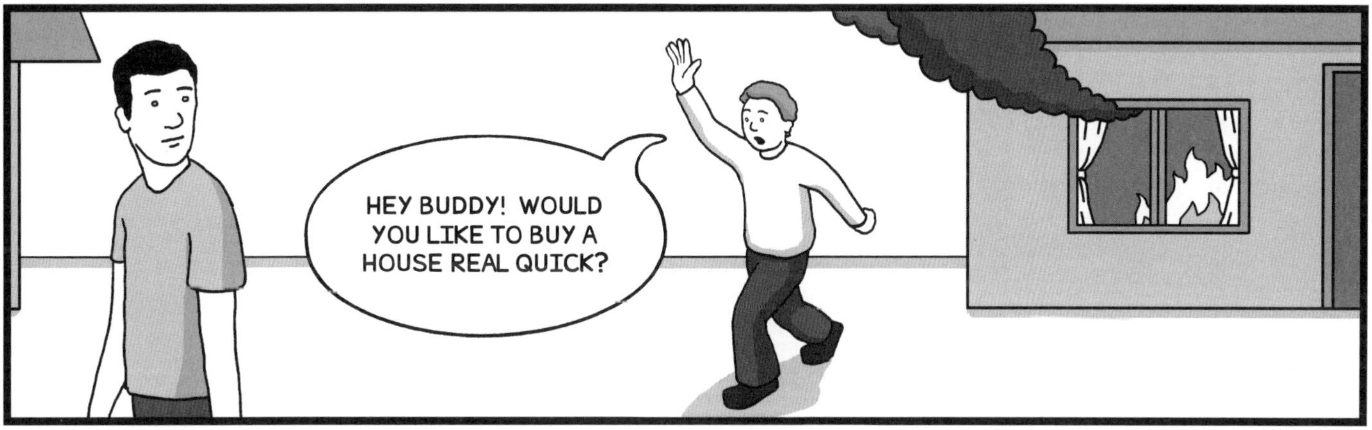
HEY BUDDY! WOULD YOU LIKE TO BUY A HOUSE REAL QUICK?

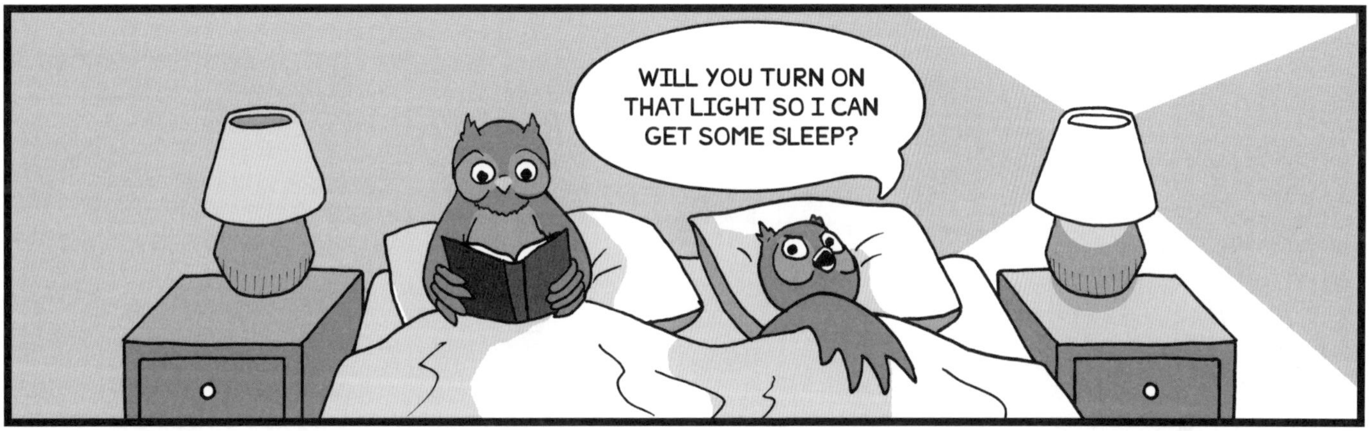
WILL YOU TURN ON THAT LIGHT SO I CAN GET SOME SLEEP?

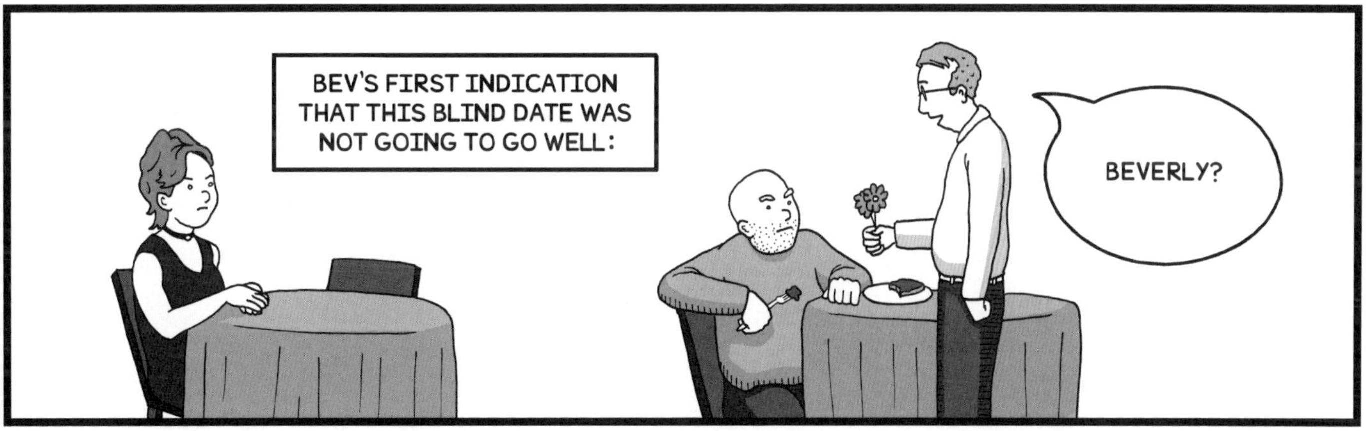
BEV'S FIRST INDICATION THAT THIS BLIND DATE WAS NOT GOING TO GO WELL:
BEVERLY?

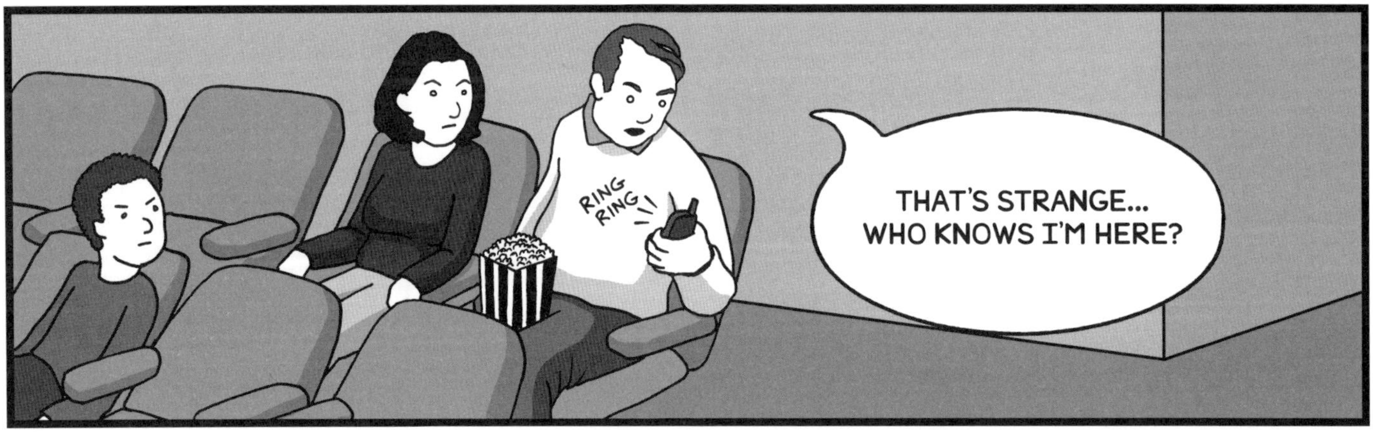
RING RING
THAT'S STRANGE... WHO KNOWS I'M HERE?

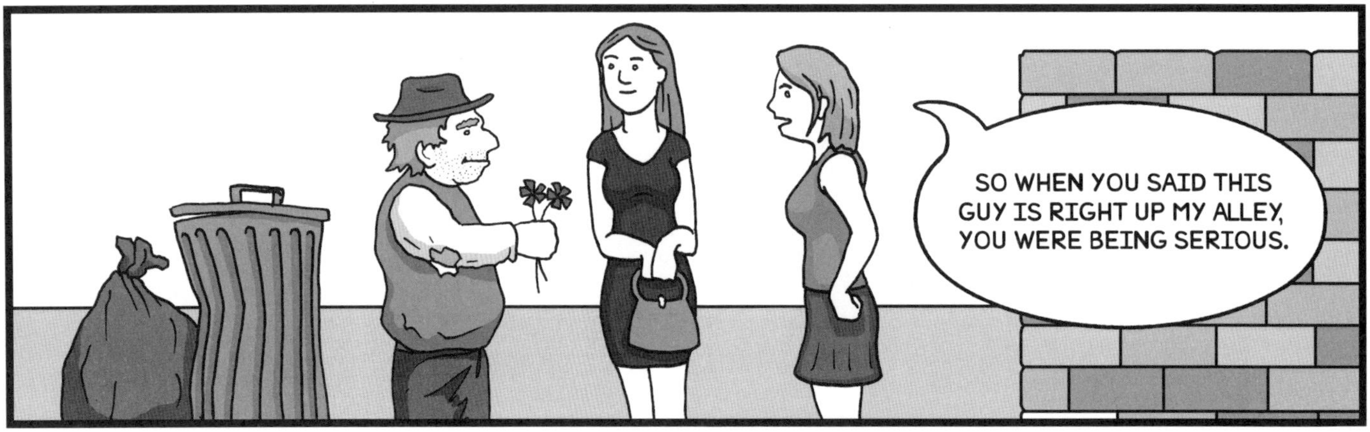
SO WHEN YOU SAID THIS GUY IS RIGHT UP MY ALLEY, YOU WERE BEING SERIOUS.

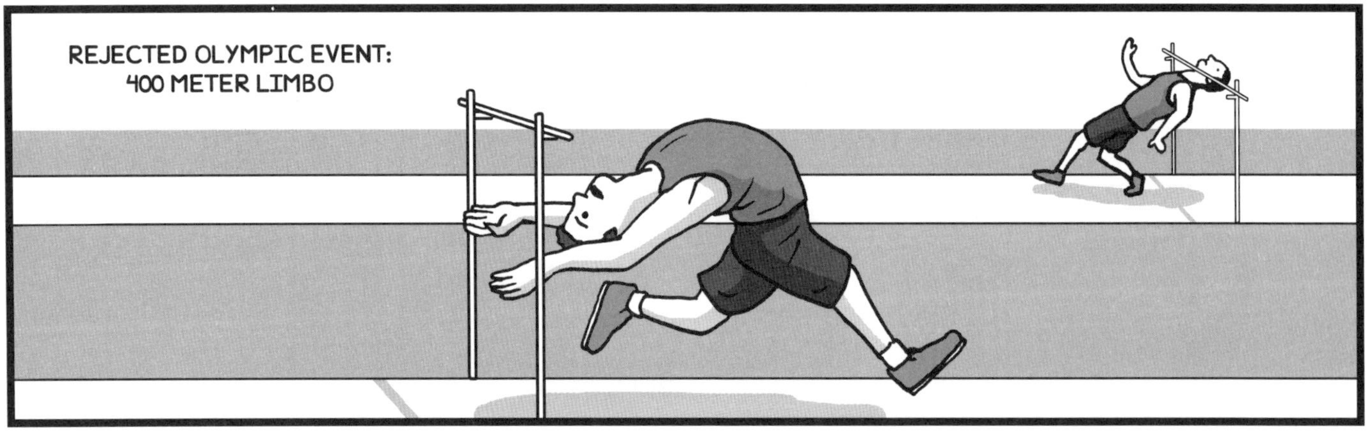
REJECTED OLYMPIC EVENT:
400 METER LIMBO

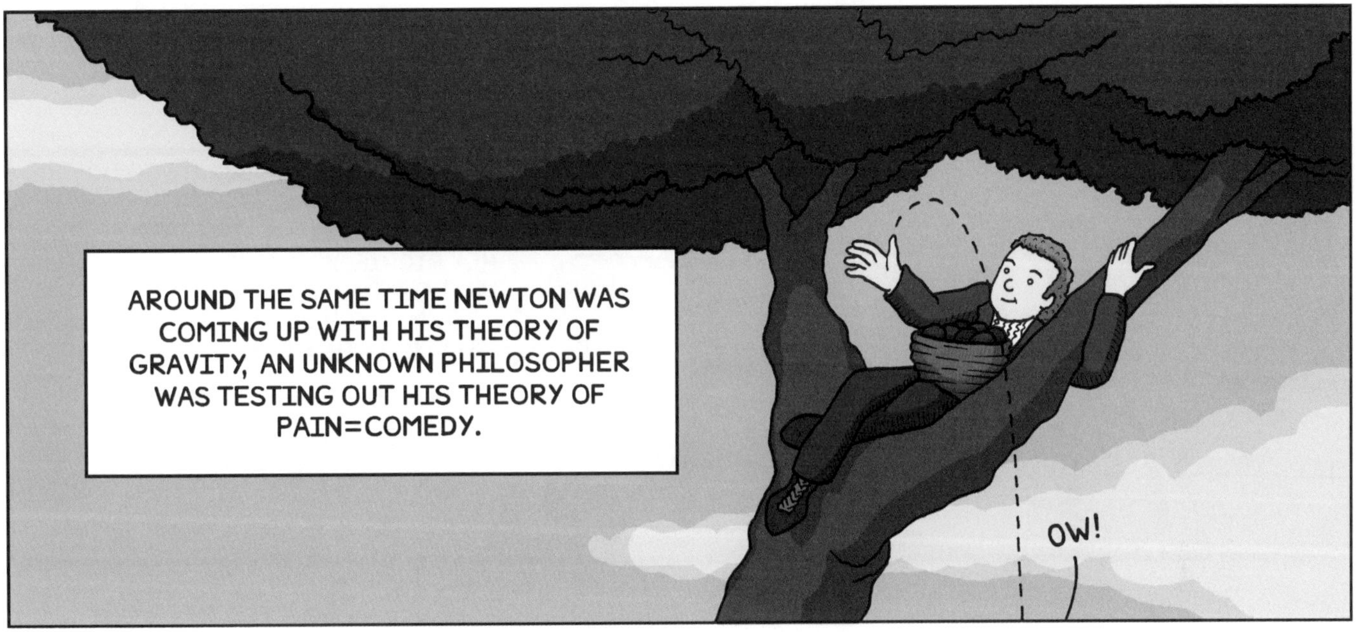
AROUND THE SAME TIME NEWTON WAS COMING UP WITH HIS THEORY OF GRAVITY, AN UNKNOWN PHILOSOPHER WAS TESTING OUT HIS THEORY OF PAIN=COMEDY.
OW!

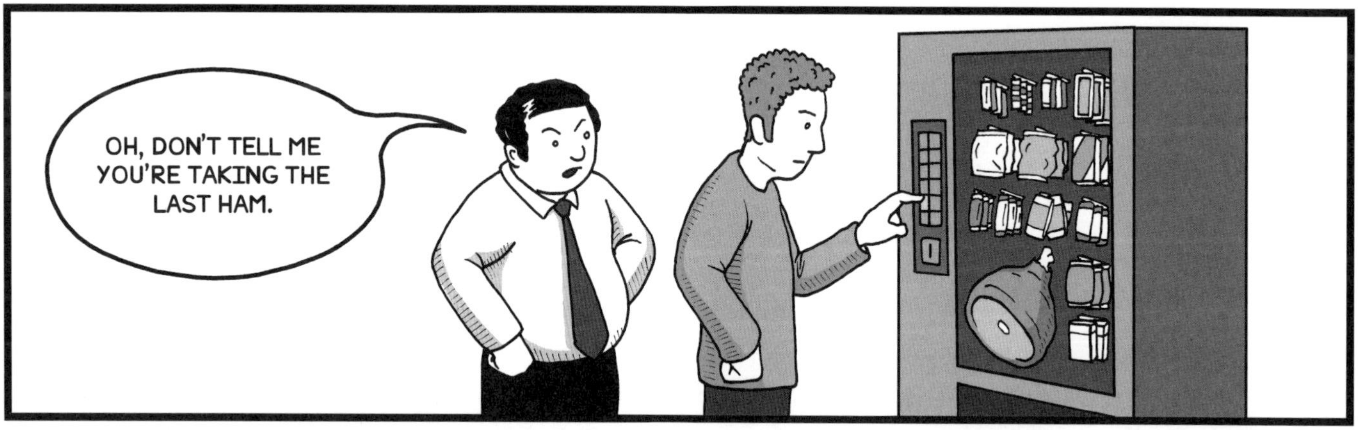
OH, DON'T TELL ME YOU'RE TAKING THE LAST HAM.

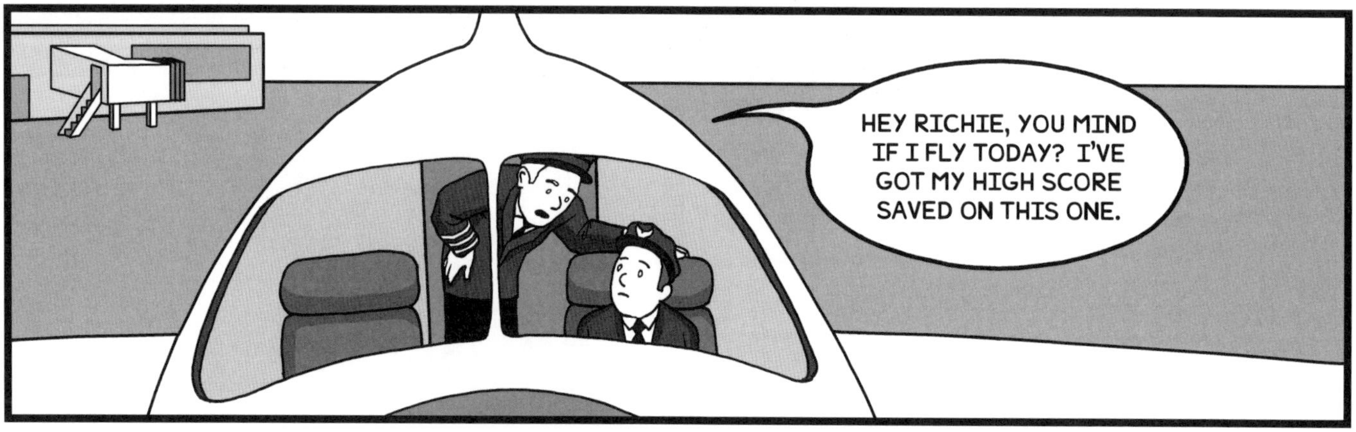
HEY RICHIE, YOU MIND IF I FLY TODAY? I'VE GOT MY HIGH SCORE SAVED ON THIS ONE.

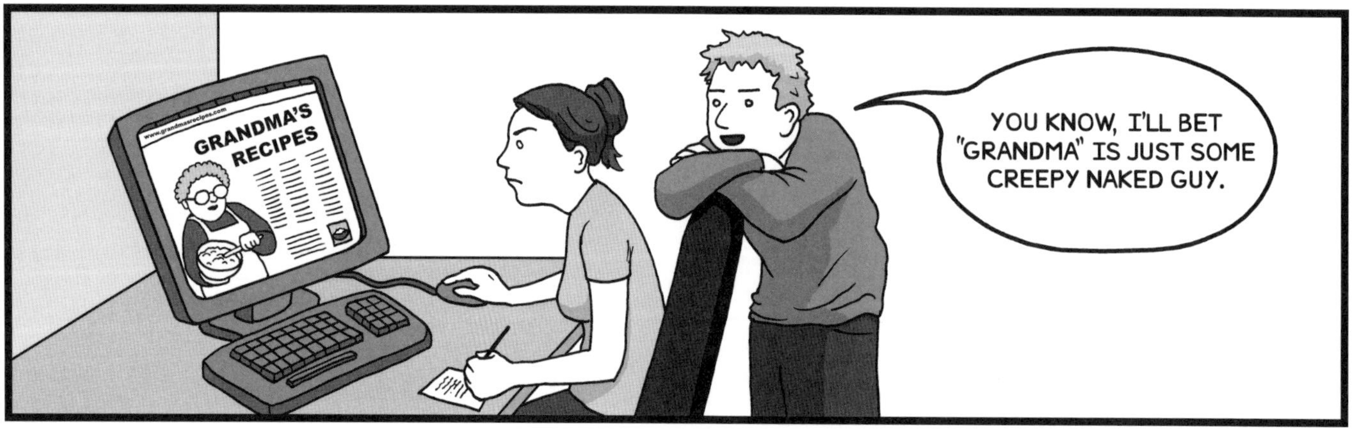
GRANDMA'S RECIPES
YOU KNOW, I'LL BET "GRANDMA" IS JUST SOME CREEPY NAKED GUY.

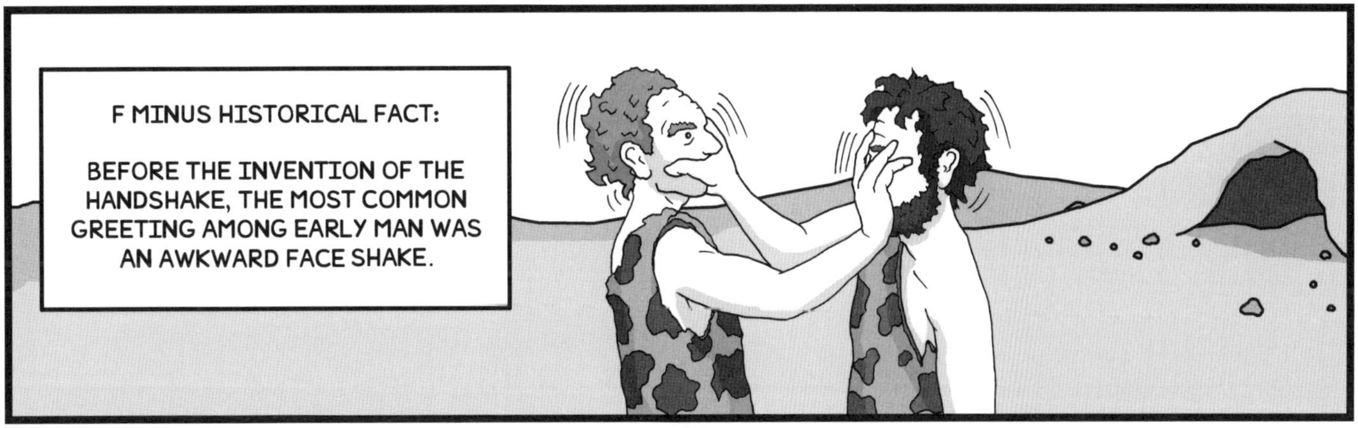
F MINUS HISTORICAL FACT:
BEFORE THE INVENTION OF THE HANDSHAKE, THE MOST COMMON GREETING AMONG EARLY MAN WAS AN AWKWARD FACE SHAKE.

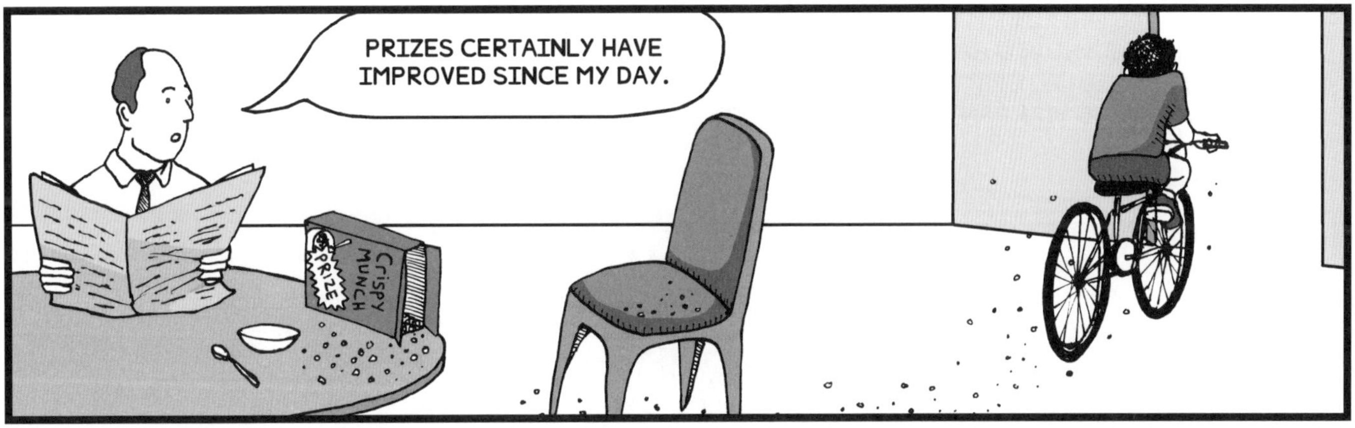
PRIZES CERTAINLY HAVE IMPROVED SINCE MY DAY.
PRIZE
Crispy MUNCH

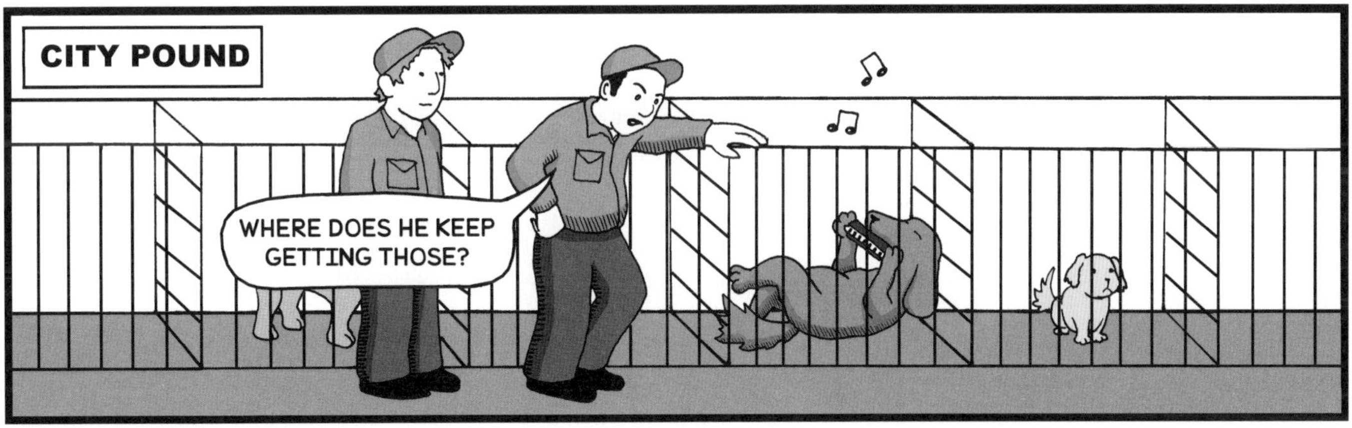
CITY POUND
WHERE DOES HE KEEP GETTING THOSE?

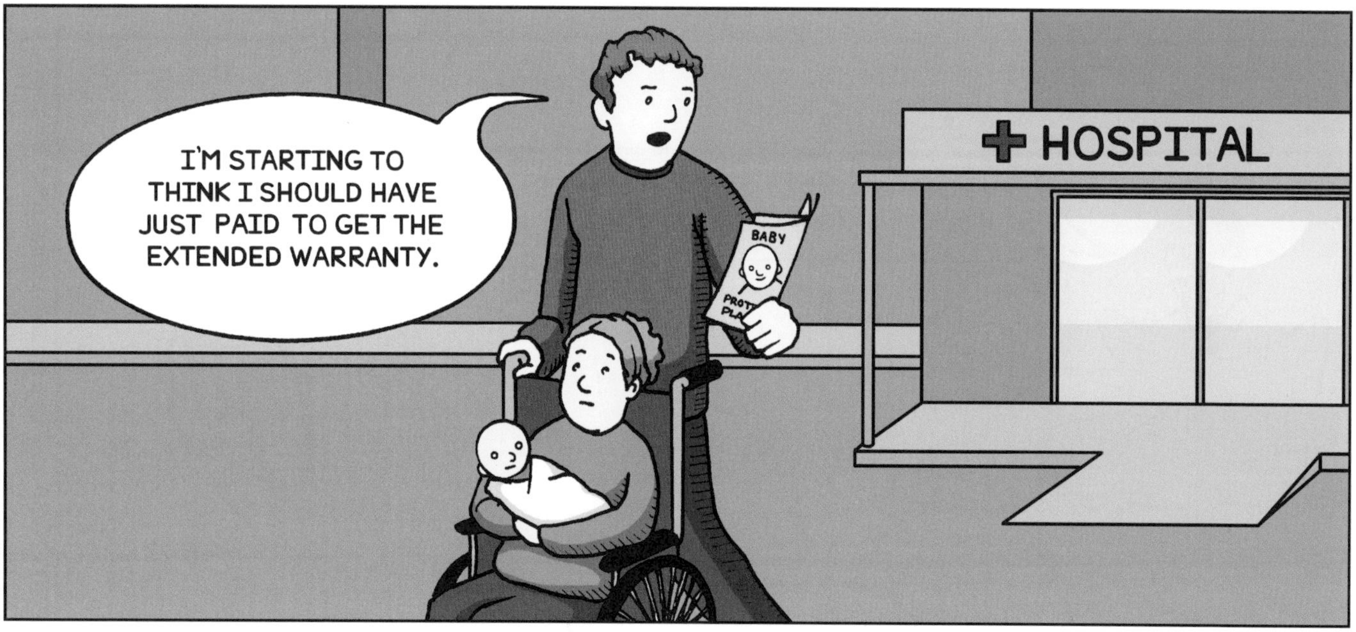
I'M STARTING TO THINK I SHOULD HAVE JUST PAID TO GET THE EXTENDED WARRANTY.
HOSPITAL
BABY

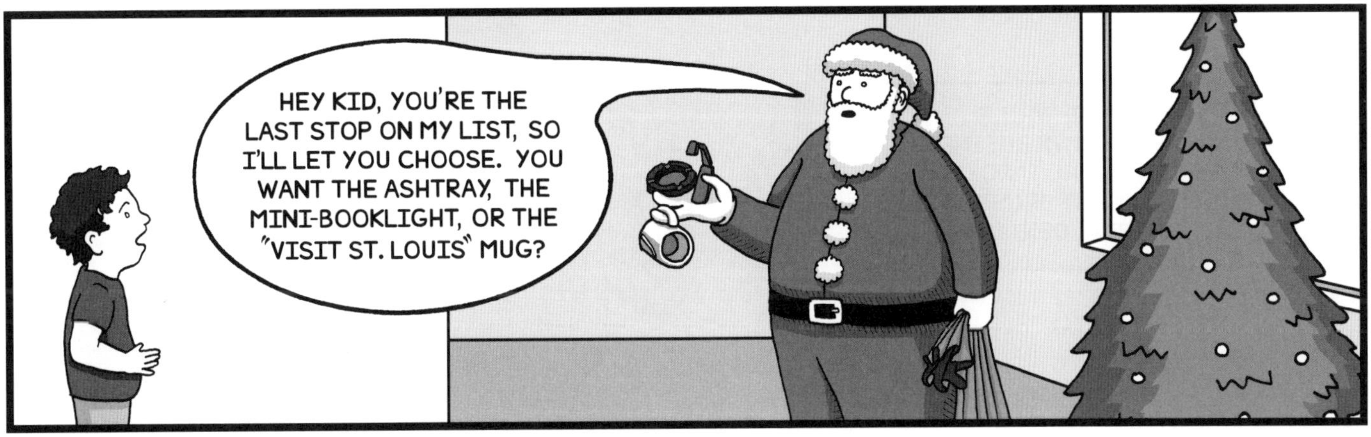
HEY KID, YOU'RE THE LAST STOP ON MY LIST, SO I'LL LET YOU CHOOSE. YOU WANT THE ASHTRAY, THE MINI-BOOKLIGHT, OR THE "VISIT ST. LOUIS" MUG?

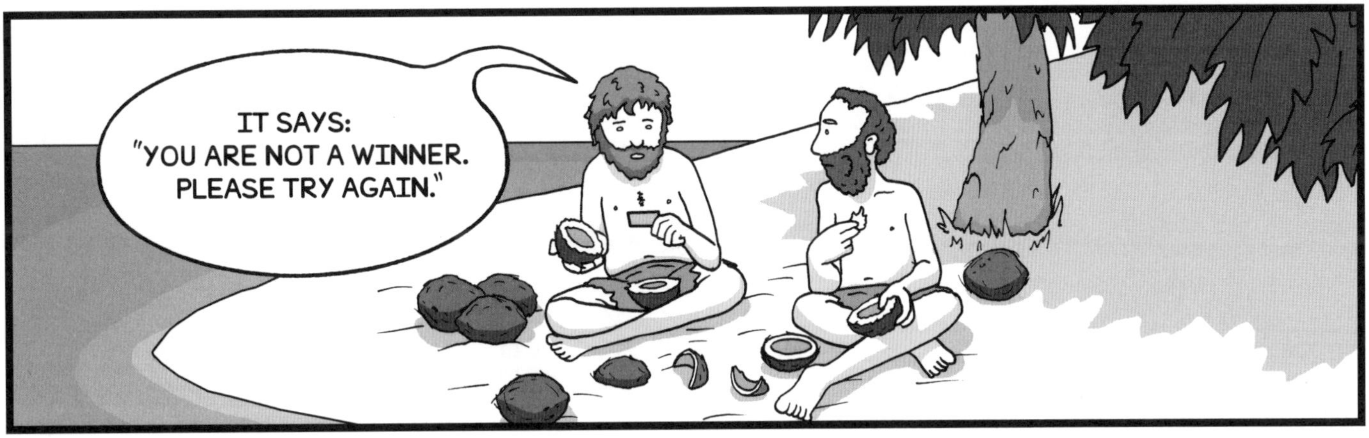
IT SAYS: "YOU ARE NOT A WINNER. PLEASE TRY AGAIN."

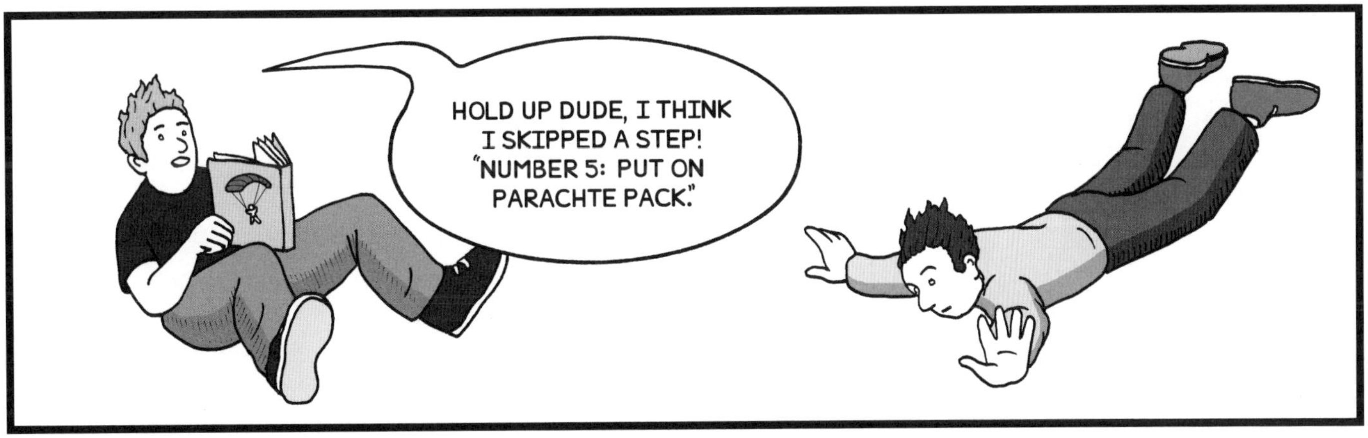
HOLD UP DUDE, I THINK I SKIPPED A STEP! "NUMBER 5: PUT ON PARACHTE PACK."

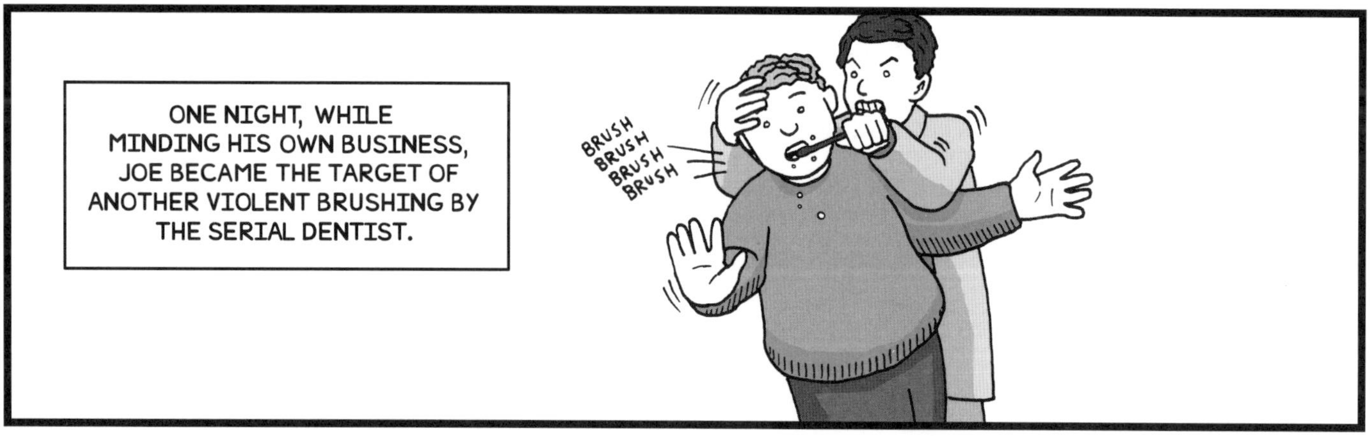
ONE NIGHT, WHILE MINDING HIS OWN BUSINESS, JOE BECAME THE TARGET OF ANOTHER VIOLENT BRUSHING BY THE SERIAL DENTIST.
BRUSH BRUSH BRUSH BRUSH

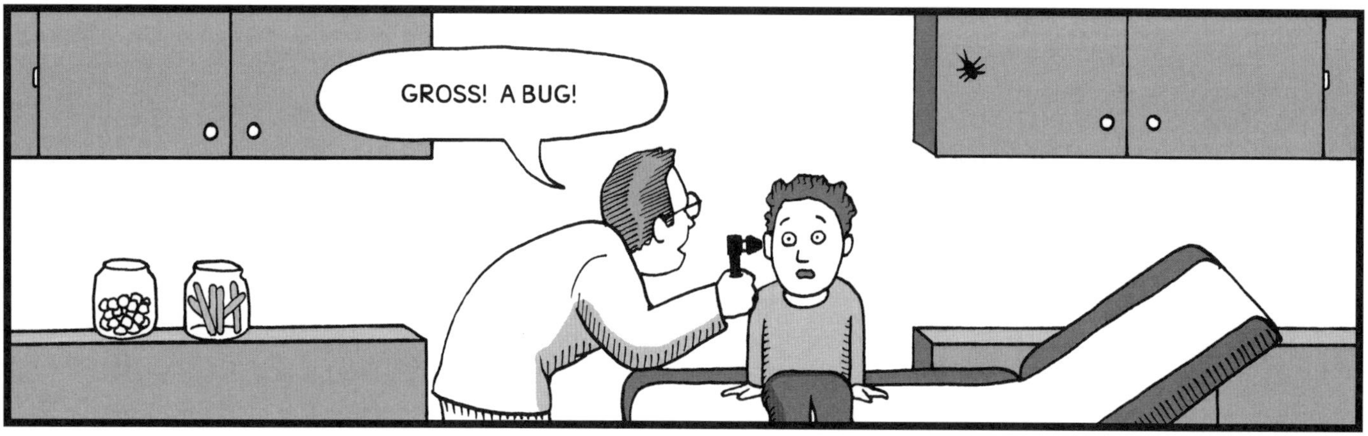
GROSS! A BUG!

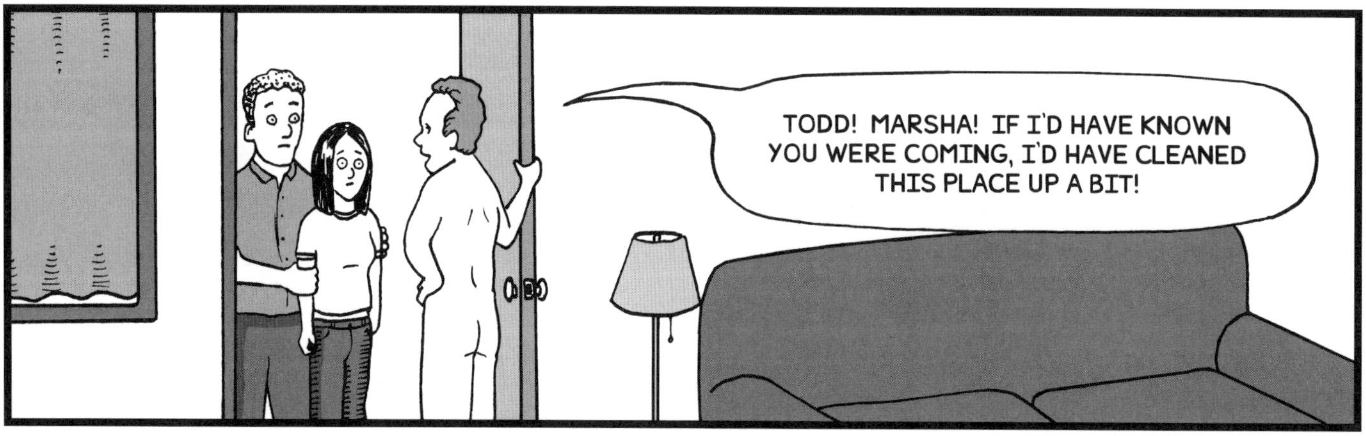
TODD! MARSHA! IF I'D HAVE KNOWN YOU WERE COMING, I'D HAVE CLEANED THIS PLACE UP A BIT!

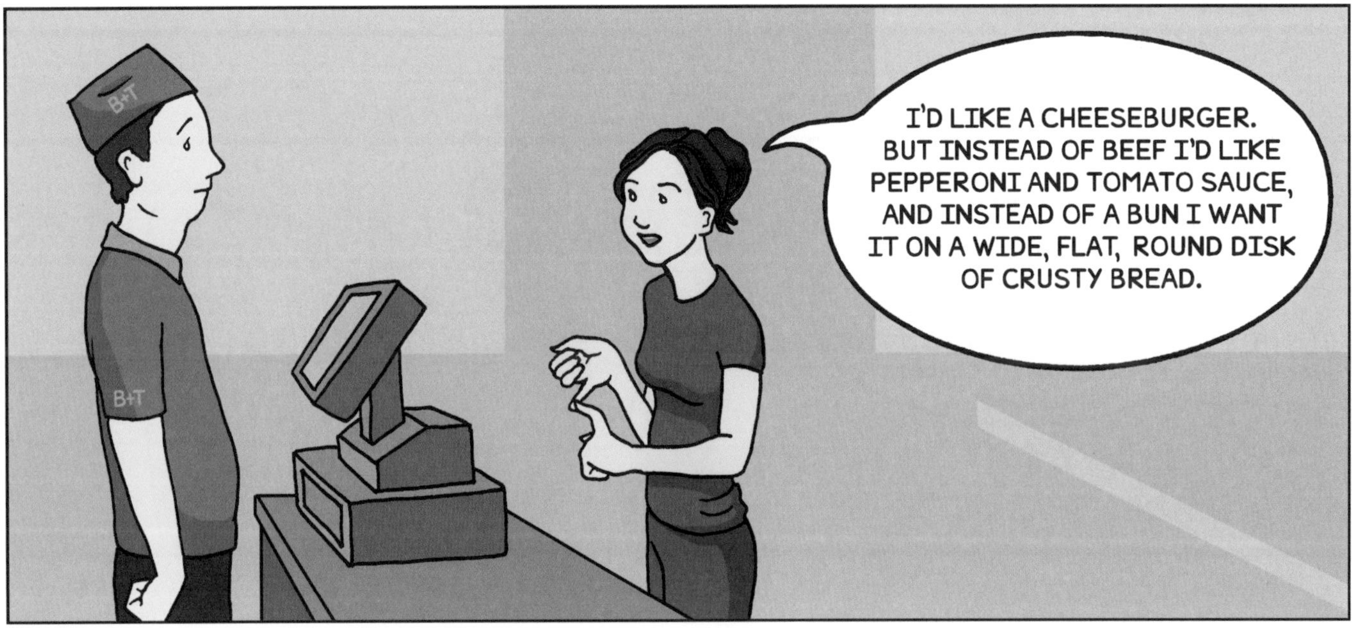
B+T
B+T
I'D LIKE A CHEESEBURGER. BUT INSTEAD OF BEEF I'D LIKE PEPPERONI AND TOMATO SAUCE, AND INSTEAD OF A BUN I WANT IT ON A WIDE, FLAT, ROUND DISK OF CRUSTY BREAD.

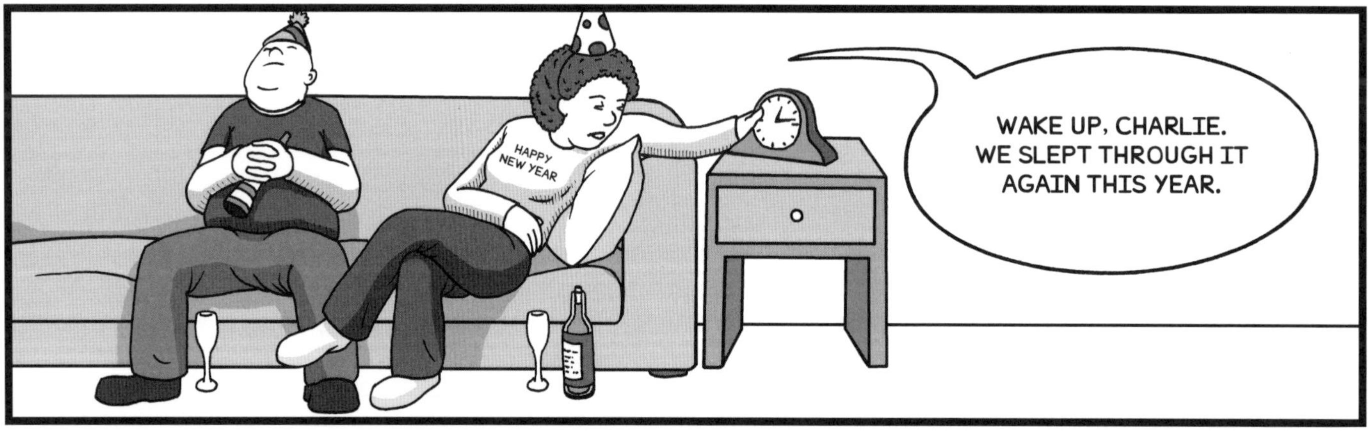
HAPPY NEW YEAR
WAKE UP, CHARLIE. WE SLEPT THROUGH IT AGAIN THIS YEAR.

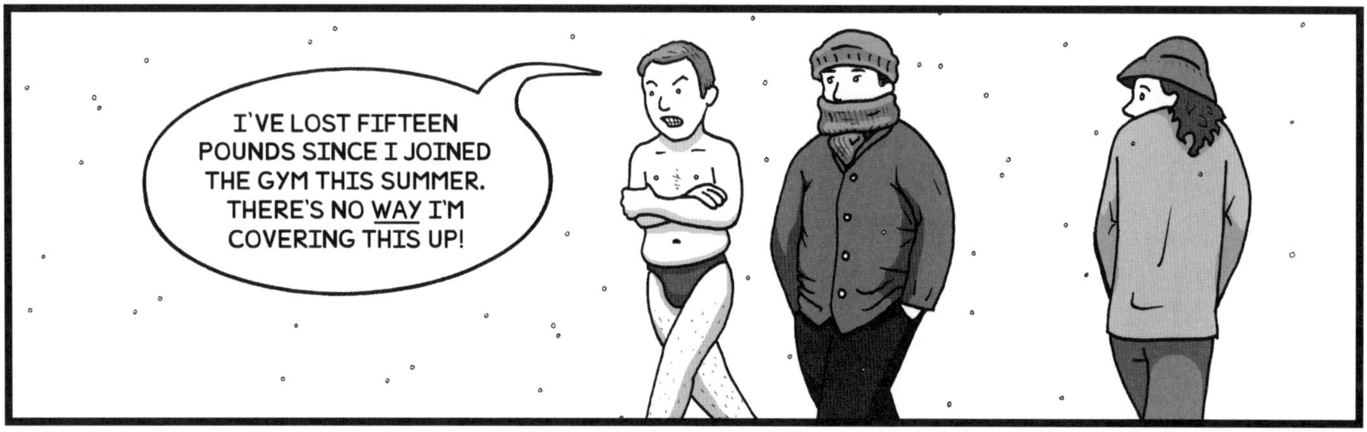
I'VE LOST FIFTEEN POUNDS SINCE I JOINED THE GYM THIS SUMMER. THERE'S NO WAY I'M COVERING THIS UP!

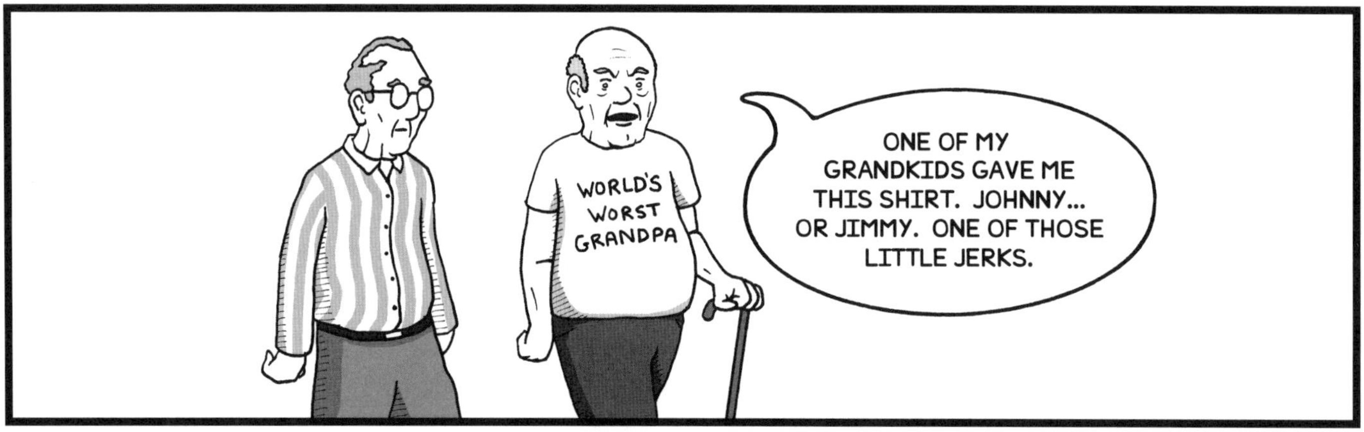
WORLD'S WORST GRANDPA
ONE OF MY GRANDKIDS GAVE ME THIS SHIRT. JOHNNY... OR JIMMY. ONE OF THOSE LITTLE JERKS.

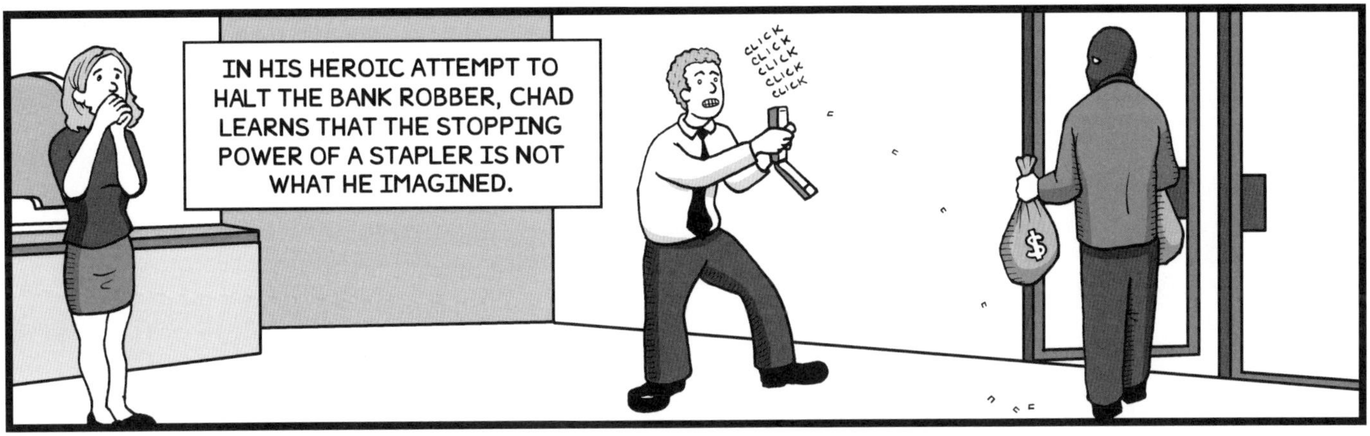
IN HIS HEROIC ATTEMPT TO HALT THE BANK ROBBER, CHAD LEARNS THAT THE STOPPING POWER OF A STAPLER IS NOT WHAT HE IMAGINED.
CLICK CLICK CLICK CLICK CLICK

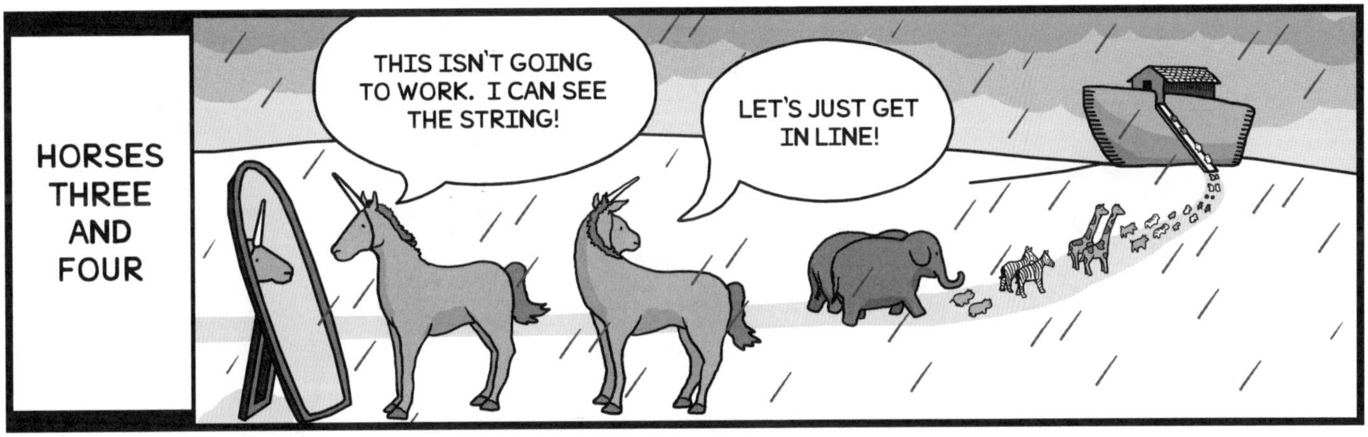
HORSES THREE AND FOUR
THIS ISN'T GOING TO WORK. I CAN SEE THE STRING!
LET'S JUST GET IN LINE!

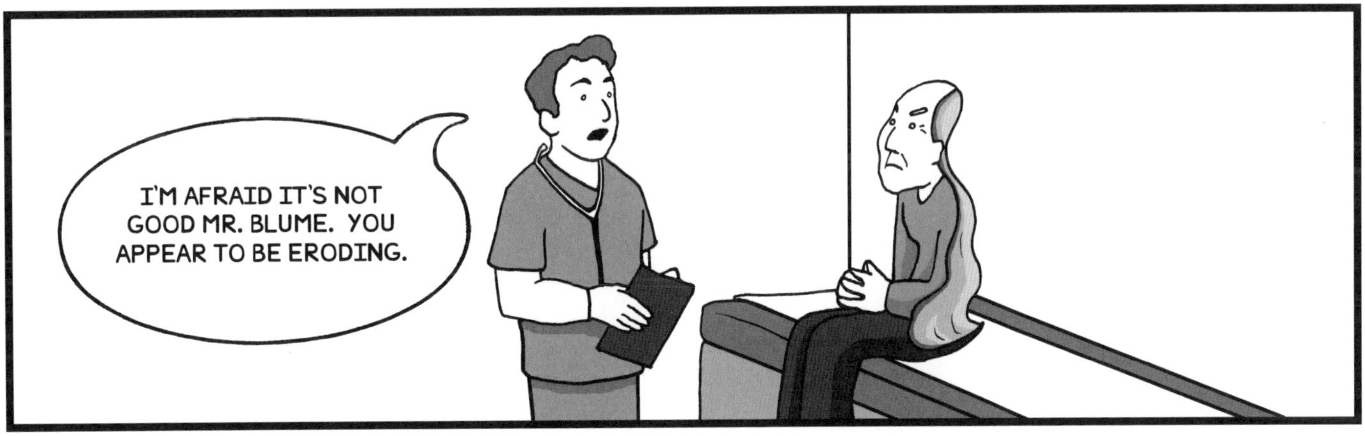
I'M AFRAID IT'S NOT GOOD MR. BLUME. YOU APPEAR TO BE ERODING.

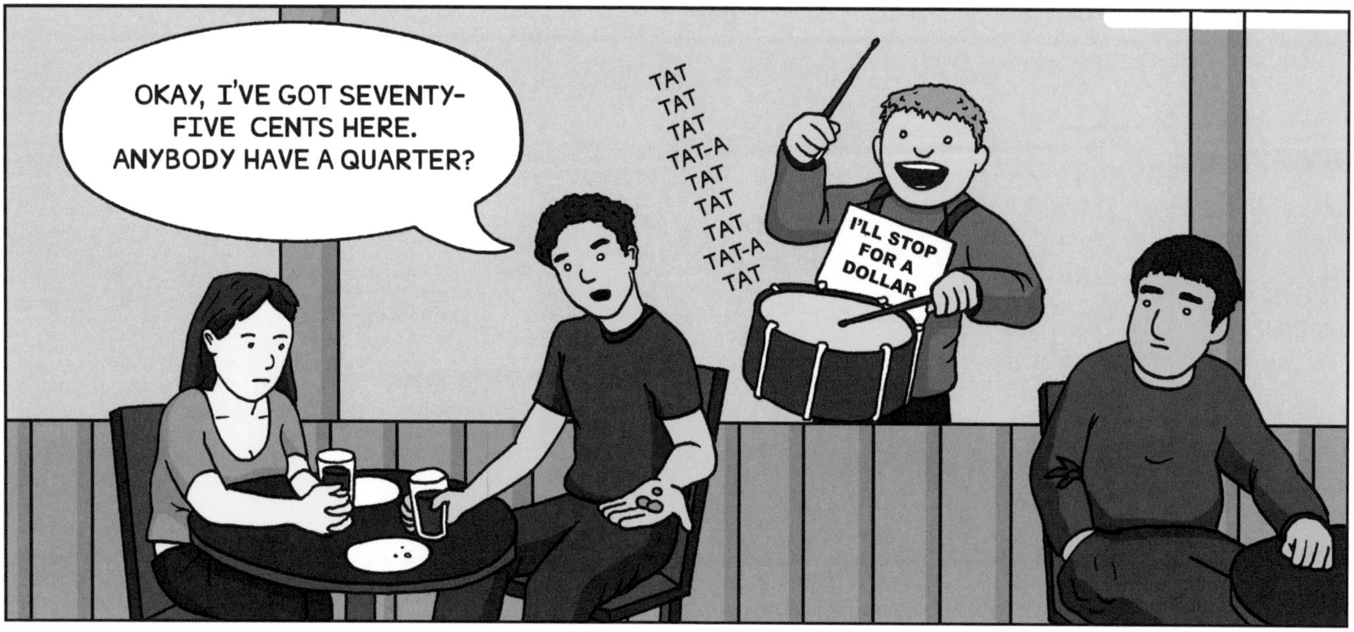
OKAY, I'VE GOT SEVENTY-FIVE CENTS HERE. ANYBODY HAVE A QUARTER?
TAT TAT TAT TAT-A TAT TAT TAT TAT-A TAT
I'LL STOP FOR A DOLLAR

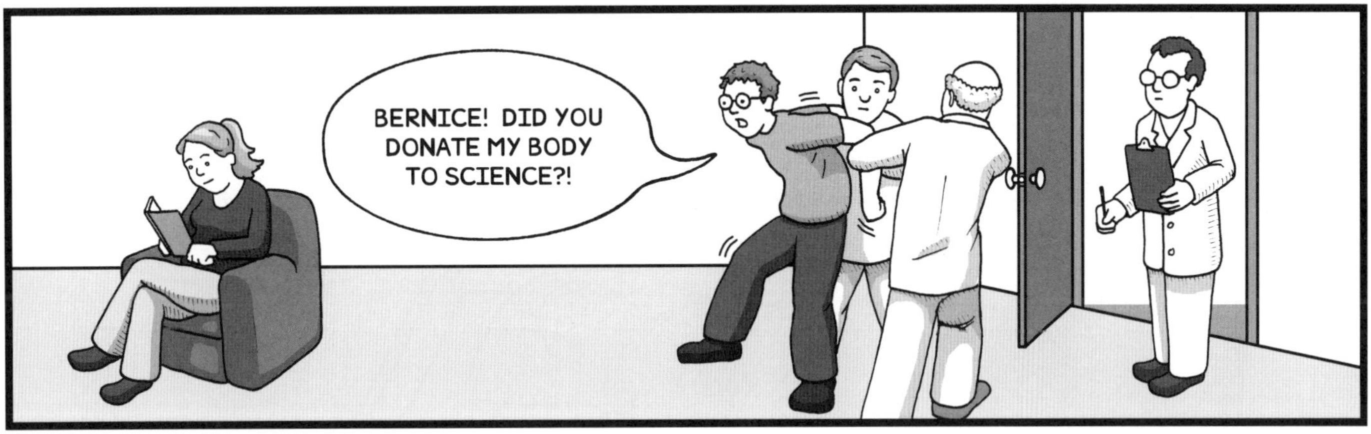
BERNICE! DID YOU DONATE MY BODY TO SCIENCE?!

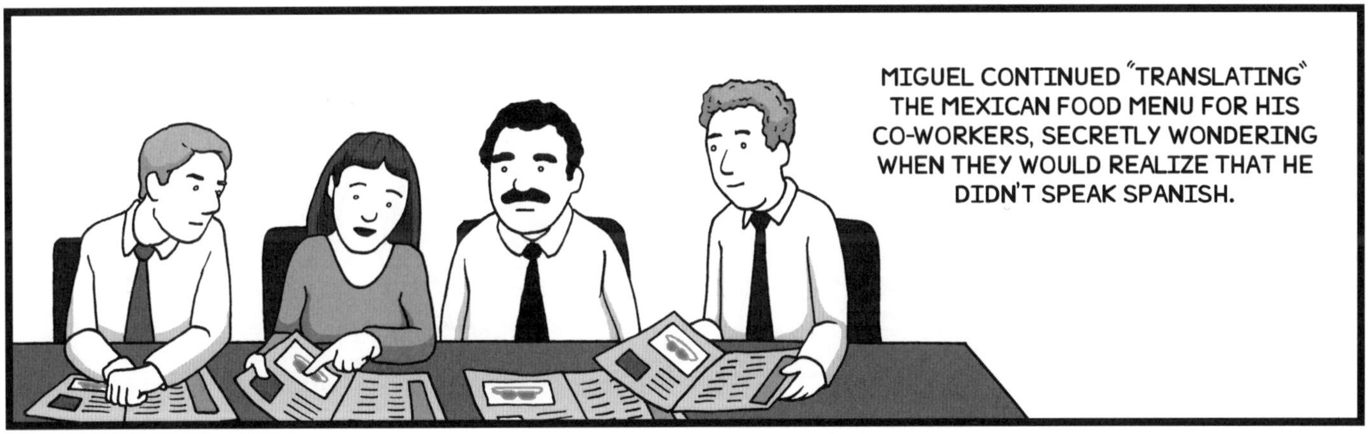
MIGUEL CONTINUED "TRANSLATING" THE MEXICAN FOOD MENU FOR HIS CO-WORKERS, SECRETLY WONDERING WHEN THEY WOULD REALIZE THAT HE DIDN'T SPEAK SPANISH.

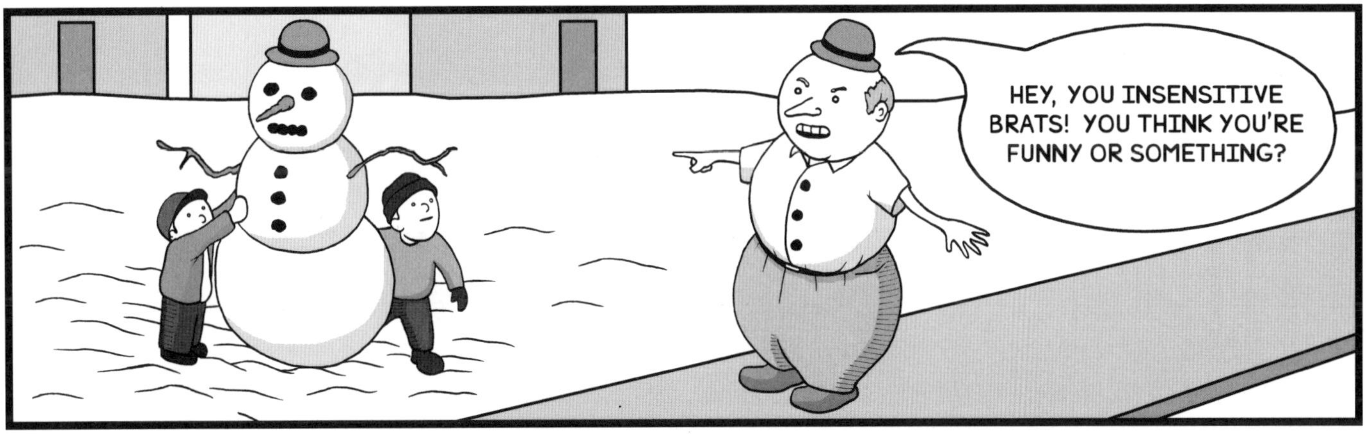
HEY, YOU INSENSITIVE BRATS! YOU THINK YOU'RE FUNNY OR SOMETHING?

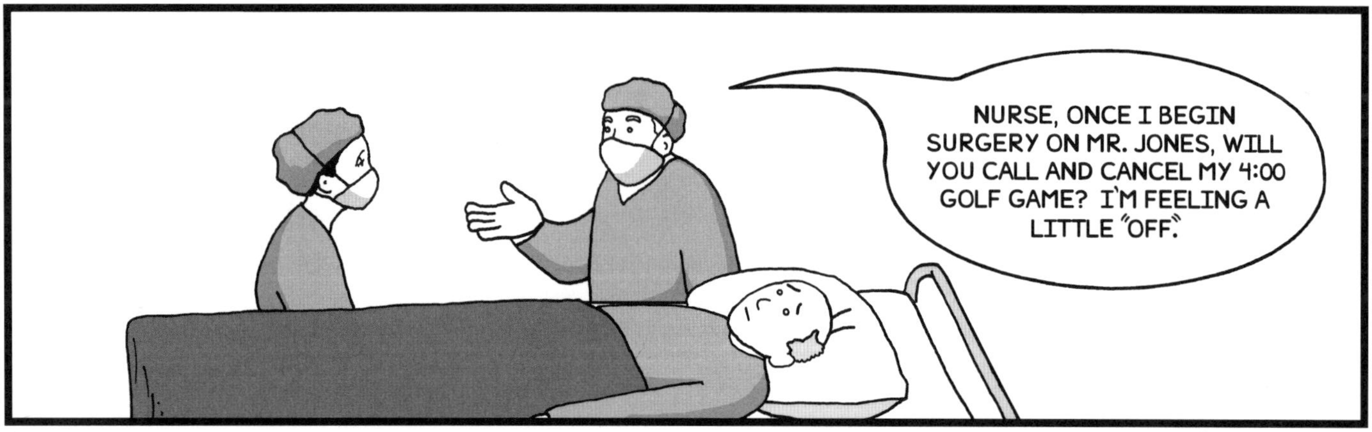
NURSE, ONCE I BEGIN SURGERY ON MR. JONES, WILL YOU CALL AND CANCEL MY 4:00 GOLF GAME? I'M FEELING A LITTLE "OFF."

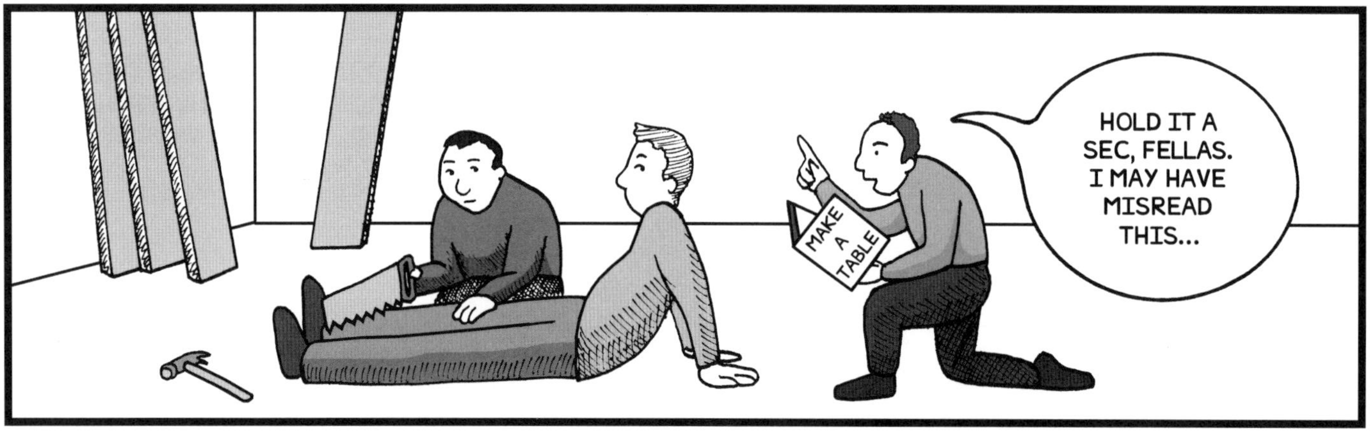
MAKE A TABLE
HOLD IT A SEC, FELLAS. I MAY HAVE MISREAD THIS...

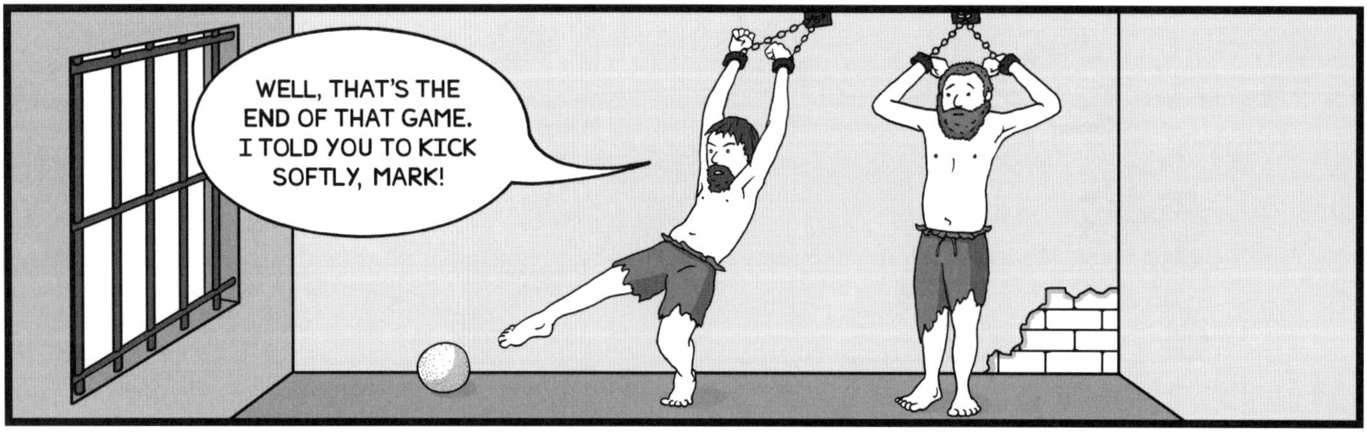
WELL, THAT'S THE END OF THAT GAME. I TOLD YOU TO KICK SOFTLY, MARK!